Essential Economics

A Guide for Business Students

guson

palgrave

First published 2002 by
PALGRAVE
Houndmills, Basingstoke, Hampshire RG21 6XS and
175 Fifth Avenue, New York, N.Y. 10010
Companies and representatives throughout the world

PALGRAVE is the new global academic imprint of
St. Martin's Press LLC Scholarly and Reference Division and
Palgrave Publishers Ltd (formerly Macmillan Press Ltd).

ISBN 0–333–96297–4

This book is printed on paper suitable for recycling and
made from fully managed and sustained forest sources.

A catalogue record for this book is available
from the British Library.

Copy-edited and typeset by Povey–Edmondson
Tavistock and Rochdale, England

10   9   8   7   6   5   4   3   2
11   10   09   08   07   06   05   04   03

Printed in Great Britain by
Creative Print & Design (Wales)
Ebbw Vale

Contents

Introduction

It is now common practice in higher education for business studies courses to be modularised. As a consequence students in their first year may study units for a relatively short time of up to 15 weeks and may not pursue these units in later parts of their course.

This publication recognises the needs of those students attending modular courses who require a basic understanding of the principles of economics and of the practical applications of economics to the business world.

This text is highly selective of the topics to be included in order to cover the requirements of most first year syllabuses. In this respect the text has the following aims.

- To give a basic understanding of the principal subject areas
- To indicate within each topic area how the theory connects with the world of business, also to indicate problems involved in viewing the business world on the basis of economic theory
- To summarise the central points within each topic area
- To indicate references to further reading which allows students to graduate their future studies according to the level of any economics course beyond this introductory stage
- To give practice questions of various types, at the end of each topic and where a written answer is required to indicate the answers from within the textbook

KEN FERGUSON

1 An introduction to the study of economics

Learning objectives

- To understand the basis for the study of economics. Scarcity leads to choice.
- To understand that the choices of people and firms and governments lead to the allocation of scarce resources.
- To understand how scarce resources are allocated. This is central, and some alternative methods are examined.
- It is important to understand that not all goods and services are viewed as the same by governments. Thus the ideas of public goods and merit goods are defined in this chapter.
- To be introduced to some basic tools of economic analysis and explanation. These need to be understood early in the study of economics, thus:
  - Opportunity Cost is the economist's way of expressing more than just the money value of any product or service.
  - The Graph is a very powerful way to explain how certain mechanisms work. To understand how to use graphs is an important skill.

1.1 Introduction

As humans most of us have a few basic needs, such as food, shelter, warmth, and water. However we also have an unlimited list of wants, the list limited only by our imaginations. The many goods and services which we want are produced by using different resources in various ways. These resources are in limited supply and therefore there is a limit to the amount of goods and services that can be produced. Herein lies the fundamental problem, we have unlimited wants and there are limited resources to satisfy those wants. Resources are *scarce*. There is therefore the logical consequence of scarcity, *choice*. Because most people have a limited amount of money, they have to choose which goods and services to buy and which to go without. Firms have to choose what they wish to produce, and how they wish to produce it. Throughout the economy there is pressure upon people, organisations and governments to *make a choice*.

When a choice is made people, organisations and governments spend their money and some of the scarce resources are allocated to producing the chosen goods and services. In the UK we are used to the idea that spending money is how most resources are allocated, but there are a number of different ways to allocate the scarce resources, other than by spending money. Economics is the study of the many complex issues which surround resource allocation.

There have been many different attempts to define the study of economics. Lord Robbins in 1932 considered economics '*a science which studies human behaviour*' and the reason for this study was in terms of '*ends and scarce means which have alternative uses.*' Other writers describe economics in various ways as a *social science* and claim that the subject seeks to explain the basis of human societies. In all these attempts to define the study of economics the authors are trying to encapsulate the wide and complex matters to be considered, and in so doing may give a less than clear view of the essence of the subject.

1.2 Different economic systems

There are two very different approaches to sharing out, or allocating scarce resources. One approach is for the government to decide what goods and services people need and should have, and to plan the use of the scarce resources in order to provide them. This is known as the *command economy* and was characteristic of the USSR and is still characteristic of countries such as North Korea. The alternative approach is to allow the markets to decide the allocation of goods and services, with minimal interference. Markets are activated by money – the ability to buy – and therefore allocation is closely related to spending power. This is known as the *market economy* and is characteristic of the USA and the UK of the 1990s. There are still a number of countries whose governments wish to exercise control over a range of goods and services – often power generation, transport, education etc.; and at the same time allow other goods and services to be allocated by the market mechanism. These are known as *mixed economies* and are characteristic of most European countries.

The command economy

The allocation of resources is decided by a centralised administrative process. Decisions are made and become *commands* from the respective planning authorities. Most people would be familiar with the reported processes of the Eastern Bloc countries prior to Gorbachev. Fewer people would realise that war-time Great Britain was very much a planned economy (command economy). During war-time the UK government ordered factories to produce weapons etc., and the Ministry of Labour directed men and women into particular occupations or the armed services.

Within the above structure shown in Figure 1.1 there were huge problems of communication between and within the various levels of decision-making. There was more emphasis upon guarding against criticism than in seeking efficiency in production and resource allocation. All economic activity was planned, including full employment. Individual choice was valid only within a narrow range of goods within the planned production. There was no emphasis nor incentive within the system to concentrate upon quality of production. The workers within the factories had no role to play other than to work in a prescribed place for the required time.

The command economy has a number of theoretical advantages.

- Resources are not wasted on competitive duplication.
- A more equitable distribution of resources can be planned, where all people have access to a standard of living according to their needs.
- Prices can be set and employment directed thus there should not be the problems of unemployment and inflation.

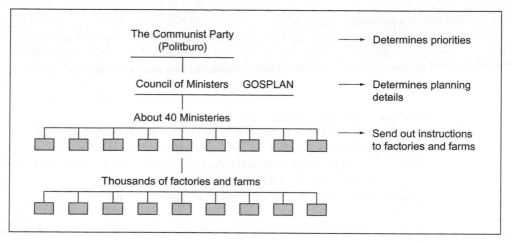

Figure 1.1   **Planning in the (old centralised) USSR**

These benefits are lost within the sheer social and political complexity of administering such a system. There is inevitably confusion within a command economy between two competing objectives. Firstly to have an equitable system responsive to people's overall welfare needs, and secondly to have an efficient system of resource allocation and production.

The market economy

The allocation of resources is accomplished by the forces of demand and supply. In the purest sense all resources; labour, land and raw materials, machinery, buildings and domestic housing, and all other goods and services; are allocated rather like a market trader sells tomatoes. This is referred to as the *market mechanism*, and will form a major part of later studies. The following example illustrates the point.

The Street Trader

Imagine that the trader has 20 boxes of tomatoes to sell on a Saturday at his market stall. He sets a price of 40p per kilo and immediately a large queue forms to buy the tomatoes. It is obvious that he has set the price too low and that he will sell out very quickly and not taking as much money as he could. So he raises his price to 80p per kilo. At this price the crowds disappear, and a steady trickle of people buy from him after visiting other stalls to compare prices and quality. If he judges that this trickle of demand will be sufficient to allow him to sell out by the end of the day then he will keep the price at 80p, if he needs to boost sales later in the day he might lower price a little to encourage sales. In this way he will have made the most money possible and allocated the resources – in this case tomatoes – to those who could afford to buy them, at the various prices.

The decision making process is mainly with the consumer in the above example. Although the trader can influence the price, he is ultimately concerned with not having boxes of tomatoes left over at the end of the day. He wants to sell the tomatoes he has bought, for a greater total sum of money than they cost him to buy; but at the least he does not want to receive less in total than the tomatoes cost. Thus it is the consumers who will choose how to spend their money, and if individually sufficient numbers of consumers hold off buying until the very last moment they may be able to force the trader to sell at or near to his cost price. It is clear from this simple example that there are a large number of different forces influencing the decisions of buyers and sellers in the market, and it is an important part of the study of economics to understand how some of these forces interact.

The market economy has a number of theoretical advantages.

- There is an automatic allocation of resources without the need for expensive, or perhaps biased, committee or government interference.
- The economy produces what consumers want, as consumers reveal their preferences by spending their money.
- The economy is efficiently allocating production resources to the areas of greatest demand.
- There is a complex signalling process wherein all parties have a vested interest in making it accurate, efficient and effective.

The advantages of the market mechanism are considerably balanced by a number of criticisms, of which three are most important.

- The market economy is activated, principally, by spending power. Thus those on low incomes, and those on fixed incomes, have very little influence over resource allocation when their social needs may even be the greatest. For example young people with young families very often have heavy family responsibilities at the beginning of their careers when they are earning relatively little. The elderly are mainly on pensions and fixed incomes and have an increased need for resources for health and support services as they get older.
- Firms in industries with little competition, can often dictate to the consumer the qualities and quantities of various products, and leave the consumers to decide who can best afford what is on offer. The production processes that develop within the economy may evolve to counteract the influence of the consumer. Thus there can develop forms of business organisation which are fundamentally against the consumers' interests.
- There is no incentive within the market economy to pay the full costs of production, including the costs of cleaning up pollution, or not producing pollution in the first place. There are many social costs associated with resource allocation, and these include lack of support for the weak or disadvantaged, as well as damage to society in general where economic factors, such as unemployment, are thought to have an influence upon social unrest, crime, illness etc. These sort of costs can never be recognised and accounted for, by a system which rewards 'low-cost' or 'value for money' as the principle for allocation.

Public goods

Public goods have two essential characteristics. Firstly, they have the characteristic of non-rivalry, which means that consumption by one person does not diminish the amount available to another person. Secondly, they have the characteristic of non-excludability, which means that once they are provided it does not make sense to exclude anyone from benefiting from the good. Pure public goods are rare, but examples might be *defence provision*, or the *Thames barriers* (flood prevention). A market economy may not provide public goods at all, because of the characteristic of non-excludability. The market mechanism seeks to exclude some consumers (and therefore to allocate) on the basis of price.

Merit goods

Merit goods are essentially the same as private goods, but the government has deemed them socially desirable for two main reasons.

1. The private benefits of consuming merit goods may not be recognised by all people. There would be under-consumption. Examples of merit goods are education, pensions, health services.
2. There are external benefits which may not be recognised or valued by consumers. There would again be under-consumption. The benefits from inoculation against serious diseases are clearly *private* as the person reduces the chance of becoming ill. The benefits are also *external* as society also benefits from the person not becoming infected and passing on the disease to others, and thus causing distress and illness. The *external* refers to the benefits beyond the *private* individual person.

It is not essential that government fully funds the provision of merit goods. The market economy will provide the goods and services – but at a price. Because of the government's wish for a wide consumption of merit goods it may seek to subsidise them to encourage consumption. Thus the examples of tax relief on private pension provision, the tax relief for private medical insurance for the over 60s (who have a greater demand for health services).

1.3 Macro and microeconomics

Economics is concerned with understanding the complexities of resource allocation, it is important to have a structure for the study. The structure adopted in economics is twofold. Firstly by looking very closely at the various components of any market within the economy, it is possible to have an idea of what is happening in detail. Secondly by looking at the economy as a whole it is possible to have an overall idea of direction and trends. The first strategy is the concern of *microeconomics* and the second is the concern of *macroeconomics*.

Microeconomics

The starting point is usually the consumer. How do consumers allocate their money, are there any guiding principles? What influences the demand for goods and services within individual markets? Are there any principles which will allow us to understand the working of markets? What are the issues and problems associated with the production of goods and services, within different markets? These are the sort of very focused questions which are considered prior to looking at both sides of the market, together.

A very important part of microeconomics is the study of how firms behave. Firm's behaviour is the subject matter of many textbooks and is very wide and complex, merging economics with business management. Thus for present purposes a few central issues will be considered, with references to further reading given at the end of each chapter.

Macroeconomics

The starting point is to understand how the total goods and services produced within the country are described and valued. A major objective of macroeconomics is to try and understand the issues surrounding topics such as inflation and unemployment, as well as understanding how functions such as banking and international trade affect the overall economy.

The ideas encountered within macroeconomics are very often those used by politicians when discussing the economy. This is no surprise as governments are mainly forced to look at the overall picture of the country. For example, politicians are frequently concerned to be seen to be attempting to produce policies aimed at reducing inflation and unemployment. Thus any serious consideration of macroeconomic topics usually includes consideration of the factors which are thought to influence various macroeconomic variables such as inflation and employment, to name but two.

1.4 Graphical representation in economics

Many students are horrified at the prospect of having to cope with mathematical or graphical presentations of ideas. It is not true that the basic economic ideas can only be understood by competent mathematicians, although it may be the case that more advanced economic concepts are easier or more clearly explained using mathematics. The representation of certain ideas by means of graphs will not involve any mathematics, but will make use of elementary arithmetic and simple statistics.

The Graph

The graph should be viewed as a picture surrounded by a picture frame. On two of the picture frame's sides will be information which helps to explain the actual picture. The rest is easy if one simple rule is remembered: **say what you see**. The following example will help to explain this idea.

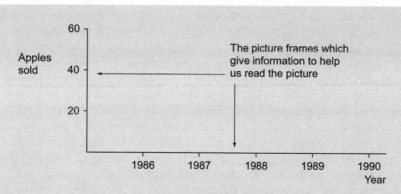

Now we add the picture, which is frequently just a line, or two.

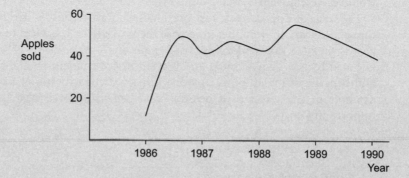

To read the picture **we say what we see**, thus: 'in 1988 more apples were sold than in 1987'. This is true because the line above 1988–1989 is higher than the part of the line above 1987–1988. We see that one is above the other and as the frame tells us that we are talking about apples sold, we can say more apples were sold. In this way we can **say what we see** anywhere in the picture. Below are some further examples of what can be seen in the graph (picture) above.

- During 1986 sales of apples went up steeply.
- During 1988 sales of apples went up steeply, reached a peak and then started to fall.
- In 1989 sales started out well above the 1987 level but during 1989 fell below the average 1987 level.

You should be sure that you can see each of the above statements in the graph. If you can then you will have no difficulty with graphs (pictures) in this book.

1.5 Opportunity cost

This is an important concept in economics and it seeks to make clear that there are costs other than just money costs. Resources are scarce. We therefore have to make choices. However in choosing to spend our money on one product we have to go without another (*which we would also have liked to buy had we enough money*). Similarly a firm can choose to use its resources in a variety of different ways, and in choosing one good to produce has to give up the prospect of producing another (*which it would also have liked to produce had it more resources*). The central idea is that in choosing one particular good or activity something else might have to be given up (alternative).

Consumers spend their money in order to obtain satisfaction from the goods they consume. If we want to spend more on some goods we have to give up some others. What is consumed is measured in terms of what was given up, as well as the money cost. A farmer can increase the production of one crop only by giving up production of another, or part of another. The local authority may wish to build a school and a car park but only have the funding for one of these. For instance, the cost of building the school, in addition to the cash, is the loss of the car parking facilities which the town would have enjoyed.

The idea of opportunity cost presumes that all resources are fully used at the time that choices are to be made, otherwise there would be less need to choose. Opportunity cost is the idea that underpins cost benefit analysis, and this is the method frequently adopted by local government and by central government to highlight the hidden costs and benefits of undertaking any one project at the expense of another. The following example of the stages of a possible cost benefit analysis clearly show the link with opportunity cost.

Cost Benefit Analysis

The basic idea is very simple. If a decision has to be made to do 'x' or not to do 'x' then the following rule applies. **Do 'x' if the benefits exceed those of the next best course of action, and not otherwise**. If this rule is applied consistently to all choices then the largest possible benefits will be generated. Another idea follows on from this. If course 'x' is taken in preference to course 'y' then we know that the benefits of 'x' outweigh the benefits of 'y'. But in choosing 'x' we lose the benefits of 'y' (i.e. we cannot have them both, perhaps because of budgetary constraints) thus the loss of benefits are also the **costs of 'x'**. The rule above is therefore modified to, **do 'x' only if its benefits exceed its costs.** We now have cost benefit analysis, but we also have a major problem, namely how to measure the various non monetary costs and benefits, and later how to compare them.

Stage 1. Identify all the benefits for any particular project. These will be benefits to individuals, firms and social/welfare benefits to the population at large. Then identify all the dis-benefits in the same categories and manner.

Stage 2. In order to be able to compare various outcomes a common unit of measure is necessary. All the benefits and dis-benefits must therefore be measured in money terms. The dis-benefits then become **costs.** The complexities of cost benefit analysis are mainly to do with how to value items which amount to 'how people feel about something'.

A Hypothetical Local Authority Project

An enquiry into the merits of replacing all existing street lights

The local authority has had a report to its Highways Committee that there is great interest in the community for the existing street lights to be replaced with new halogen lights which cost less to run and give out 12 times the light of the existing lights. Furthermore the producers of halogen lights are a local company.

A comparison of some costs and benefits

Some benefits might be.

- Reduced accidents from much clearer driving conditions.
- Reduced crime in certain areas, such as car thefts, mugging etc.
- People living near the road may feel more secure, as their houses are bathed in light.
- The manufacturers of halogen lamps will make a profit and may employ more workers.
- The existing workers will feel more secure with the extra demand for their product.
- The existing and extra workers will spend more in the local community.
- Old people and females may feel safer when out late at night.

Some dis-benefits (costs) might be.

- The present suppliers of lighting will lose business and may be forced to close.
- The workers for the present suppliers face unemployment or reduced wages.
- Some people may have expensive alarm systems and may not want this level of lighting.
- Some people may feel that to light their houses allows the burglar a better chance to evaluate.
- Local home security specialists may find they lose business.
- There will be community dis-benefit from any unemployment or loss of wages.

The example above raises the major problems in cases like this. How might money values be put to each of the above categories? How accurate or valid is the money value in each case? Is there a better way of doing the exercise? There are no 'correct' answers to these questions. In the above example the local authority must come to its own decision. Cost benefit analysis can draw attention to the non-financial issues but is not designed to resolve them.

1.6   Summary

The objective of this first chapter has been to introduce the subject. It has been important to introduce some basic ideas which show the way that economists seek to explain the business world.

   The idea of cost benefit analysis is directly related to the idea of Opportunity Cost. It is very important because many local authorities and large corporations, as well as government departments, use the technique to evaluate alternative investment plans.

Test your understanding

(Answers are provided at the back of the book.)

1. A mixed economy may be defined as one in which resources are

    A   allocated to meet the needs of both consumers and producers
    B   used partly to produce consumer goods and partly to produce capital goods
    C   allocated partly by market forces and partly by the state
    D   used for the production of both goods and services
    E   allocated by the spending decisions of firms

2. *In principle* which of the following is an advantage of a planned economy

    A   decisions are taken on the basis of social costs and benefits
    B   the government can always balance its budget
    C   patterns of production will reflect consumer preferences
    D   production is efficient as only the goods needed are produced
    E   there is effective communication between the workers and government

3. The winner of a TV show is offered a choice of either £1000 or the contents of one or other of two sealed boxes. She is told that one box contains £2500 and the other box is empty.
    What is the opportunity cost to the individual of opting for the £1000 prize?

    A   a 50% chance of winning £2500
    B   a 50% chance of winning £1500
    C   a 50% chance of losing £1500
    D   a 50% chance of losing £2500
    E   a 50% chance of losing £1000

Questions 4 and 5 refer to the graph on the opposite page.

4. Which of the following statements are correct?

    A   Sales fell in January but were still above the July sales
    B   Sales were rising in April but still below October levels
    C   Goods sold in September were priced between £10 and £12
    D   April was the best month
    E   Most money was taken at Christmas time

5. Which of the following statements are correct?

    A   Total income in July was the same as November
    B   On some days in July the total revenue taken was the same as some days in November
    C   £10 000 was taken on some days in March, May, August, September and October
    D   £10 000 was taken on some days in February
    E   None of the above

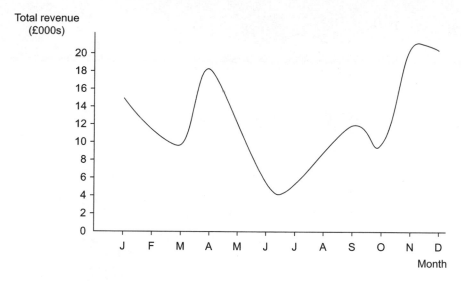

Graph for Questions 4 and 5

6. In a paragraph of 150 words or less explain the connection between 'opportunity cost' and 'cost benefit analysis'?

7. List three advantages of a command economy, and in 150 words or less explain why these advantages are not always able to be realised.

8. List three advantages and three disadvantages of a market economy.

9. Public goods have two **essential** characteristics, which are:

   A ....

   B ....

   Explain these characteristics in 250 words or less, giving at least one example.

10. Give two examples of private merit goods.

    A ....

    B ....

    Give one example of an external merit good.

    C ....

11. Taking the illustrated example of the 'street lights' cost benefit analysis (page 9) explain how money amounts might be allocated to each of the bulleted costs and benefits. (i.e. how would you work out a money amount to represent each item).

PART I

Microeconomics

2 Consumer theory

Learning objectives

- To understand how consumers might exercise their choices
- To understand the analysis known as the equi-marginal principle.
- To understand the way in which indifference curve analysis helps to explain consumer behaviour.
- A major objective is to become acquainted with the terminology of consumer theory.
  - Rational behaviour
  - Ordinal measurement
  - Cardinal measurement
  - Utility
  - Rate of substitution

2.1 Introduction

How consumers decide to spend their money is a question which has fascinated both economists and psychologists. Do most consumers try to get the best value (to them) for each pound they spend? Do they spend on impulse? Are consumers manipulated or at least heavily influenced by media, especially television, advertising? Whilst this last point may throw some doubt upon the amount of control some people have over their methods for deciding their priorities, there is little doubt that most people undertake a series of complex processes prior to spending their money. (NB These processes may be wholly or mainly sub-conscious). By studying consumer behaviour economists are able to gain important insights into the mechanisms which influence market demand.

A starting point is to make clear a major assumption. It is assumed that consumers are rational. This means that people will spend their money on items which give them the most satisfaction.

An example of irrational behaviour

A person went into a butcher's shop and bought some steak and upon leaving the shop was stopped by someone doing consumer research. The conversation might go something like the following.

'Is this steak for your family'?
'Yes'
'Is your family particularly fond of steak'?
'No, we are vegetarians'.

> We are unable to understand this behaviour as there appears to be no rationality behind the spending pattern. This is perhaps an extreme example, but if most people habitually bought goods they did not like or did not want, the market place would be more chaotic than it sometimes appears.

The ordinal and the cardinal approaches.

Ordinal measurement is for example, *first, second, third, fourth, etc.* It is concerned with ranking, and is the way in which 'best seller' book lists or 'pop charts' are compiled. It does not tell you how many of each were sold or how many calories were burned in the excitement of reading or listening to the product concerned.

Cardinal measurement is for example, *one, two, three, four etc.* It is concerned with value, and is used to give a precise numerical value to something. Thus one book is more expensive than another or one book sells more copies than another.

The early studies of consumer behaviour were mainly *cardinal*. Marshall introduced a fictitious unit of measurement for a person's level of satisfaction, he called it the *util*. The word utility, in its economic usage, can be directly replaced with the word satisfaction, thus the util was derived from the idea of utility. The idea was that as people spent their money they would get more and more utility (satisfaction), and that by allocating a certain number of utils to each product bought, economists could study consumer behaviour. This approach is studied as **marginal utility theory.** There is an obvious problem with this approach, namely that to allocate fictitious levels of utils to spending patterns is methodologically unsound.

The *ordinal* approach has no need to allocate numbers to spending patterns as it is not concerned with how much utility (satisfaction) a consumer derives from a particular product. The *ordinalist* is concerned with ranking the spending habits. Thus it is enough to know that the consumer gets more utility from *A* than from B, and we would expect *A* to be bought in preference to B. This approach to consumer theory is methodologically sound, but slightly more complex and is studied with **indifference curve analysis.**

Both approaches give identical results, and both are considered in this chapter.

2.2 Marginal utility theory

The basic idea is that as the consumption of a particular product increases there will come a point where the additional utility gained from each additional unit bought will decrease. Because this theory makes use of cardinal units, utils, it is best illustrated by way of a table of figures (Table 2.1).

Total utility increases as more of the product is consumed, until the 8th unit when total utility finally falls. The important measure from the point of view of the economist is the **Marginal utility.** Marginal utility is the *extra* utility gained from consuming *one more* unit of the product. It is the difference in total utility between the first and second units consumed, the second and third units consumed, the third and fourth units consumed and so on.

Table 2.1 Total and marginal utility gained from consuming various units of a product X

Quantity of Product X consumed in 1 week	Total utility 'utils' per week	Marginal utility
0	0	0
1	45	45
2	83	38
3	106	23
4	118	12
5	127	9
6	131	4
7	132	1
8	127	−5

Marginal utility is always falling in the above example, and eventually becomes negative. This is explained by the fact that the consumer gets most satisfaction from the first unit, and although there is high satisfaction from consuming units 2 and 3 there is never as much as in consuming the first unit. Therefore as consumption increases **marginal utility diminishes.**

The above data can be represented in picture form (a graph) where the relationship between total utility and marginal utility can be illustrated (Figure 2.1).

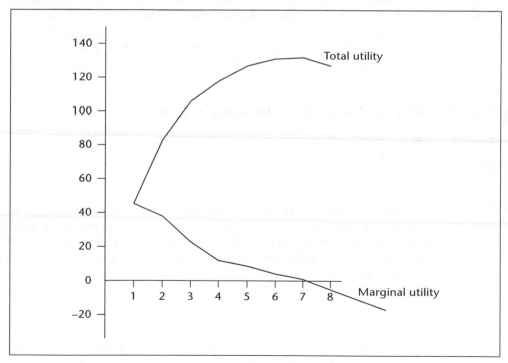

Figure 2.1 The relationship between total utility and marginal utility

In Figure 2.1 some important relationships can be seen. Even as the total utility is rising quite steeply the marginal utility is falling. Marginal utility equals zero (crosses the quantity axis) directly below the highest point on the total utility curve. Therefore when marginal utility equals zero total utility is at its maximum. From the above relationships is derived the idea of *consumer equilibrium* or the *equi-marginal principle*.

Consumer equilibrium (the equi-marginal principle)

It has been shown that as the consumption of any product increases the extra utility (satisfaction) gained from the additional consumption falls. For example you might buy a new fashionable shirt and get 50 utils of satisfaction from owning it. If you bought a second shirt this might give an additional 40 utils of satisfaction, a third shirt 30 utils and so on. Although each shirt gives successively less utils the total utility rises, and it may be nice to have a wardrobe full of fashionable shirts, but probably one or two could suffice. The real question here is how many shirts should one buy? The answer is that one should buy the number of shirts to maximise total utility, given the limited budget. An example will allow this concept to be developed.

An example of consumer decision making

For the sake of simplicity only two products will be considered, but the principles established work equally for any number of products. Let us assume that you have a budget of £100 for various clothes and entertainment items each month. Further assume that the two products being considered this month are shirts and CDs. A shirt costs £20 and a CD costs £10. It is possible to buy 5 shirts or 10 CDs or any combination of the two, given the budget. Table 2.2 summarises the position.

Table 2.2 **What could be bought for the budget of £100**

Shirt @ £20	5	4	3	2	1	0
CD @ £10	0	2	4	6	8	10

Table 2.2 shows what *could* be bought for the budget of £100, but we need to understand what *should* be bought in order to maximise total satisfaction. This question cannot be decided on the information given. It is necessary to know how many utils of satisfaction will be gained from each unit of the above two products. If we know this then we can deduce the correct levels to purchase. Table 2.3 extends the pricing information to include utils.

Remember Marginal utility values are given in terms of the 'util', the fictitious measurement of satisfaction.

Table 2.3 Utils (satisfaction) gained per pound (£) spent on each product

Shirts			CDs		
(1) Quantity	(2) Utils gained from each item purchased	(3) Utils per £ spent	(4) Quantity	(5) Utils gained from each item purchased	(6) Utils per £ spent
0			0		
1	90	4.5	1	60	6.0
2	78	3.9	2	51	5.1
3	66	3.3	3	42	4.2
4	54	2.7	4	33	3.3
5	42	2.1	5	24	2.4
			6	15	1.5
			7	6	0.6
			8	3	0.3

What to buy to maximise total utility for the given budget?

Columns (3) and (6) in Table 2.3 show the utils (satisfaction) to be gained per £ spent on each of the products. Thus the first shirt bought gives 4.5 utils per £ whereas the first CD bought gives 6 utils per £. In this case the first CD is the 'best buy' as it gives the most utils per £ spent. If this idea is carried forward the consumer will buy in the following order:

1st CD   2nd CD   1st shirt   3rd CD   2nd shirt   3rd shirt   4th CD

The consumer has maximised total utility (only the highest marginal utilities were chosen, so they must add up to the greatest total) and has spent the budget of £100 by buying 3 shirts and 4 CDs.

Notice, in Table 2.3, that the MU per £ of the third shirt equals the MU per £ of the fourth CD. A rule can be stated from this example. **A consumer will spend on any product until the last penny (or pound) spent brings the same marginal utility as the last penny (or pound) spent on any other product.** This is known as the equi-marginal principle and is usually written in shorthand or algebraic form as:

$$\frac{Mua}{Pa} = \frac{Mub}{Pb} = \frac{Muc}{Pc} = \frac{Mud}{Pd}$$

This reads: the marginal utility of good *A* divided by the price of good *A* equals the marginal utility of good *B* divided by the price of good *B* equals the marginal utility of good *C* divided by the price of good *C* equals the marginal utility of good *D* divided by the price of good *D*. This is exactly what was done to decide upon the purchase of shirts and CDs in the above example. By equating the utility gained per £ on one product with the utility gained per £ on any other products the consumer **maximises total utility within the budget constraint.**

Indifference curve analysis

This is an alternative approach to the analysis of consumer behaviour. The issue is still how to maximise total utility within a given budget. It is no longer necessary to use the cardinalist device of allocating utils to a product. This is the ordinalist approach which relies on the idea of ranking, i.e. something is bigger than something else, or higher or better etc., the actual numbers are not required.

It is still a central assumption that people are rational, and are able to decide what products they prefer. They must be able to choose between 'bundles' of goods. But may decide that there are packages (or bundles) of goods of equal preference so that they are happy with all bundles and would not want to choose between them.

The indifference curve

It is possible to have combinations of different products between which the consumer is indifferent; i.e. gets the same satisfaction so does not mind which combination is purchased. A table of combinations might be as shown in Table 2.4.

Table 2.4 **Combination of product X and product Y which give equal satisfaction**

Combination	Product X (units)	Product Y (units)
A	8	36
B	16	19
C	24	12
D	32	8
E	40	7

It is assumed that combination A (8X + 36Y) gives the same satisfaction as all the other combinations and therefore a consumer would not choose between any of the combinations. The consumer would be **indifferent.** The combinations in Table 2.4 can be plotted on the graph in Figure 2.2. Once an indifference curve has been plotted it will show how much of product X has to be given up if the consumer wants more of product Y.

Example Assume that the consumer starts with a combination of 20X and 15Y. (These are the approximate values on the graph above). Now assume he wants to buy 5 more of product Y. The indifference curve will show how many of product X has to be given up so that when 5 more of product Y are purchased **the total level of utility does not change,** that is the consumer is still indifferent between the old combination (20X + 15Y) and the new combination 15X + 20Y.

In other words the indifference curve shows how the products can be **substituted** for each other.

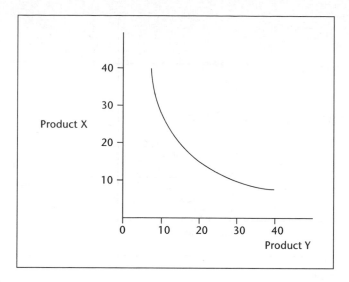

Figure 2.2

An indifference curve represents the **marginal rate of substitution between products.** In this case the margin refers to giving up one unit of X or one unit of Y and seeing how much of the other product is substituted.

Some important properties of indifference curves

- Each represents a given level of utility
- The further from the origin the higher the utility
- Convex to the origin
- Never touch or cross

Indifference curves representing all possible combinations make up an indifference map. An indifference map might look something like Figure 2.3.

In Figure 2.3 there are a large number of indifference curves and as each one gets further from the origin it represents combinations of good X and good Y which give higher levels of satisfaction than the previous indifference curve. This is all that is necessary for the analysis. It is not necessary to know how much satisfaction each indifference curve represents, merely that IC6 represents more satisfaction than IC5. The idea is to consume a combination of goods on the highest possible indifference curve. The only constraint upon consumers buying what they want is their budget, that is, people have limited money to spend. This idea must be introduced in diagram form before the analysis can be attempted.

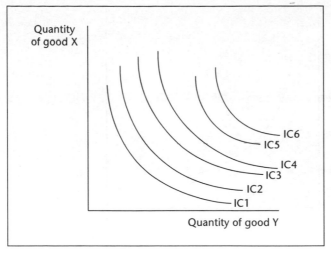

Figure 2.3 **An indifference map**

The budget line

Assume that a consumer has £50 to spend and that good X costs £2 each and good Y costs £5 each. If all the £50 was spent on good X then 25 could be bought. If all the £50 was spent on good Y then only 10 could be bought. To buy some of good X and some of good Y means that 2.5X have to be given up to be able to afford 1Y. This can be shown diagrammatically, as in Figure 2.4.

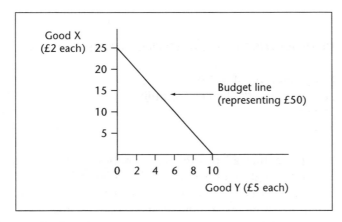

Figure 2.4 **The budget line**

By drawing a straight line between the maximum of good X that can be afforded (25) and the maximum of good Y that can be afforded (10) the line will give all other combinations of good X and good Y that can be bought for £50. For instance, if only 15 of good X were bought then 4 of good Y could be afforded.

You should plot various prices and budgets accurately on graph paper and read off the answers. This will help you to see that any straight line that joins two sides of a graph, automatically gives all the different combinations, for what is plotted on the sides of the graph.

Exercise

You have a budget of £100. You have two products: *trainers* and *CDs*. The trainers cost £20 each and the CDs cost £10 each. Draw a graph to represent this situation and then *from the graph* read off how many CDs can be bought together with 2 pairs of trainers.

How many CDs do you have to substitute for each extra pair of trainers?

The budget line and indifference curves

We now have two important pieces of information.

1. We know how much the budget is worth, and can show this on a diagram (graph).
2. We know that to maximise consumer satisfaction combinations of goods must be bought – on the highest indifference curve.

Putting these two ideas together on the same graph will allow some conclusions to be drawn. The indifference map is reduced to a few indifference curves (ICs) and the budget line is drawn between the two axes.

In Figure 2.5 it can be seen that the budget line touches two different indifference curves. It actually cuts IC1 at points A and C. It just touches IC2 at point B. The combinations of goods X and Y at points A, B and C can all be afforded, so it just remains to see which combination gives the most satisfaction. IC2 is higher than IC1 and therefore represents a higher level of satisfaction for all its combinations, than any combination on IC1. Thus points A and C represent combinations on IC1 and these must give less satisfaction than the combination represented by B which is on IC2.

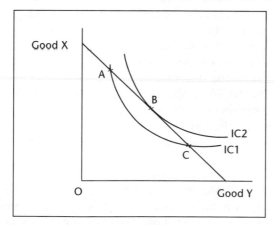

Figure 2.5 **Budget line and indifference curves**

When a straight line just touches a curve, such as at point **B**, it is said to be at a **tangent** to the curve. The consumer is in **equilibrium**, *that is obtains the highest level of satisfaction that the budget (income) allows*, when the budget line is a tangent (or just touches) to an indifference curve.

The effect of changes in income

If a consumer's income rises then clearly there is a greater budget to spend. This is shown on the graph by drawing a new budget line **parallel and to the right** of the existing budget line. This is shown in Figure 2.6.

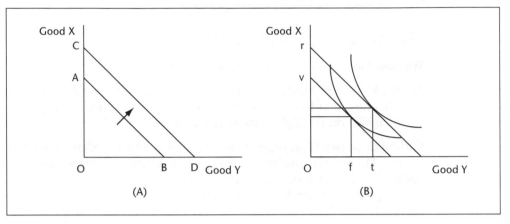

Figure 2.6   **The effect of an income use on the budget line**

In Figure 2.6 (A) the old budget is shown by the line AB. The new budget, after the increase in income, is shown by the new budget line CD. It should be noticed that in the same way that indifference curves represent higher levels of satisfaction, the further they are from the origin, so also budget lines represent higher levels of spending the further they are from the origin. This is the reason for moving the new budget line to the right of the old budget line – as the new budget line has to be further from the origin to represent the higher spending (income). Figure 2.6 (B) shows the effect of the increase in income. The new budget line is able to touch an even higher IC than before and this represents a new combination of goods giving an even higher level of satisfaction. The original budget allowed OV of good X plus OF of good Y to be purchased. The increase in income has resulted in OR of good X plus OT of good Y to be purchased – more of both goods.

This example has shown an increase in income, but if there had been a decrease in income then the budget line would have moved parallel and to the left of the original budget line. The analysis is similar but less of both goods would have been bought and satisfaction would have reduced. You should be sure that you understand this point.

Reminder

- An increase in income requires a new budget line parallel and to the right of the original budget line.
- A decrease in income requires a new budget line parallel and to the left of the original budget line.
- The further from the origin the budget line lies, then the greater the budget it represents.
- The closer to the origin the budget line lies, then the smaller the budget it represents.

The effects of changes in the prices of products

It is not just income changes that can increase or decrease the amount of goods that a consumer can purchase. If the price of a good goes up then less of that good can be bought for the same budget, and vice versa if the price falls more of the good can be purchased for the same budget. It is in this way that **rises and falls in the prices of goods can have the same effect as an increase or decrease in the budget.** Reductions in prices are shown graphically in Figure 2.7

In Figure 2.7 (A) the first diagram the original budget line is GH. If the price of good Y falls and the price of good X stays the same, then more of good Y can be bought for the same amount of money. The budget line will stay the same at point G (because the price of good X has not changed and if all the budget was spent on good X then OG could be bought). The budget line on the other axis will move from point H to the new point K. As good Y has become cheaper OK of good Y can now be bought if all the budget was spent on this good. To represent this the budget line pivots from point G to

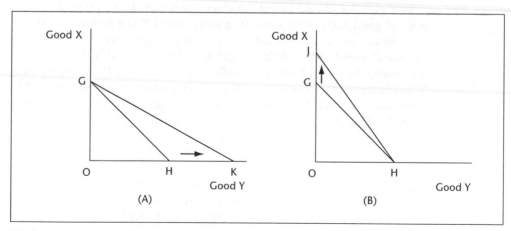

Figure 2.7   **Reductions in prices**

the new point K. This gives a different slope to the budget line and will probably mean that it will touch a new indifference curve, giving higher levels of satisfaction.

Figure 2.7 (B) represents a fall in the price of good X rather than good Y. In this case the original budget line GH pivots on point H (as the price of good Y is unchanged) and joins the new point J. The movement from point G to point J shows how much more of the cheaper good X can be bought for the same budget. Just as in Figure 2.7 (A), the new budget line HJ will probably touch a new (higher) indifference curve representing the higher satisfaction gained as the result of the effect of lower prices.

If prices were to rise then less of the good would be able to be purchased for the existing level of budget. The budget line would again move to reflect this. Figure 2.8 shows price rises in both good X and good Y.

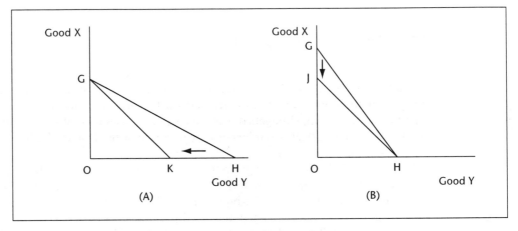

Figure 2.8   **Rises in prices**

In Figure 2.8 (A) the original budget line is GH. If the price of good Y rises and the price of good X stays the same, then less of good Y can be bought for the same amount of money. The budget line will stay the same at point G (because the price of good X has not changed and if all the budget was spent on good X then OG could be bought). The budget line on the other axis will move from point H to the new point K. As good Y has become more expensive OK of good Y can now be bought if all the budget was spent on this good. To represent this the budget line pivots from point G to the new point K. This gives a different slope to the budget line and will probably mean that it will touch a new indifference curve, giving lower levels of satisfaction.

Figure 2.8 (B) represents a rise in the price of good X rather than good Y. In this case the original budget line GH pivots on point H (as the price of good Y is unchanged) and joins the new point J. The movement from point G to point J shows how much less of the more expensive product can be bought for the same budget. Just as in Figure 2.8 (A), the new budget line HJ will probably touch a new (lower) indifference curve representing the lower satisfaction gained as the result of the effect of increasing prices.

Example analysis

Figure 2.9 shows an example of an analysis using the ideas introduced in this chapter.

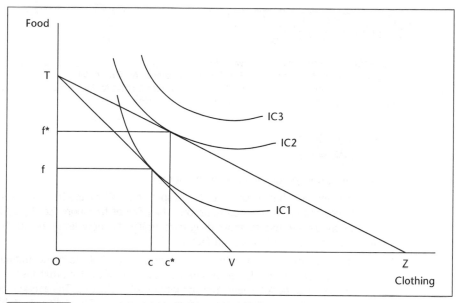

Figure 2.9   **Household budget analysis**

A household has a budget of £100 for food and clothing and this is represented by the budget line TV. With this level of spending they are able to obtain the level of consumer satisfaction associated with IC1 by purchasing Of level of food plus Oc level of clothing. The prices of some of the items of clothing fall as various retailers put on their summer sales, and this means that the household budget will stretch even further. The new budget line TZ represents the fall in price of clothing. The household now is able to obtain an even greater level of consumer satisfaction by purchasing the new combination of goods represented by the new (higher) indifference curve; namely Of* level of food plus Oc* level of clothing.

More food and more clothing can be purchased as the result of some price reductions. The same effect as if there was an increase in income.

Summary

Before looking at the way in which markets work, it has been the objective of this chapter to introduce the basic ideas behind consumer theory. It is necessarily difficult, as much of consumer behaviour is psychological and not available to public scrutiny. But it is individuals who collectively decide how markets behave. In this respect the equi-marginal principle is important, because people do try to maximise their 'value for money'.

Indifference curve analysis helps us to see the effect that changing prices can have upon consumers as they substitute cheaper goods for some of the more expensive goods in order to increase their total satisfaction. (Marginal rate of substitution).

Further reading

ANDERTON, A., *Economics,* Causeway Press.
BEGG, D., FISCHER, S. and DORNBUSCH, R. *Economics,* McGraw-Hill.
HARDWICK, P., KHAN, B. and LANGMEAD, J. *An Introduction to Modern Economics*, Longman.
ISON, S. *Economics*, M&E: Pitman Publishing.

Test your understanding

(Answers are provided at the back of the book.)

1. A consumer has a budget of £150. This is spent on clothes and transport, such that OC is spent on clothes and OT is spent on transport. The price of transport rises by 50 per cent.

    You should be able to show diagrammatically the new levels of purchases and make an assessment as to the level of satisfaction.

2. You are given the following information. A person has £146 to spend and has decided to spend it on clothes and videos. There are a number of items of clothing that she wants. Also she would like to buy a number of videos. She cannot buy all she wants. The average price of clothing per item is £22.50p and the average video price is £14. The following table summarises the quantities of each commodity and the marginal utility that she would get from each item.

    How many of each item should she buy to maximise her total utility?

Clothing		Videos	
Quantity (Q)	Marginal utility (MU)	Quantity (Q)	Marginal utility (MU)
0		0	
1	90	1	60
2	78	2	51
3	66	3	42
4	54	4	33
5	42	5	24
		6	15
		7	6
		8	3

3. Explain, in 150 words or less, how the following formula indicates how consumers should spend their money if they wish to maximise their total utility.

    $$\frac{Mua}{Pa} = \frac{MUb}{Pb} = \frac{MUc}{Pc} = \frac{Mud}{Pd}$$

4. Give a brief explanation (no more than 75 words) as to why indifference curves can never touch or cross each other.

5. Which of the following statements are correct
    A   Marginal utility is total utility divided by the number of units consumed
    B   Average utility will always rise because total utility is always increasing
    C   As total utility is always rising it follows that marginal utility is always rising
    D   Marginal utility is the extra utility gained from consuming one more unit
    E   Average utility is always higher than marginal utility when marginal utility is rising

6. Referring to the diagrams below, which of the following statements are correct?

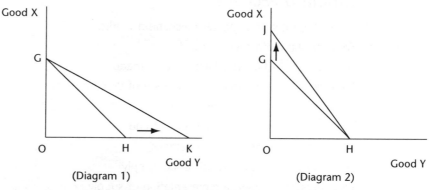

(Diagram 1)   (Diagram 2)

    A   Good X is cheaper in diagram1 and more expensive in diagram 2
    B   Good Y is cheaper in diagram1 and more expensive in diagram 2
    C   Good Y is more expensive in diagram 1 and good X is cheaper in diagram 2
    D   Good X is more expensive in diagram 1 and good Y is cheaper in diagram 2
    E   Good Y is cheaper in diagram 1 and good X is cheaper in diagram 2

7. Referring to the diagram below, which of the following statements are correct?

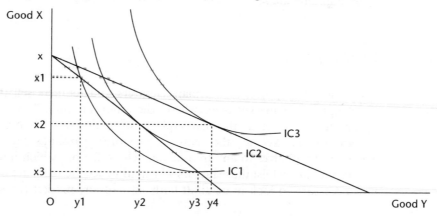

    A $0x1+0y1$ and $0x2+0y2$ and $0x3+0y3$ are all combinations of good X and good Y that
        can be afforded within the given budget.
    B $0x2+0y2$ are the combination giving the highest total satisfaction before the price of
        good Y fell.
    C $0x1+0y1$ and $0x3+0y3$ are combinations which give the same levels of total
        satisfaction.
    D   The price of good X has not changed.
    E   After the price of good Y falls the same amount of good X is bought but more of good Y
        is bought.

3 The market

Learning objectives

To understand how the market mechanism works.

- To understand effective demand
- To be aware of factors which affect demand
- To understand graphical representation of demand
- To be able to distinguish between:
  - Expansion and contractions of demand
  - Increases and decreases in demand
- To be aware of factors which affect supply
- To understand graphical representation of supply
- To be able to distinguish between:
  - Expansion and contractions of supply
  - Increases and decreases in supply
- To be able to explain the idea of market equilibrium by representing demand and supply on the same graph

3.1 Introduction

Consumers buy products and manufacturers and retailers sell their products in the 'marketplace'. A market is anywhere where buyers and sellers communicate. Thus a telephone line is often the marketplace for mail order shopping, whilst the more recognisable markets are the many shops, stores, warehouses and even market stalls. There are two halves to any transaction. Those factors which influence the buyer are on the one side, whilst those factors which influence the seller are on the other side. It is now necessary to look in detail at both sides of any market transaction.

3.2 The theory of demand – the buyer's side

In the last chapter we looked at how individual consumers behave to maximise their satisfaction from spending their income. We now turn attention to those factors which influence many individuals in their collective demand for any product. We are now looking at the demand for beef, or chicken, or small motor cars, or houses or any other product or service; and so on.

Demand defined

Just because a person would like a product, or wishes for a product, is not what the economist calls demand. The person who is 'window shopping' but has no money does not have demand in the economic sense. Demand is a want backed by the ability to pay. *In this sense demand is* effective demand.

Factors which affect demand

For each individual there are many factors to be taken into consideration before the budget is spent. Many of the most influential factors are concerned with how a person feels and other psychological states. As a starting point the economist takes some of the more observable factors and tries to assess their influence. This is done by an analytical method called *comparative statics*. One fixed position is compared to another fixed position, and this will become clear as the analysis proceeds.

The quantity demanded of any product will depend upon, and will therefore be a function of, among other things, the price of the product, the prices of all other products, income available, wealth and general tastes.

This is a bit of a mouthful to keep repeating so it will be reduced to a few symbols, rather like a code. Once we know what the symbols stand for we can use them instead of sentences.

$$Qd = f(Pg, Pn \ldots Pn - 1, Y, W, T)$$

This is a *functional relationship* and it is code for the paragraph in italics above. It is not mathematics. It is rather like a foreign language, once you know what the symbols stand for you can understand and speak the language – so it is with economic code.

Qd	stands for the quantity demanded of a product
$= f$	stands for 'depends upon' or 'is a function of'
Pg	stands for the price of the good
Pn...n − 1	stands for the prices of all other goods
Y	stands for income. *In economics this letter invariably stands for income*
W	stands for wealth
T	stands for tastes. In this usage anything which makes a consumer 'feel' positive or negative about a product is thought of as 'tastes'

These factors will now be considered in detail.

Pg – the price of the good

The price of a product is thought to be the single most influential factor which consumers take into consideration.

Pn . . . n − 1 − the prices of all other goods

Consumers spend their money on a variety of goods, often referred to by economists as 'baskets of goods'. Thus if the prices of some goods go down this means that there is more money, in the budget, to be spent on other goods. Similarly if prices of goods rise, there is less to spend on other goods. It is by this reasoning that the prices of other, unrelated goods, will have an effect upon the demand for any product. This effect was seen in Chapter 2 – indifference curve analysis – where changes in the prices of unrelated goods caused the budget line to move.

Example

What is the relationship between the price of butter, eggs, milk, bread; and the demand for certain clothes, or the demand for entertainment.

For people on a restricted budget, and most budgets are restricted in some degree, if the prices of the basic foods rise then there may be insufficient left in the weekly budget to pay for the necessary schoolclothes, or to pay for the weekly trip to the cinema. Many families on low incomes are often faced with this prospect, and have to postpone the purchase of necessary items because the prices of some unrelated goods have risen.

The price rise which affects almost everyone's budget is the mortgage, or rent on one's house.

Y − income

In general terms, as consumers' incomes rise these consumers will demand more of many products. They may also switch from buying some products to others which they previously could not afford. People who have low incomes often buy products which they consider to be 'inferior' to other products which they would prefer, but which they cannot afford. A good example of this would be black and white televisions. Most people consider colour televisions to be 'normal' but for those who cannot afford a colour television a black and white one may be an affordable, though inferior, option.

W − wealth

There can be little doubt that wealth has some effect upon demand, but the precise connection is often unclear. Wealth is defined as **the value of everything one owns**. The most valuable possession for most people is their house. There are reported to be many older people on small fixed pensions who live in houses worth many hundreds of thousands of pounds. Because they are seen to be living in 'well-to-do circumstances' they can often obtain credit from local shopkeepers and businesses. These people often have difficulty finding the income to support their spending patterns, and this type of situation is an example where wealth directly influences demand, even when income is very restricted. The other point to be made here is that wealth can often be converted into spending power, the only question being how quickly?

T – tastes

This is a catch-all category and arguably the most important influence upon demand. Tastes include the ideas people have about 'value' and often centre upon issues such as 'quality', 'fashion', 'political influence', 'morality' and straightforward 'preferences'. Tastes are inextricably bound up with our psychological influences and these play a major role in determining what products we are prepared to buy. This role is not diminished because we do not fully understand the mechanisms by which people choose to demand some products whilst avoiding others. The importance of the price of the good, referred to above, comes after a consumer has decided what is preferred and what is not wanted, *at any price*.

Some examples of how TASTE influences demand

1. Many people who support animal welfare issues will not eat meat. Their **taste** is to avoid meat and they therefore will not have a demand for meat. This **taste** decision will however affect their demand for vegetarian foods.

2. Many people will not buy products which are made in certain countries where human rights are abused. This would be an example of a political or moral influence upon **tastes.**

3. Many people demand products which have been produced in an environmentally friendly manner, or which have not been tested upon animals. There may be many complex psychological reasons underpinning these **tastes.**

4. In various research findings the single most important factor which consumers look for in any product is quality. The consumer's perception of quality is therefore a powerful influence in their **taste** for or against a product.

The graphical representation of demand

In all elementary economics texts demand is represented by a downward sloping straight line. Why this is so, and what the line represents, will now be explained.

Just considering the price of a product, it is usually true that as the price goes up demand falls, and as the price falls demand rises. Demand and price are moving in opposite directions, and therefore **demand is said to be inversely related to price**. If this relationship was not correct then there would be no point in retailers reducing prices for sales, for the purpose of a sale is to sell more products *because* the price has fallen. The line which establishes this relationship is one that slopes downwards from left to right, as in Figure 3.1.

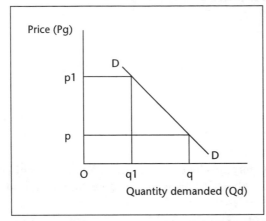

Figure 3.1 **The relationship between the price of a normal good and the demand for that good**

In Figure 3.1 if we start with price Op we see that Oq quantity will be demanded at that price. If price now rises to Op1 quantity demanded will fall to Oq1. If we started with a price of Op1 then quantity demanded would be Oq1. If price now falls to Op demand will rise to Oq. It is the demand curve DD which establishes this relationship.

It will be noticed that in Figure 3.1 two of the factors in the functional relationship appear on the axes of the graph. The price of the good (Pg) is measured on the vertical axis and the quantity demanded (Qd) is measured on the horizontal axis. The question arises, how are all the other factors represented? All the other factors $(Pn\ldots Pn-1, Y, W, T)$ are assumed to be unchanging and are represented by the demand curve itself. Thus all the factors which help to determine a consumer's demand are incorporated into the demand curve, and held constant (or unchanging). The only two factors, from the above functional relationship, which change freely are quantity demanded (Qd) and the price of the product (Pg). By changing the price and holding all other factors constant, economists can theorise as to how demand will change in response to changes in price.

The DEMAND FUNCTIONAL RELATIONSHIP

$$Qd = f(Pg, Pn\ldots Pn - 1, Y, W, T)$$

Holding factors constant is rather like taking a snapshot. The snapshot only applies truly for the precise moment it is taken, after which things change. It is the same for these factors which help to influence demand. They are only a particular value at any instant, after which they are constantly changing. With constantly changing values

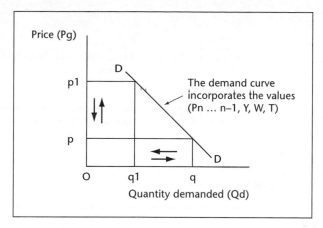

Figure 3.2 **The demand functional relationship**

economists would find it impossible to have a theoretical model which they could use to examine the mechanisms that make the market work. Thus they simplify reality by assuming that a number of important factors are constant or unchanging *at any one time*. This assumption is known as the ***ceteris paribus*** assumption.

Figure 3.2 represents the position arrived at so far. The quantity demanded will change depending only upon how the price of the product changes, all other factors *ceteris paribus*.

Changes in the price of the good (Pg)

If the price of the product changes the result of this change is measured by changes in quantity demanded. Notice that in order to register the change in quantity demanded there is a movement **along the existing demand curve.** This movement along an existing demand curve is called either an **expansion** of demand or a **contraction** of demand.

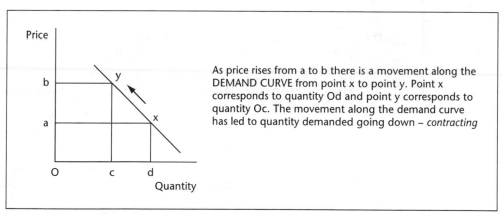

Figure 3.3 **Contraction of demand**

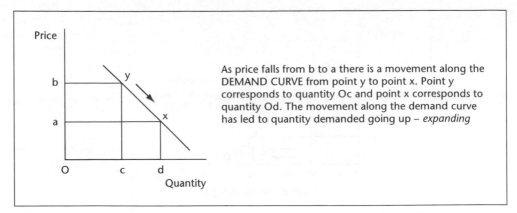

As price falls from b to a there is a movement along the DEMAND CURVE from point y to point x. Point y corresponds to quantity Oc and point x corresponds to quantity Od. The movement along the demand curve has led to quantity demanded going up – *expanding*

Figure 3.4 **Expansion of demand**

Changes in any of the factors held constant (*ceteris paribus*)

If any of the factors which have been held constant change then the whole demand curve shifts. We said earlier that the demand curve represented all of the other factors *ceteris paribus*. Therefore if any of the factors change, there will have to be a new demand curve to represent the new level of these factors – this new level once more held constant. Every time that we wish to acknowledge a change in **Pn...Pn-1** or in **Y** or in **W** or in **T** or even a change in all of these at the same time, a new demand curve is necessary. If, say, income increases then demand is likely to **increase** and the new demand curve will be placed to the **right** of the old demand curve; that is further away from the origin. If, say, tastes changed and a product went out of fashion then demand is likely to **decrease** and the new demand curve will be placed to the **left** of the old demand curve; that is closer to the origin. If any factor other than the price of the product changes, there is a new demand curve and demand either **increases** or **decreases.**

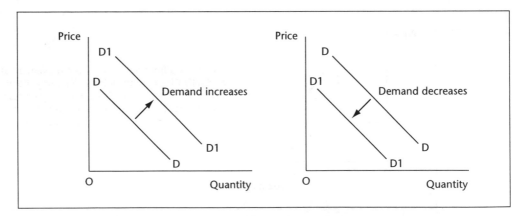

Figure 3.5 **The graphical representation of increases and decreases in demand**

A decrease or an increase in demand is distinguished from a contraction or an expansion. The main distinction is that one is a movement **along** a demand curve, whilst the other involves a movement **of** the demand curve. The use of these different words allows economists to be precise when emphasising forces which may be influential in any market situation.

$$Qd = f (\boxed{Pg} \quad \boxed{Pn \ldots Pn-1, \ Y, \ W, \ T})$$

A change in this factor leads to either an EXPANSION or a CONTRACTION in the quantity demanded (Qd).	A change in any of these factors leads to either an INCREASE or a DECREASE in the quantity demanded (Qd).

3.3 The theory of supply – the seller's side

Market supply refers to the quantities of any particular product which individual firms (suppliers) are collectively willing to make available at the various prices.

The quantity supplied of any product will depend upon, and will therefore be a function of, among other things, the price of the product, the prices of all other component products, the prices and availability of the factors of production, the current state of technology, the availability of storage to provide for buffer stocks, and other unspecified variables.

As this is a bit of a mouthful to keep repeating it will be reduced to a few symbols, rather like a code. Once we know what the symbols stand for we can use them instead of sentences.

$$Qs = f (Pg, \ Pc \ldots Pc - 1, \ Pfp \ldots Pfp - 1, \ Tech, \ St, \ A)$$

This is a *functional relationship* and it is code for the paragraph in italics above.

Qs	stands for the quantity of a product which suppliers are willing to supply
$=f$	stands for 'depends upon' or 'is a function of'
Pg	stands for the price of the good
Pc ... c − 1	stands for the prices of all component products
Pfp ... Pfp − 1	stands for the prices of the various factors of production
Tech	stands for the current state of technology
St	stands for the available level of storage or buffer stocks
A	stands for all other factors which influence the quantity which suppliers are willing to supply

These factors will now be considered in detail.

Pg – the price of the good

The prices which consumers are willing to pay for any product are likely to have a major influence upon the amount of that product supplied to the market. If prices are high and are expected to remain high, or keep rising, then suppliers will be anxious to supply more of the product so as to capture the increased revenue which results from higher prices. If the market prices are low, or are falling, then suppliers will not be as anxious to supply the market and may even consider restricting production of the product in favour of alternative products, which would sell for better prices and generate higher income.

The suppliers (the various firms producing for the market) are interested in producing revenue from the sale of their goods. They have already incurred the costs of production, and in order to recover these costs they will be attracted by higher prices, which generate higher revenues. They will be less attracted by low prices which may leave them in danger of not recovering their costs.

Pc . . . Pc – 1 – the prices of all component products

Very few products are produced from the pure natural raw materials, steel is perhaps one of the few. Most products require a variety of semi-manufactured products or semi-finished products as inputs before a final good can be produced. Clearly the availability of these various inputs is an important constraint upon any supplier. The prices of the inputs may form a major part of the cost structure of the final product.

An example is the car industry. The major car manufacturers buy in many hundreds of components. These include the body shells, the engines, the wheels, the tyres, the seats, the glass, the electrical parts, the upholstery, the wipers and rubber wiper blades, and many other parts. If there is a problem with the supply of any of these components there will be a knock-on effect in the supply of the finished product in the retail car market. Similarly if the prices of these components are rising there will be pressure for car manufacturers to look for increasing prices in the retail market.

Pfp . . . Pfp – 1 – the prices of the factors of production

Labour and machinery are among the factors of production. (The factors of production are considered in detail in the next chapter). The costs (wages, salaries etc.) of skilled workers will have a direct effect upon the costs of production, and therefore on the costs of the final product.

Tech – the current state of technology

This is a very important factor underpinning the supply curve. Most products are manufactured with a view to producing as much as possible as cheaply as possible. Production efficiency depends upon a number of factors but one of the most important is the state of technology. If a new technique for producing CDs is discovered, such that it becomes very much cheaper to produce increased quantities, then firms not employing this new technology will not be able to compete in the market. Not all technology is part of the public knowledge. Some firms spend vast sums of money on research and development and may wish to keep secret any technical developments they make, so that they can gain a market advantage. This is particularly the case with the major drug companies who can protect their research discoveries from the competition by means of patents.

St – the availability of storage or buffer stocks

It is easy to assume that if the market price of a product rises then more will be supplied. This is not always the case. Only where a manufacturer can respond flexibly to produce more of the product, or has more of the product in storage, can there be a reasonably fast response to price. It is clear that in the case of agricultural produce, there are severe limits on what extra can be supplied at any price. As the crop takes a period of time to grow, and only a finite amount was planted or sown, it follows that flexibility of supply is severely limited. Where manufacturers are producing products which are not too perishable and which can be stored for a reasonable period of time, they often have a system of warehouses so as to be able to respond swiftly to changes in market demand or market price. However, storage costs are high and increasingly seen as an unjustifiable overhead. It depends upon how important it is to be flexible as a market supplier.

The graphical representation of supply

Supply is represented by an upward sloping straight line. Why this is so, and what the line represents, will now be explained.

Just considering the price of a product; it is usually true that as the price goes up suppliers wish to sell more and as the price falls they wish to sell less. The price of the product and supply are moving in the same direction, and therefore **supply is said to be directly related to price**. The line which establishes this relationship is one that slopes upwards from left to right, as in the following example.

In Figure 3.6 if we start with price Op we see that Oq quantity will be supplied at that price. If price now rises to Op1 the quantity supplied will rise to Oq1. If we started

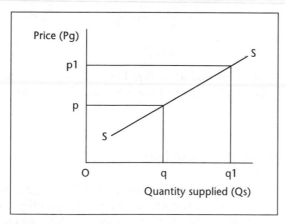

Figure 3.6   **The representation of supply**

with a price of Op1 then quantity supplied would be Oq1. If price now falls to Op the quantity supplied will fall to Oq. It is the supply curve SS which establishes this relationship.

It will be noticed that in Figure 3.6 two of the factors in the functional relationship appear on the axes of the graph. The price of the good (Pg) is measured on the vertical axis and the quantity supplied (Qs) is measured on the horizontal axis. All the other factors (Pc ... Pc − 1, Pfp ... Pfp − 1, Tech, St, A) are assumed to be unchanging and are represented by the supply curve itself. Thus all the factors which help to determine a firm's market supply are incorporated into the supply curve, and held constant (or unchanging). The only two factors, from the above functional relationship, which change freely are quantity supplied (Qs) and the price of the product (Pg). By changing the price and holding all other factors constant, economists can theorise as to how supply will change in response to changes in price.

The SUPPLY FUNCTIONAL RELATIONSHIP

$$Qs = f\,(Pg,\ Pc \ldots Pc - 1,\ Pfp \ldots Pfp - 1,\ Tech,\ St,\ A)$$

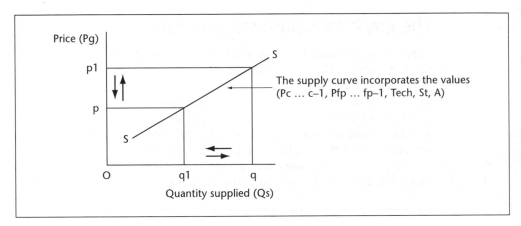

Figure 3.7 Supply functional relationship

Figure 3.7 represents the position arrived at so far. The quantity supplied will change depending only upon how the market price of the product changes, all other factors *ceteris paribus*.

Changes in the market price of the good (Pg)

If the market price of the product changes the result of this change is measured by changes in quantity supplied. In order to register the change in quantity supplied there is a movement **along the existing supply curve.** This movement along an existing supply curve is called either an **expansion** of supply or a **contraction** of supply.

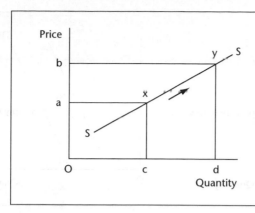

As price rises from a to b there is a movement along the SUPPLY CURVE from point x to point y. Point x corresponds to quantity Oc and point y corresponds to quantity Od. The movement along the supply curve has led to quantity supplied going up – *expanding*

Figure 3.8   **Expansion of supply**

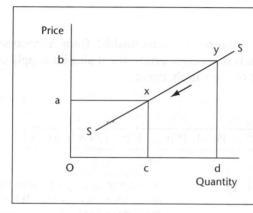

As price falls from b to a there is a movement along the SUPPLY CURVE from point y to point x. Point y corresponds to quantity Od and point x corresponds to quantity Oc. The movement along the supply curve has led to quantity supplied going down – *contracting*

Figure 3.9   **Contraction of supply**

Changes in any of the factors held constant (*ceteris paribus*)

If any of the factors which have been held constant change then the whole supply curve shifts. The supply curve represents all of the other factors, *ceteris paribus*. Therefore if any of the factors change, there will have to be a new supply curve to represent the new level of these factors. This new level once more held constant. Every time that we wish to acknowledge a change in **Pc … Pc-1,** or in **Pfp … Pfp-1,** or in **Tech,** or in **St,** or in **A** or even a change in all of these at the same time, a new supply curve is necessary. If, say, technology changes and leads to improved productivity then supply is likely to **increase** and the new supply curve will be placed to the **right** of the old supply curve, to represent the new conditions of supply. If, say there were excessive wage claims, or there was a shortage of input components leading to higher prices, then supply is likely to **decrease** and the new supply curve will be placed to the **left** of the old supply curve, to represent these new conditions affecting the suppliers. If any factor other than the market price of the product changes, there is a new supply curve and supply either **increases** or **decreases.**

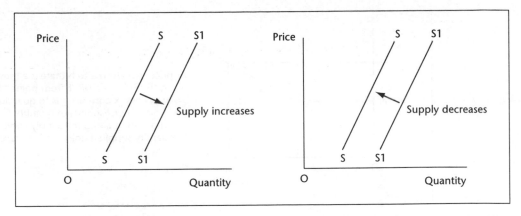

Figure 3.10 **The graphical representation of increases and decreases in supply**

A decrease or an increase in supply is distinguished from a contraction or an expansion. The main distinction is that one is a movement along a supply curve, whilst the other involves a movement of the supply curve.

$$Qs = f(\;\boxed{Pg}\;\boxed{Pc \ldots Pc-1,\; Pfp \ldots Pfp-1,\; Tech,\; St,\; A}\;)$$

A change in this factor leads to either an EXPANSION or a CONTRACTION in the quantity supplied (Qs).

A change in any of these factors leads to either an INCREASE or a DECREASE in the quantity supplied (Qs).

3.4 The market – where buyers and sellers communicate

So far demand and supply have been treated separately. However they have a number of features in common; they are both illustrated in graphs with price (Pg) and quantity (Q) on the axes, and they both have all the other factors held constant (*ceteris paribus*) in the curves themselves. It is now possible to illustrate both these curves on the same graph, and thus represent both sides of the market.

Figure 3.11 represents the market. There is only one point where the quantity that consumers wish to buy, at the price they are prepared to pay, is equal to the quantity that suppliers are willing to supply at that same price. This is where the two curves intersect – they are equal at this point.

Thus Oq quantity is demanded and supplied at price Op. This unique market position is called **market equilibrium.**

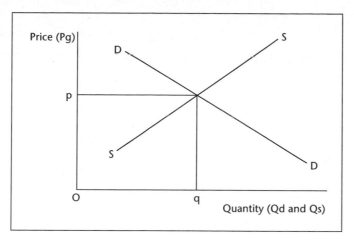

Figure 3.11 The representation of supply and demand – the market

Market equilibrium

There is a tendency for the market price to remain at the equilibrium level. The market forces – that is the pressure of demand and supply – act together to make this so. This important conclusion is illustrated below.

Assume that the market price in Figure 3.12 is Op1, which is above the equilibrium price of Op. At the price of Op1 quantity Oq1 is demanded and quantity Oq2 is supplied. Oq2 is greater than Oq1 and so there is an excess of supply over demand. This is not surprising as demand will fall as price rises, but suppliers will be anxious to supply more as price rises. As there is excess supply the price will have to fall, if suppliers are to sell their stocks. Again, this is not surprising as consumers are only prepared to demand more if the price falls. The conclusion is:

> that for any market price above the equilibrium price there will be pressure for price to fall towards the equilibrium price.

Now, assume that the market price in Figure 3.12 is Op2, which is below the equilibrium price of Op. At the price of Op2 quantity Oq4 is demanded and quantity Oq3 is supplied. Oq4 is greater than Oq3 and so there is an excess of demand over supply. This is not surprising as demand will rise as price falls, but suppliers will not wish to supply very much to a market with low or falling prices. As there is excess demand the price will have to rise as consumers compete to buy the products in short supply. The conclusion is:

> that for any market price below the equilibrium price there will be pressure for price to rise towards the equilibrium price.

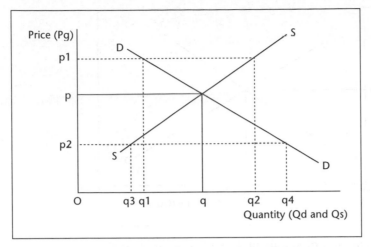

Figure 3.12 Pressures for prices to move towards the equilibrium market price

REMEMBER

Price higher than equilibrium price ⟶ *pressure for price to fall*
Price lower than equilibrium price ⟶ *pressure for price to rise*

Only at the market equilibrium price is there no pressure for price to either rise of fall. At this unique price consumers and suppliers agreee.

Changes in conditions of demand or supply

There are other factors, within the demand and supply functions, which can change. These are those factors held, *ceteris paribus*. If any of these factors change then, as has already been discussed a new demand or supply curve is necessary to represent the new factors. In Figure 3.13 both the conditions of demand and supply have changed.

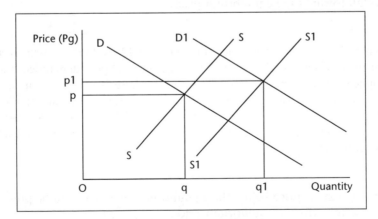

Figure 3.13 The effect of changes in conditions of supply and demand

In Figure 3.13 demand has increased from D to D1 and supply has increased from S to S1. The original equilibrium price was OP and the equilibrium quantity OQ. The new equilibrium price has risen slightly and this reflects the willingness of consumers to pay more for what they see as a more attractive product – *for whatever reasons*. The equilibrium quantity has also risen, reflecting the new demand conditions and the willingness (and ability) of suppliers to offer more for sale at higher prices. The following example shows a sequence of events which might have led to the above situation.

EXAMPLE

Assumptions

Let us assume that it is the market for fish.

Assume as an example that there have been a series of reports in the press concerning the health risks associated with eating beef and lamb. In addition to these negative reports nutritionists have been widely publicising the benefits of eating more fish and fruit.

Assume as an example that there have been reports of two significant benefits to the UK fishing fleet. Firstly the quota of fish tonnages that may be landed, have been raised by 20 per cent. Secondly a new type of net is being used, which allows small fish to escape whilst catching more of the marketable size of fish. The result of these two benefits is that the fishing industry expects to be more profitable.

Analysis of Example

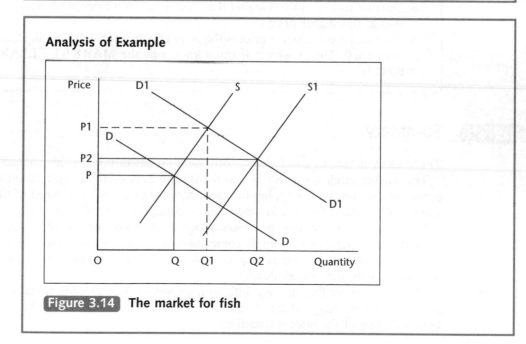

Figure 3.14 The market for fish

Starting point

The market is in equilibrium with OQ quantity of fish being demanded and supplied at price OP. At this stage there is no pressure for price or quantity to change.

Conditions of demand change

The reported health risks associated with meat eating and the advertised benefits from fish have had the effect of changing consumer's tastes. People are prepared to consume more fish *even if it costs them a little more*. The extra demand for fish is represented by the new demand curve D1. Under these new conditions consumers are prepared to pay very much higher prices OP1 for a small increase in quantity supplied OQ1.

Conditions of supply change

The fishermen want to bring more to market to benefit from the higher prices and increased demand, but are initially restricted by the amount they can catch and land. With the new quotas and the new net technology they are able to catch very much more fish, and therefore can increase their supply to the market. This they do, represented by the new supply curve S1. As more is now brought to market the consumers are prepared to consume the extra fish only if the price falls a little. The new equilibrium price is thus P2 and at this price all the extra supplies of fish are sold.

Conclusions

- The new market price is higher than the old market price, and much more is sold at this higher price.
- The market equilibrium price is the price at which the market will clear all it has to sell. This is why it is often known as the MARKET CLEARING PRICE.

3.5 Summary

The student should be comfortable with the ideas introduced in this chapter.

The market mechanism will be put forward in part or total explanation for many economic situations. This applies to macro-economics as well as the rest of this micro-section. When the term 'market mechanism' is applied it is often a shorthand way of referring to the adjustment processes which have been introduced in this chapter. Increases in demand and in supply come about for a number of reasons and it is often the reasons which are made explicit followed by a statement such as; 'market adjustment will bring prices down'.

The theory of the firm, money, inflation, employment and international trade are all areas of future study where it will be assumed that the student has a familiar understanding of the price mechanism.

The student should be particularly familiar with:

- How various conditions of demand move the demand curve. Either an increase or decrease in demand. Remember: CHANGES IN THE PRICE OF THE GOOD DO NOT MOVE THE DEMAND CURVE.
- How various supply conditions can change the supply curve. Either an increase or decrease in supply. CHANGES IN THE PRICE OF THE GOOD DO NOT MOVE THE SUPPLY CURVE.
- When price is established above or below the market equilibrium price, there will be an adjustment process bringing pressure on the market to return to equilibrium. The same process operates if demand and supply are out of balance for any reason. THIS IS AN IMPORTANT PROCESS TO UNDERSTAND.
- The prices of all goods will have an effect upon any single product market. Especially the prices and conditions of demand and supply for SUBSTITUTES and COMPLEMENTS.

Further reading

ANDERTON, A., *Economics,* Causeway Press.
BEGG, D., FISCHER, S. and DORNBUSCH, R. *Economics,* McGraw-Hill.
GRIFFITHS, A. and WALL, S. *Applied Economics,* Longman.
HARDWICK, P., KHAN, B. and LANGMEAD, J. *An Introduction to Modern Economics,* Longman.
ISON, S. *Economics,* M&E: Pitman Publishing.

Test your understanding

(Answers are provided at the back of the book.)

1. List 4 factors, in each of the following cases, which might have an influence on a consumer's demand for
   A   Fish
   B   Summer clothes
   C   Overseas holidays.

2. In 75 words, or less, explain why a normal demand curve slopes downwards from left to right.

3. *Ceteris paribus* is an assumption made because:

   i   The use of Latin improves the credibility of the subject.
   ii   In comparative static analysis all variables move at the same time.
   iii   In comparative static analysis only the influence of one variable can be examined at any one time.

4. Complete the following sentences.

   An increase in demand is where . . . .
   A contraction of demand is where . . . .
   A decrease in demand is where . . . .
   An expansion of demand is where . . . .

5. List 4 factors which affect the supply of:
   A   Fish
   B   Vegetables
   C   Fashion clothes

6. In the market illustrated by the diagram the price is fixed at OP. The Trade Association agrees to buy up any quantity left unsold at that price. Which area in the graph represents the amount of money the Trade Association will have to spend?

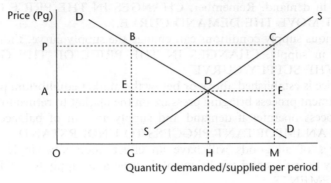

Quantity demanded/supplied per period

7. The following diagram shows the original market equilibrium position, in the fish market, at point K (where demand (D) equals supply (S)). The various other points represent movements along the demand and supply curves and shifts in the demand and supply curves.

    If fishing quotas are halved by the government, to conserve fish stocks, and the latest medical research indicates that if people ate twice as much more fish they would be protected against heart disease: what would be the new market equilibrium?

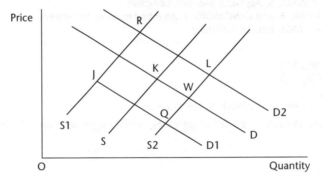

8. Refer to the diagram in question (7).

    Starting at point K. What point would represent an increase in supply followed by a contraction of demand?

9. In the diagram the market price of OP will have to rise? Explain why this is so, and explain in detail the mechanism by which price is likely to rise.

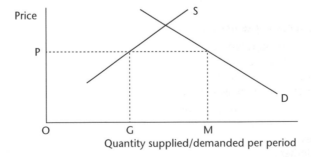

Quantity supplied/demanded per period

4 Elasticity

Learning objectives

- To understand the concept of elasticity and to be able to use the concept to explain the pricing decisions of businesses.
- To understand that elasticity is defined in terms of changes in total revenue.
- To be able to explain and distinguish between:
  - Price elasticity of demand
  - Income elasticity of demand
  - Cross price elasticity of demand
- To be aware of the factors which determine the various levels of demand elasticity for different products and services.
- To be able to define and distinguish between normal, inferior and superior goods.
- To be able to calculate elasticity values from basic data.

4.1 Introduction

The demand curve slopes downward from left to right. It therefore follows that as the price of a product falls more will be demanded. This is known as an expansion of demand. It is at this point that an interesting question arises, namely how much will the quantity demanded change in response to given changes in the price of the product? This is an important question for firms who want to know if they can put the price of their products up, without risking the loss of too many customers. Similarly, if they put their prices down, will enough extra demand be created to make it worthwhile. Firms are concerned with increasing their total revenue. Therefore to know how their pricing decisions will affect their total revenue is of crucial importance.

> **NOTE** It is often assumed that firms only seek to maximise their profits. This has frequently been an assumption to simplify much of the analysis, and this idea will come up again in future chapters. However, firms have many different objectives and in most cases it is not inconsistent with the various objectives for firms to wish to increase their revenue.
>
> A fuller discussion of the various objectives of the firm is given in Chapter 6.

Elasticity defined

The idea of elasticity refers to the **responsiveness** of demand. Demand will respond to changes in any of the variables discussed on page 19. The more responsive demand is, the more elastic it is said to be; and the less responsive it is, the less elastic it is said to be. There are different types of elasticity and each is defined in terms of the demand variable, which causes the change in demand. Thus if price (Pg) of the product is the cause of the demand changing then the elasticity measured is **price elasticity.** If demand changes because there has been a change in consumer's income (Y) then the elasticity measured is **income elasticity.** If demand changes because there has been a change in the prices of other goods (Pn...Pn1) then the elasticity measured is **cross price elasticity**. Each of these elasticities will be examined in turn.

4.2   Price elasticity of demand

This is the responsiveness of quantity demanded as the result of changes in the price of the product (see Figure 4.1).

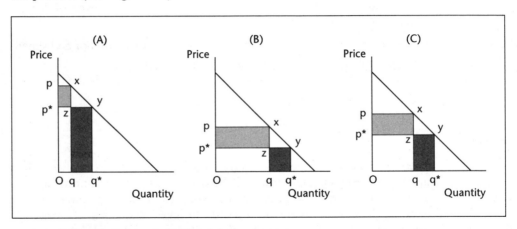

Figure 4.1   **Quantity demanded as a result of price changes**

TOTAL REVENUE

Total revenue is the quantity sold multiplied by the price at which it is sold. Thus in the diagrams above this is Op multiplied by Oq – or Op* multiplied by Oq*. In Figure 4.1(A) the rectangle that represents Op multiplied by Oq is Opxq. In Figure 4.1(B) the rectangle that represents Op* multiplied by Oq* is Op*yq*.

In diagram (A) price has fallen from p to p* and this has led to an increase in quantity demanded from q to q*. When price was at p the total revenue was represented by the rectangle Opxq. When price fell to Op* the total revenue was represented by the rectangle Op*yq*. Rectangle p*pxz shows the total revenue lost by reducing the price for the original quantity demanded of Oq. Rectangle qzyq* shows the total revenue gained from the expansion of demand to Oq*. It is clear that total revenue has increased.

Where a reduction in the price of the product leads to an increase in total revenue, demand is said to be PRICE ELASTIC.

In diagram (B) price has fallen from p to p* and this has led to an increase in quantity demanded from q to q*. When price was at p the total revenue was represented by the rectangle Opxq. When price fell to Op* the total revenue was represented by the rectangle Op*yq*. Rectangle p*pxz shows the total revenue lost by reducing the price for the original quantity demanded of Oq. Rectangle qzyq* shows the total revenue gained from the expansion of demand to Oq*. It is clear that total revenue has decreased.

Where a reduction in the price of the product leads to a decrease in total revenue, demand is said to be PRICE INELASTIC.

In diagram (C) price has fallen from p to p* and this has led to an increase in quantity demanded from q to q*. When price was at p the total revenue was represented by the rectangle Opxq. When price fell to Op* the total revenue was represented by the rectangle Op*yq*. Rectangle p*pxz shows the total revenue lost by reducing the price for the original quantity demanded of Oq. Rectangle qzyq* shows the total revenue gained from the expansion of demand to Oq*. In this case the amount of total revenue lost is the same as the amount of total revenue gained and therefore total revenue remains unchanged.

Where a reduction in the price of the product leads to no change in total revenue, demand is said to be PRICE UNIT-ELASTIC.

PRICE ELASTICITY AND TOTAL REVENUE

Price elasticity is determined by CHANGES IN TOTAL REVENUE

The following table summarises the various price elasticities of demand and their effect upon total revenue.

PRICE ELASTICITY OF DEMAND AND TOTAL REVENUE

Price Elasticity of Demand	Price change	Effect upon Total Revenue
Elastic	Price falls	Total revenue increases
Inelastic	Price falls	Total revenue decreases
Unit Elasticity	Price falls	Total revenue remains unchanged
Elastic	Price rises	Total revenue decreases
Inelastic	Price rises	Total revenue increases
Unit Elasticity	Price rises	Total revenue remains unchanged

Measuring price elasticity

Price elasticity of demand is measured by the following formula:

$$\frac{\text{The percentage change in quantity demanded}}{\text{The percentage change in the price of the product}}$$

The reader will often see this calculation represented by symbols. The above will now be transformed into a symbol format. Just as in earlier chapters, there is no mathematics introduced, it is just a matter of understanding the symbols and doing some elementary repositioning.

Symbols defined

ΔQ = difference in quantity demanded, between the original quantity and the new quantity.

q = the original quantity demanded.

ΔP = difference in price, between the original price and the new price.

p = the original price.

The calculation can now be turned into symbols:

The percentage change in quantity demanded – can be written:

$$\frac{\Delta Q \times 100}{q}$$
this is the difference in quantity demanded as a fraction of the original quantity demanded multiplied by 100 to turn it into a percentage.

The percentage change in price of the product – can be written:

$$\frac{\Delta P \times 100}{p}$$
this is the difference in price as a fraction of the original price multiplied by 100 to turn it into a percentage.

$$\frac{\text{The percentage change in quantity demanded}}{\text{The percentage change in the price of the product}} \text{ now becomes } \frac{\dfrac{\Delta Q}{q} \times 100}{\dfrac{\Delta P}{p} \times 100}$$

This can be simplified by dividing both the top and the bottom by 100 and by rewriting, thus:

$$\frac{\Delta Q}{q} \div \frac{\Delta P}{p}$$

In algebra it is possible to change a divide sign into a multiply sign by inverting the term that follows the divide sign. Thus:

$$\frac{\Delta Q}{q} \div \frac{\Delta P}{p} \text{ is identical to } \frac{\Delta Q}{\Delta P} \times \frac{p}{q}$$

The formula in symbols for calculating the price elasticity at any point on the demand curve is:

$$\frac{\Delta Q}{\Delta P} \times \frac{p}{q}$$

The object of both the formula in words and the symbol formula is to reduce the price elasticity of demand to a single number. It is this number which tells us whether demand is price elastic, price inelastic or of unit price elasticity. An example will make this point clear.

Example

The price of a return economy airfare to the USA is £350 and at this price an airline sells 1000 seats. However the airline has 500 seats spare and in order to try and sell these, it advertises its airfare to the USA at £290. In response to this advertising campaign the airline receives a total demand for 1500 seats, thus achieving its objective.

Is demand elastic or inelastic?

By using either formula the single value can be calculated:

$$\Delta Q = 500 \quad \Delta P = -£60 \quad q = 1000 \quad p = £350$$

$$\text{Thus } \frac{500}{-60} \times \frac{350}{1000} = -2.9$$

$$\frac{\text{The percentage change in quantity demanded}}{\text{The percentage change in the price of the product}}$$

$$= \frac{500 \text{ divided by } 1000 \text{ multiplied by } 100}{-60 \text{ divided by } 350 \text{ multiplied by } 100}$$

$$= \frac{50}{-17.1} = -2.9$$

The answer is that the price elasticity of demand is a value of -2.9

Price elasticity values

0 to under 1   Demand is inelastic
exactly 1   Demand is of unit elasticity
over 1   Demand is elastic

(Note: It will be noticed that the reduction in the seat prices gives a minus figure for ΔP and this would make the final answer a minus number. **All demand elasticities are minus numbers** but for convenience the minus signs are sometimes ignored. It is whether the final number is over 1 or below 1 that is important. Thus -1.4 is over 1 and -0.8 is below 1.)

Price elasticity represented graphically

A starting point is Figure 4.1 on page 50. The illustration showed three different values of elasticity, elastic, inelastic and unit elasticity. If illustrations (A) and (B) are now superimposed on one graph a very important conclusion can be drawn.

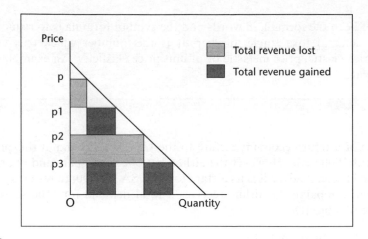

Figure 4.2

In Figure 4.2 it is clear that for price movements between p and p1 – that is at the top of the demand curve – demand is elastic. For price movements between p2 and p3 – that is at the bottom of the demand curve – demand is inelastic. For any straight line demand curve the elasticity of demand will change as we move along the curve. If elasticity is moving from elastic (i.e. a number greater than 1) to inelastic (i.e. a number less than 1) it follows that there must be a value of exactly 1 somewhere between these high and low values. This conclusion is illustrated in Figure 4.3.

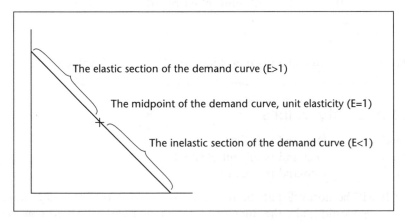

Figure 4.3 **Different values of elasticity on a straight line demand curve**

Special cases of price elasticity of demand

There are two special cases where a straight line demand curve does not have varying elasticity values throughout its length. These are a **perfectly elastic** demand curve and a **perfectly inelastic** demand curve. Both are illustrated and explained below.

Perfectly elastic demand

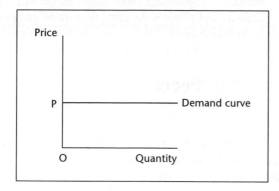

Figure 4.4

In Figure 4.4 the demand curve is a horizontal straight line and is perfectly elastic ($E = \infty$). In this case at price OP as much as can be supplied will be demanded. If price goes above OP then nothing will be demanded. Price is unlikely to fall below OP as suppliers know they can get OP for all they can produce. In the case of perfectly elastic demand the elasticity value ($E = \infty$) is the same throughout the whole curve.

Perfectly inelastic demand

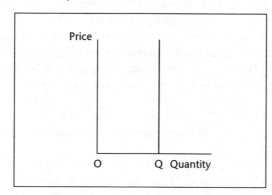

Figure 4.5

In Figure 4.5 the demand curve is a vertical straight line and is perfectly inelastic ($E = 0$). In this case the fixed quantity of OQ will be demanded, **no matter what the price.** Clearly suppliers will be able to charge as high a price as they wish without the risk of demand contracting. In the case of perfectly elastic demand the elasticity value ($E = 0$) is the same throughout the whole curve.

Elastic or inelastic – the determinants

If there are alternative choices to any product or service then the consumer may choose the cheapest, so each producer will be aware of the consumer's responsiveness to unfavourable changes in price. Demand would be elastic. In general terms, where the consumer has **choice** demand is elastic. The choice is between **substitute products** and a product is only a substitute if it performs the same **function** as the alternative product.

There are a number of commercial situations where producers can limit the availability of substitute products. Pharmaceutical companies patent their products, which may be the result of many years research. These products may then be unique in the market and consumers have little choice, they either want the product or are prepared to go without. Some products require very large-scale enterprises in order to be produced in commercial quantities, and at acceptable costs. Cement manufacture, large engineering products and steel making are examples. Very often the sheer size and costs of production will leave the market open to one or two producers, and consumers will have little choice. In all these case the consumer has **little choice** and therefore will have inelastic demand. The choice very often is between buying the product and not buying any product, and this is a defining feature of inelastic demand.

There are a number of products which are habit forming or are addictive, examples are cigarettes and alcohol. Demand for these products is inevitably inelastic.

Practical applications of the theory

Example 1

The various rail companies put their fares up on a regular basis, usually in early January each year. The commuters, who often pay for season tickets, face the highest fares increases whilst people who travel during the daytime often face little or no increases. Whilst commuters groan about the situation they continue to pay the higher fares.

Explanation

Commuters are those who travel to work, usually before 0930 each morning. There are two main alternatives to train travel, namely bus and car travel. The congestion on the roads during rush hours, and the problem of parking in many city centres convinces many rail travellers that there is no acceptable alternative to rail travel. Thus they have inelastic demand for their rail travel. *It should be noted that it is irrelevant that there is an alternative to rail travel, what counts is what the consumer thinks – and if the consumer does not count road transport as an alternative to rail transport then that is the actual position.* The rail companies know that commuter travellers have inelastic demand for the service and therefore they can raise the fares and increase their total revenue.

This is not the case with those who travel outside peak hours. They have a variety of choices such as road, bus and even not to travel at all. These travellers have elastic demand for their rail travel. The rail companies have to try and encourage these travellers to use the train, and recognising the alternatives available to the consumer they will use price as their main competitive weapon. Thus there are a variety of incentive fares, many return fares are under half the normal single fare. Whether the rail coaches are full or empty they have to run to a timetable and it is in the interests of the rail companies to take some money rather than no money. Thus it makes sense to encourage leisure travellers to pay a little, knowing that with realistic alternatives available they will be price sensitive.

An important feature of this analysis is to recognise that the rail transport market is not a uniform market. There are two distinct markets, and each is treated according to its main features. One is a market with price inelastic demand whilst the other is characterised by price elastic demand. The rail companies will maximise their revenue by raising price in one market and by lowering price in the other.

Example 2

Each year the Chancellor of the Exchequer puts up the duty payable on cigarettes. The rationale is that the government is trying to encourage people to understand the health risks and by putting up the price of cigarettes they are making it more difficult for people to smoke. It is also recognised that a very large amount of revenue is generated from tobacco smokers.

Explanation

Tobacco has long been recognised as habit forming, and many smokers find it difficult to stop smoking. In this case the consumer's demand for cigarettes is inelastic but the consumer may seek a brand of cigarettes which is cheapest. Demand for any one brand of cigarettes may be elastic, whilst demand for cigarettes as a general product will be inelastic. Thus the Chancellor views the market for tobacco as a single uniform market and levies the duty and taxes accordingly. He knows that demand is inelastic and that the various price rises will generate increased total revenue. The consumer views the market as a variety of different brands, some of which are preferable to others. The consumer – whilst accepting the overall situation that tobacco is expensive and will become increasingly more expensive – will seek to buy the preferred brands as cheaply as possible. Thus to the various cigarette producers they may be able to increase their total revenue by assuming that smokers have elastic demand for various brands, and therefore lowering the prices of some brands.

A similar analysis can be applied to alcohol. The interesting feature of alcohol is that whilst overall demand for alcohol is inelastic, the demand for alcohol from any particular outlet is very elastic. Thus the search for cheaper sources of alcohol has led to cross channel excursions and the exploitation of differing rates of taxation in France and the UK.

4.3   Income elasticity of demand

This is the responsiveness of quantity demanded as the result of changes in consumer's incomes. As income increases consumers tend to increase demand for most products. Thus the patterns of demand, and the levels of demand for various products will in large part depend upon income.

Measuring income elasticity

To establish a measure of how changing income will affect demand all the factors in the demand functional relationship, except income, are held to be constant (*ceteris paribus*). When income changes a new demand curve is necessary to reflect the increase or decrease in demand *as a result of* the changing income. Income elasticity of demand is measured by the following formula:

$$\frac{\text{The percentage change in quantity demanded}}{\text{The percentage change in income}}$$

The calculation will result in a single number. This will be either positive (above 0) or negative (below 0). The responsiveness of demand will define the type of product as **normal** or **inferior.** A normal good has an income elasticity of demand greater than 0. An inferior good has an income elasticity of demand less than 0. The normal good has two further sub-divisions which are important to understand, and the descriptions and values are given in the following table.

INCOME ELASTICITY OF DEMAND

Income elasticity of demand value	Type of good (definition)	Effect of a 3% increase in income upon quantity demanded
Positive (greater than zero)	Normal	Increases quantity demanded
Larger than 1	Superior (luxury)	Demand increases by more than 3%
Between 0 and 1	Necessity	Demand increases by less than 3%
Negative (less than zero)	Inferior	Decreases quantity demanded

Superior goods tend to be high-quality, higher-priced goods, for which there are lower-priced lower-quality substitutes, but which function perfectly adequately. Examples of superior goods might be BMW or Jaguar motor cars. There are a number of smaller, less prestigious and cheaper cars which would be considered normal products.

Inferior goods tend to be low-quality products for which there are higher-quality higher-priced substitutes. Examples of inferior goods might be the cheaper cuts of meat, bread and cereals or synthetic material in clothing and shoes. As consumer incomes rise there may be a permanent switch away from the inferior goods towards the higher-priced better quality alternatives.

NOTE

Any particular good is not **inferior** or **superior** *per se*. Goods become inferior or superior when consumers show by their demand patterns whether they want more or less of them, as they become higher income earners. Thus it is perfectly reasonable for rich households to continue to purchase cheaper low-quality goods and not switch to the higher quality alternatives. In this case *this household* would view the particular product as normal and not inferior. In this way individuals can define for themselves how they view the various products and services available in the economy.

It is the spending patterns of all consumers which defines whether a product is inferior or superior. If as aggregate income rises, aggregate spending on a product falls, then by definition consumers (in general) have defined that product as inferior. Similarly, if as aggregate income rises, aggregate spending on a product increases by more than the percentage rise in income, then by definition consumers (in general) have defined that product as superior.

Applications of the theory

The key to understanding the usefulness of the income elasticity value is given in the above note. Consumers, in aggregate, define the categories of products by their spending patterns. Thus if producers know the income elasticity values for various products, they know how the demand for their products is likely to change, over time, as incomes in the economy rise. Some interesting examples and conclusions can be derived from the data in Table 4.1.

Table 4.1 **Estimates of income elasticities of demand in the UK**

Broad categories of goods	Income elasticity of demand	Narrower category of goods	Income elasticity of demand
Tobacco	−0.5	Coal	−2.02
Fuel and Light	0.3	Bread and cereals	−0.50
Food	0.45	Dairy produce	0.53
Alcohol	1.14	Vegetables	0.87
Clothing	1.23	Travel abroad	1.14
Durables	1.47	Recreational goods	1.99
Services	1.75	Wines and spirits	2.60

Source: A. Deaton (1975) 'The measurement of income and price elasticities', *European Economic Review*, Vol. 6.

Let us assume that over the next 2 years incomes will rise, on average at 4 per cent per annum. Tobacco manufacturers can expect a reduction in demand for their products of 4 per cent over the two-year period. This is just in response to the increasing incomes and does not affect any tax changes, or health reasons for further changes in demand.

The calculation

The formula is:
$$\frac{\text{The percentage change in quantity demanded}}{\text{The percentage change in income}} = \text{Elast. Y}$$

$$\frac{\text{The percentage change in quantity demanded}}{8\%} = -0.50$$

$$\text{The percentage change in quantity demanded} = -0.50 \times 8$$

$$= -4$$

The answer shows the percentage change in demand, i.e. minus 4%.

By a similar calculation clothing manufacturers can expect a 9.8 per cent increase in demand for their products over the next two years. It is interesting to note that businessmen in the broadly defined Fuel and Light industries might be looking forward to modest increases in demand of 2.4 per cent over the next two years.

However, if they were in the coal-producing sector of the Fuel and Light category they would be facing a decrease in demand of 16.2 per cent over the next two years. It can not be assumed that all elements within any category will be affected in the same way, and this points to the importance of market research within as narrow a market definition as is practicable. Although these are old figures (mid 1970s) it is interesting to note that within 'Food' bread and cereals are considered to be inferior goods whilst vegetables are a much higher rated normal good (.87).

Firms will use information like income elasticities to assess the growth prospects of the markets in which they compete. These assessments will determine future investment and market strategies. Knowledge of future demand trends in one industry may lead to decisions in another. For example, if there is an expected downward trend in demand for tobacco then airlines may review their smoking versus non-smoking accommodation.

> The trend over recent years to make aircraft, trains, coaches, offices, etc. non-smoking only, is perhaps a reflection of expected future trends in demand for tobacco products.

The close relationship between level of income and the ownership of various consumer durables can be seen from Table 4.2.

Table 4.2 **Income and percentage of households owning particular consumer durable goods**

	Usual gross weekly income (£)		
	0–60	**100–120**	**350 or more**
Deep freezer	39	65	91
Washing machine	53	79	95
Microwave oven	5	14	39
Dishwasher	1	1	22
Telephone	63	74	98
Video	7	21	65
Black and White TV only	26	9	2

Source: Social Trends, HMSO, 1989.

Income elasticity graphically represented

In Figure 4.6 the original demand curve is D and quantity demanded is q. When income rises, as in the above text, by say 4 per cent p.a. then income elasticity is measured by the horizontal shift in the demand curve. In this case the shift from point x to point c shows a lower elasticity value than the shift from point x to point d. The further the horizontal shift to the right the greater the income elasticity value, i.e. the

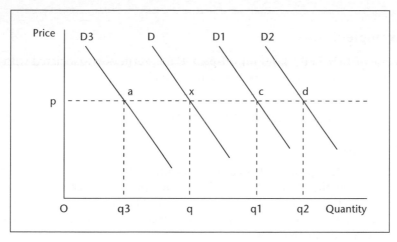

Figure 4.6 **Income elasticity**

more likely it is that the product is a superior good. Where the demand curve moves to the left of the original position, as in the above example from point x to point a, this indicates a negative elasticity value and an inferior good.

4.4 Cross price elasticity of demand

Cross price elasticity of demand is often abbreviated to cross elasticity of demand.

Cross price elasticity measures the change in demand for one product as the result of changes in the price of a related product. In the demand function (see page 31) there was a symbol representing the prices of all other goods – *Pn...Pn–1*. By holding all other factors constant (*ceteris paribus*) and varying just the prices of related goods we can understand whether the related products are substitutes or complementary goods.

Measuring cross price elasticity

The measurement of cross price elasticity is similar to other measures of elasticity, except that the calculation involves two different products. Thus:

$$\frac{\text{The percentage change in quantity demanded of good X}}{\text{The percentage change in the price of good Y}}$$

This calculation will generate a number which will be either positive or negative. If the number is negative then the product whose price has changed is a **complementary** good to the other good. If the number is positive then the product whose price has changed is a **substitute** good to the other good. Two examples will make this measurement clear.

61

Example 1

A rise of 10% in the fares for off-peak train journeys is associated with an 18% increase in demand for coach and bus travel.

$$\frac{\% \text{ rise in demand for coach and bus travel}}{\% \text{ rise in price of train travel}}$$

$$= \frac{18}{10} = 1.8$$

As the result is positive it is certain that these are substitute services. It would be expected therefore that any change in price of either service will have a direct effect upon the demand for the other. Thus just as a rise in price of one service leads to a rise in demand for the other, a fall in price of one service will lead to a fall in demand for the other.

Example 2

A rise of 10% in chartered airfares may be associated with a 4% reduction in demand for overseas package tours.

$$\frac{\% \text{ fall in the demand for overseas package tours}}{\% \text{ rise in the price of chartered airfares}}$$

$$= \frac{-4}{10} = -0.4$$

As the result is negative it is certain that these are complementary services. It would be expected therefore that any change in price of either service will have an inverse effect upon the demand for the other. Thus just as a rise in price of one service leads to a fall in demand for the other, a fall in price of one service will lead to a rise in demand for the other.

4.5   Summary

The idea of elasticity is importantly connected to TOTAL REVENUE. For this reason firms are interested in trying to estimate all three elasticity values.

- *Price elasticity* – This is important for firms as they need to know whether they will lose or gain total revenue if they put prices up. The wrong decision will affect revenue and profits.
- *Income elasticity* – This is equally important to firms as they will want to make future production schedules well ahead of time. They will also want to chart their marketing strategy a number of years ahead. All of this may involve future investment (or dis-investment) and it is very useful to know the estimated income elasticities for various products and product ranges.

- *Cross price elasticity* – This measure has less prominence, in texts, than the previous two measures. It is however important in a number of respects. Firms are usually trying to distinguish their products in the eyes of the consumer. In effect trying to show that their product is different. Although substitutes are defined in terms of 'function', it is the consumer who finally defines whether one product is a substitute for another, or not. The measure of the cross price elasticity will help to define for the manufacturer or supplier the degree of substitutability – or in his terms how successful he has been in distinguishing his product among all other similar products.
- *The concept of elasticity* – particularly price elasticity – will be referred to, and employed, many times throughout the book. It is less important for the student to be able to calculate the value of the various elasticities, than to understand the practical application of the ideas.

Further reading

ANDERTON, A. *Economics*, Causeway Press.
BEGG, D., FISCHER, S. and DORNBUSCH, R. *Economics*, McGraw-Hill.
COOK, M. and FARQUHARSON, C. *Business Economics*, Pearson Education Limited.
GRIFFITHS, A. and WALL, S. *Applied Economics*, Longman.
HARDWICK, P., KHAN, B. and LANGMEAD, J. *An Introduction to Modern Economics*, Longman.
SLOMAN, J. and SUTCLIFFE, M. *Economics for Business*, Prentice Hall.

Test your understanding

(Answers are provided at the back of the book.)

1. The price of a product rises by 10% and total revenue rises by 5%. It follows that
   A   The price elasticity of demand is less than 1.0
   B   The price elasticity of demand is 1.0
   C   The price elasticity of demand is greater than 1.0*
   D   The price elasticity of demand is 0

2. A coach company has a capacity of 450 seats on its eight coaches. It charges a fare of £30 for a return trip from London to Bristol and attracts 350 customers. In order to try and increase the seat occupancy the company reduces the price per return trip to £25. At this price the 450 seats are all sold.
   The price elasticity of demand for coach seats is:
   A   −1.7
   B   2
   C   −2
   D   1.7

The following 2 questions refer to the table below. The price of *The Times* newspaper was reduced from 45p to 30p in the county of Kent on 31 July 1993. The table shows sales at the time of the reduction (Week 1) and four weeks later (Week 4). Sales figures of *The Guardian* newspaper are also given for the same two weeks.

Broadsheet newspaper sales

Title		Net sales
The Times	(Week 1)	11 565
	(Week 4)	13 266
The Guardian	(Week 1)	9009
	(Week 4)	8474

Source: *The Independent*, 3 September 1993.

3. From this information the cross elasticity of demand for *The Guardian* in relation to *The Times* price reduction appears to be

   A 0
   B between 0 and +0.5
   C between 0 and −0.5
   D between +0.6 and +1.0
   E between −0.6 and 0

4. From this information it appears that the price elasticity of demand for *The Times* in the period concerned was

   A between 0 and −0.5
   B between −0.5 and −1.0
   C −1.0
   D between −1.0 and −1.5
   E between −1.5 and −2.0

5. A firm sells 5000 units of a product at 60p per unit. The directors believe that the price elasticity of demand for the product is −0.8. The directors raise the price by 20p, to see if total revenue will increase.

   Assuming that the price elasticity is −0.8 will the firm sell more or less units, and what will be the difference in total revenue?

6. The board of directors of a large package tours company have been told by the market research department that the income elasticity of demand for package tours abroad (in general) is 1.75. They are aware that the various economic statistics and projections are forecasting that incomes will rise at about 3% per annum. Taking the available data into account, what strategies might the board of directors consider when planning their business over the coming year? Explain your reasoning in detail.

7. A fall of 20% in the weekday first class fares on Eurostar, to Paris is associated with a 30% decrease in demand for seats on British Airways London to Paris daily shuttle.

   Calculate the cross price elasticity of demand for travel to Paris. What does the figure calculated mean?

5 Production

Learning objectives

- To recognise the contributions, to the production process, of the various factors of production. To recognise the rewards to the factors of production.
- To understand the concepts of the short run and the long run.
- To be able to explain and distinguish between:
  - Total physical product
  - Average physical product
  - Marginal physical product
- To understand the relationships between total, average and marginal product.
- To be able to define and explain the law of diminishing marginal returns.
- To be able to explain and distinguish between:
  - Short run total costs
  - Short run average costs
  - Short run marginal costs
- To understand the idea of normal profit.
- To be able to explain long run average costs
- To be able to explain economies of scale and diseconomies of scale in terms of the long run.

5.1 Introduction

In order to supply some of the consumer's unlimited wants, factors of production are combined in various proportions to produce goods and services. The quantity of output that can be produced with different proportions of the factors of production is of major interest to the economist. A further important consideration concerns the costs of these factors.

5.2 The factors of production

There are three factors of production; land, labour and capital. However there has been debate, over the years, as to the legitimate existence of a fourth, namely the entrepreneur. Whilst not entering the debate here, the entrepreneur will be considered separately.

Land

In normal usage the word land means the 'earth' or the 'surface of the ground'. To the economist however, land includes not only the surface of the land on which factories, shops, houses, etc., are built, but also all the resources that are contained within the land. Land therefore includes fishing, oil, agriculture and farming, mining, sunlight, air, water, etc.

Capital

In normal usage the word capital usually denotes money. The idea that one needs capital to start a business, or sufficient capital to retire, emphasises the money aspect. This is not how the term is used in economics.

In economics, capital refers to the plant and machinery and the various tools and machines which are used to produce consumer goods. Capital can take many forms, for example a drilling rig, a fishing rod, a microchip. These different forms of capital have one feature in common – they are all manufactured means of production. Resources have been allocated to produce **producer goods** (capital) so that they in turn can produce consumer goods.

Labour

Labour refers to human resources. This includes all workers, no matter how they earn their rewards; weekly, monthly or even yearly. Labour also refers to the mental skills of workers as well as the physical work done by them. Thus knowledge and intelligence – aspects of research, is part of what is meant by the term labour.

The entrepreneur

There is a category of worker, unlike other workers, which is often referred to as the fourth factor of production; the entrepreneur.

The entrepreneur organises the various factors, in their various proportions, then arranges for the necessary financial and market support in order to produce goods and services. The entrepreneur receives a profit if the venture succeeds and loses any investment if it fails. He therefore takes a risk, or bears the uncertainty of the venture, and he is paid nothing until a profit is made. Some would argue that these circumstances do not constitute a fourth factor of production, but merely a special case of the existing category, namely labour. Others point out that all workers, except for entrepreneurs (the self-employed) receive regular secure wages or salaries and take no risk with their personal wealth. Thus without the willingness of the entrepreneur to bear the uncertainty of any venture there would be no secure paid work for others to do. For present purposes it is not important whether there are three or four factors of production – the debate has been declared.

5.3 Physical production

The amount of goods and services that can be physically produced is limited by the amount of resource inputs available (factors of production) and the state of technology. **Technology is important.** It is very important to understand that it must be technically possible to combine these factors so that production can take place. The **production function** specifies the various technically efficient methods of combining inputs to produce outputs. Producers will seek to minimise the cost of production.

There are two separate elements: *technical production* and the *cost of production*.

Technical production

Different combinations of the factors of production can be used to produce a specified output. Where large amounts of capital are supported by a minimal number of workers production is *capital intensive*. Computer controlled production, using robots, such as the latest car manufacturing plants are examples of this type of capital intensive process. Where large amounts of labour are supported with relatively little investment in capital, production is *labour intensive*. Most production processes are capable of being undertaken by large numbers of workers taking the place of machinery. In developing economies, where labour is very cheap, labour intensive production is frequently the chosen method. As standards of living rise in an economy the labour force becomes better educated, expectations rise, and the cost of labour rises. It is at this point, when labour becomes more versatile and more expensive, that technical efficiency is very important. An example of a labour intensive industry, in the UK, is particular aspects of the 'rag trade'. Large numbers of workers, each with a sewing machine, are employed to finish or alter a wide variety of clothing. What makes this operation so susceptible to being labour intensive is the need for flexibility of working practice. A worker with a sewing machine can be sewing labels into a garment one minute and assembling a new range of clothing the next. A machine would need to be programmed and re-programmed which would be time consuming and costly.

Any firm must decide upon an efficient production function. In the planning stages of production this will involve consulting various experts such as engineers, designers, marketing experts and existing competitor's operations. The possibilities open to the firm will depend upon the length of time over which the firm is planning. Economists have defined time periods in terms of two planning periods: the **long run** and the **short run.**

TIME PERIODS

Short run   A period of time in which the quantity of at least one input is fixed, whilst the quantity of other inputs can be varied. Thus the firm can only partially adjust to changing market conditions.

Long run   A period of time in which quantities of all inputs can be varied. Thus the firm can fully adjust to changing market conditions.

With time defined in this way, there is no period of days, months or years that can be said to correspond with the short run or the long run. The short run in some industries could be many years, as with for example the nuclear generation of electricity. It takes some 15 or 20 years to commission a new generating plant. The short run in the example of the 'rag trade' given above, might be 20 minutes – the time it takes to get an additional worker (from the agency) and a new sewing machine. For a shipping line to add to its fleet may take years, as the process of building new ships is lengthy.

> **ALL FIRMS OPERATE IN THE SHORT RUN AND PLAN IN THE LONG RUN**

Short run production

If a firm wishes to increase output in the short run then it must increase the quantity of an input. Technology will dictate how much of the variable input is needed to increase output. The ability to vary output in the short run is now considered in terms of: *total product, average product and marginal product.*

Total product

Table 5.1 **Production schedule – total product**

Labour employed (per day)	Output in units (per day)
0	0
1	21
2	50
3	69
4	76
5	80

The total amount produced is called *total product*. For present purposes it will be assumed that capital is the fixed factor in the short run, and that labour is increased in order to increase output. Table 5.1 gives an imaginary production schedule showing how much output will increase for each extra worker employed.

With the data in Table 5.1 a total product curve can be constructed.

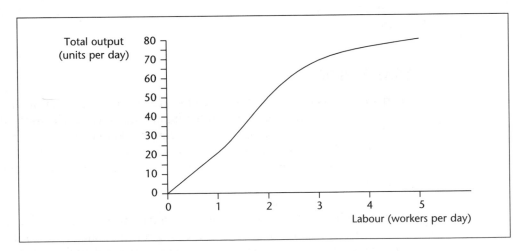

Figure 5.1 **Total product curve**

Average product

This measures the total production averaged over the number of workers who made it. Thus a third column is added to the original table, and each level of total output is divided by the number of workers employed.

Table 5.2 **Average product**

Labour employed per day	Total output (units per day)	Average output per worker
0	0	0
1	21	21
2	50	25
3	69	23
4	76	19
5	80	16

With the data in Table 5.2 an average product curve can be constructed.

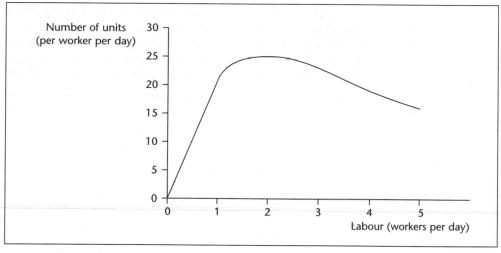

Figure 5.2 **Average product curve**

It is interesting to note, at this stage, that the total product curve (Figure 5.1) continues to rise indicating that total output is **rising.** However the average product curve indicates that after the second worker was added, average output per worker began to fall. To see this effect more clearly and to establish some important relationships it is necessary to examine marginal production.

Marginal product

This is defined as the increase in total output as the result of employing one more worker. It is each worker's **actual contribution** to total output. It is measured by

69

Table 5.3 Marginal product

Labour employed per day	Total output (units per day)	Average output per worker	Marginal output per worker
0	0	0	0
1	21	21	21
2	50	25	29
3	69	23	19
4	76	19	7
5	80	16	4

deducting the total output of two workers, from the total output of the first worker; and by deducting the total output of four workers, from the total output of three workers, etc.

Table 5.3 shows an extra column added to show each worker's marginal product.

There are some interesting relationships in Table 5.3. Both average output and marginal output rise at first and then fall; **but it is marginal output that influences average output, at first pulling the average up and then pulling it down.** Notice that when marginal output is rising it is above average output, and when it is falling it is below average output. The marginal output has a direct effect upon the total output. When marginal output is at its greatest the total product curve is at its steepest. When marginal output is falling the total product curve gets more and more shallow. These relationships are more clearly seen when the marginal product is graphed, and then compared to the total product graph and the average product graph (Figure 5.3).

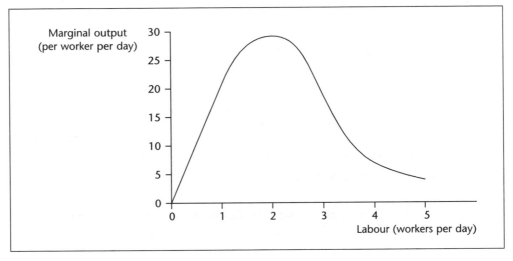

Figure 5.3 Marginal product curve

Relationships

The relationship between marginal product and average product, described above under the table of figures, can now be shown by placing both marginal and average

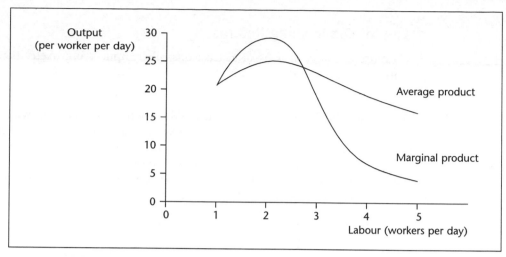

Figure 5.4 The relationship between average and marginal product curves

product on the same graph. This is shown in Figure 5.4. Notice the influence of the marginal product curve when it is above the average product curve, it pulls it up. Conversely, notice how when it is below the average product curve it has the effect of pulling average product down. A further important relationship is that marginal product cuts the average product curve from above – as marginal product is falling – at the highest point of the average product curve.

These relationships between average and marginal product curves are a general feature of the relationship between any average and marginal values of any variable. This is particularly important when we come to consider costs in the next section.

Increasing marginal returns

This occurs when the marginal product of an additional worker is greater than the marginal product of the previous worker. In the above diagram worker two produces more (29 extra units) than worker one (21 units). Thus the curve rises steeply to indicate this.

Diminishing marginal returns

This occurs when the marginal product of an additional worker is less than the marginal product of the previous worker. In the above diagram worker three produces less (19 extra units) than worker two (29 units); and worker four produces less (7 units) than worker three. All production processes eventually will reach a point of diminishing returns, *in the short run*. This is because, in the short run, not all inputs can be varied and as extra workers are added they eventually become inefficient without the support of the extra capital or land. This situation has led to the 'law' of diminishing returns.

71

Law of Diminishing Returns

As more of an input is used, at least one other input being fixed, its marginal output will eventually diminish.

The relationship between total product and marginal product is shown in Figure 5.5. Notice that in Figure 5.5(a) the largest boxes (these represent the largest marginal output or product) are on the steepest part of the total product curve. The largest boxes – the steepest part of the total product curve – are directly above the largest columns in the histogram in Figure 5.5(b). The columns in Figure 5.5(b) represent the size of the marginal output of each worker.

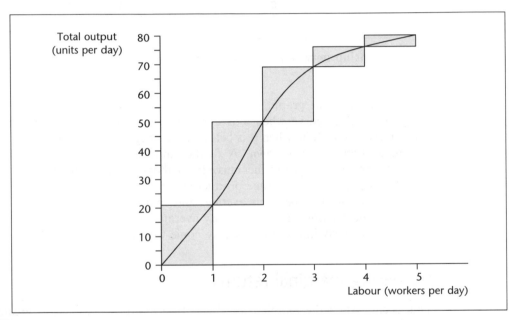

Figure 5.5(a)   **Total output**

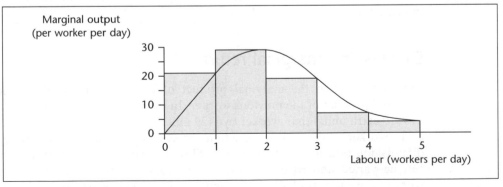

Figure 5.5(b)   **Size of the marginal output per worker**

5.4 The cost of production

The costs of production are the costs of all the inputs needed to produce an output. The costs include the rewards to all the factors of production plus the costs of manufactured and part-manufactured material inputs.

Rewards to the factors of production

The cost of *land* is *rent*.
The cost of *capital* is *interest*.
The cost of *labour* is *wages, salaries, fees*, etc.

The reward for the *entrepreneur*, and therefore the cost of the entrepreneur, is *profit*. Whether the entrepreneur is a part of labour or a special fourth factor is less important than the fact that **the cost of the entrepreneur is part of the normal costs of production.** The profit that is part of normal costs is known as **normal profit.** The concept of normal profit is explained below as it is important to understand why, in economics, profit is counted as part of costs.

The concept of NORMAL PROFIT

The entrepreneur assembles the various factors of production, plus any part manufactured inputs, and combines them in various combinations to produce an output. This output is then sold to consumers. The income from selling the output must be sufficient to repay the cost of production, or the entrepreneur will lose money. Clearly there is a major risk that consumers will not buy the products in sufficient quantities, or even that the price charged is higher than the consumers wish to pay.

It is the entrepreneur who bears this risk. He has to arrange the necessary finance to pay for the factors of production on a weekly or monthly basis, and only receives his reward after the product is sold.

The entrepreneur could safely invest his money in a bank or building society at the prevailing rates of interest, and earn an income free of any risk. Thus if he is to risk his money he must **at least** receive a reward equal to the return he could receive, risk free, by putting his money in a bank. This is his normal profit. The 'normal' refers to the profit necessary to keep the entrepreneur investing in production and not depositing his money in a bank. This is why it is considered to be a cost of production.

Short-run and long-run costs

The concepts of the long and short run have been explained on page 67. Because in the short-run at least one factor is fixed it follows that production will become more and more inefficient as output expands. There will be diminishing marginal returns. The extra workers will produce less and less each as the supply of tools and other capital necessary cannot be increased in the short term. These extra workers will also be costing more because the increased demand for workers is likely to drive up wages. Thus the diminishing returns will be costing more and more to produce. In the long-run all factors can be varied, and therefore modern technologies can be embraced which often means increased output at lower total cost. Also, in the long-run, new factories can be built, new capital produced and newer production processes employed. In this way a firm can build up to a scale of production where sheer size will produce economies of scale. All of these possibilities exist in the **long-run** but the firm must operate in the short run. The actual costs of production are always short-run costs, even if a firm is planning to reduce them in the long-run.

5.5   Short-run costs

Total cost

This is the sum of all the costs of all the inputs used in the production process. Total cost is divided into two separate elements; total fixed costs and total variable costs.

Total fixed costs	These are the costs which are incurred whether, or not, any output is produced. This would include the cost of a factory, the costs of maintaining land, etc.,
Total variable costs	These are the costs which vary with output. As more is produced then more raw materials are used; more labour may be used; more electricity, fuel and other consumables will be used.

Thus in symbols total cost (TC) equals total fixed cost (TFC) plus total variable cost (TVC):

$$TC = TFC + TVC$$

In Table 5.4 the first two columns reproduce figures from the production section (p. 68), and the additional three columns give the various elements of total cost. Fixed cost is the same at all levels of output, whilst variable cost rises with output. These figures are then shown in a graph in Figure 5.6.

Table 5.4   **Elements of total cost**

Labour employed (per day)	Total output (per day)	Total cost	Total fixed cost (TFC)	Total variable cost (TVC)
0	0	150	150	0
1	21	328	150	178
2	50	525	150	375
3	69	695	150	545
4	76	841	150	691
5	80	966	150	816

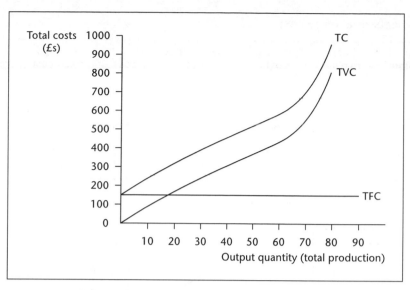

Total costs
(£s)

Figure 5.6   **Elements of total cost**

In Figure 5.6 the TC curve is the same shape as the TVC curve. This is because the TFC curve is fixed at all levels of output and is therefore a straight line at £150. The TVC curve is £0 at zero output but rises steeply as output increases. As TC = TFC + TVC the TVC curve is added to, or placed on top of the TFC curve, and therefore the TC curve is the same shape as the TVC curve but higher by £150 in the graph. This graphical way of representing the relationships is useful in showing the effect of variable costs.

Average cost

This is the total costs divided by the total quantity of units produced – (TC/Q). Average cost is divided into two separate elements; average fixed costs and average variable costs.

Average fixed costs	These are the total fixed costs divided by the total quantity of output produced.
Average variable costs	These are the total variable costs divided by the total quantity of output produced.

Thus in symbols average cost (AC) equals average fixed cost (AFC) plus average variable cost (AVC):

AC = AFC + AVC

Table 5.4 showing the total costs of production is now amended as in Table 5.5 to show an additional three columns with average costs. The average costs are then shown in graphical form in Figure 5.7.

In Figure 5.7 the AFC curve falls continuously as the total fixed cost is spread over an increasing quantity of output. Thus the fixed cost per unit gets less and less as output increases. The AVC falls at first and then rises continuously. This reflects the

Table 5.5 Elements of average cost

Labour employed (per day)	Total output (per day)	Total cost (TC)	Total fixed cost (TFC)	Total variable cost (TVC)	Average cost (AC)	Average fixed cost (AFC)	Average variable cost (AVC)
0	0	150	150	0			
1	21	328	150	178	15.6	7.1	8.5
2	50	525	150	375	10.5	3.0	7.5
3	69	695	150	545	10.1	2.2	7.9
4	76	841	150	691	11.1	2.0	9.1
5	80	966	150	816	12.1	1.9	10.2

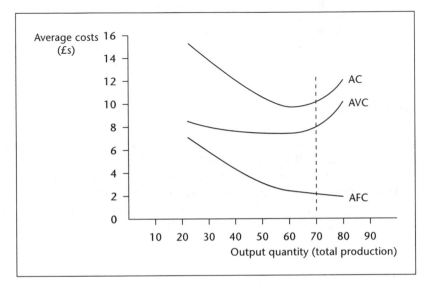

Figure 5.7 Elements of average cost

production process, where the second worker adds more than the first worker to the total output but that successive workers become more inefficient. This inefficiency shows in costs: as productivity falls the average variable cost of each unit produced is rising. The AC curve is the addition of the other two curves. Thus where AFC and AVC are both falling the AC curve will also fall – but not so fast as AFC as it will take the average shape of the AFC and AVC curves. Even where the AVC curve is rising (such as at an output of 70 units) the falling AFC curve has the opposite effect on the AC curve. Where the AVC curve is rising steeply and the AFC curve is falling gently the combined effect is for the AC curve to rise. Thus the AC curve will fall at first (reflecting the initial increasing marginal returns of production) and will then rise (reflecting the diminishing marginal returns of production).

Marginal costs

The marginal cost of production is the **addition to TOTAL COST of producing one more unit of output.** The relationship of marginal cost to average cost is one of the more

Table 5.6 Relationship between marginal cost and average cost

Labour employed (per day)	Total output (per day)	Total cost (TC)	Total fixed cost (TFC)	Total variable cost (TVC)	Average cost (AC)	Average fixed cost (AFC)	Average variable cost (AVC)	Marginal cost (MC)
0	0	150	150	0				
1	21	328	150	178	15.6	7.1	8.5	8.5
2	50	525	150	375	10.5	3.0	7.5	6.8
3	69	695	150	545	10.1	2.2	7.9	9.0
4	76	841	150	691	11.1	2.0	9.1	20.9
5	80	966	150	816	12.1	1.9	10.2	31.1

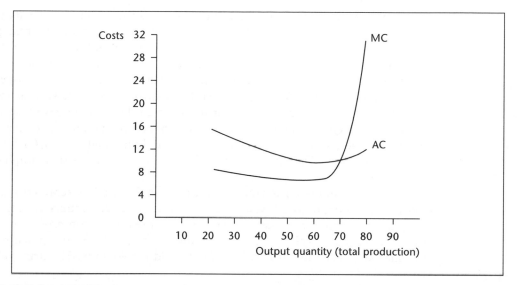

Figure 5.8 Relationship between marginal cost and average cost

important relationships in economics and is therefore shown in Figure 5.8. In Table 5.6 the marginal cost column has been added.

NB To calculate marginal cost in the above example requires two steps. First take the difference between the total cost of one level of output and the total cost of the next level of output, e.g. the difference in total cost of producing 50 units of output rather than 21 units of output, which equals $375 - 178 = 197$. This marginal cost is the marginal cost of producing an extra 29 units of output – i.e. 50 minus 21 = 29. Thus dividing 197 by 29 will give 6.8 which is the marginal cost per unit of the second level of output. **This is the extra total cost of producing one extra unit of output.**

There are two very important relationships in Figure 5.8, which are axiomatic.

1. The marginal cost curve cuts the average cost curve from below. All the time that marginal cost is below average cost then average cost will be falling. Even when marginal cost is rising, so long as it is still below average cost then average cost is falling.

2. The marginal cost curve cuts the average cost curve at the lowest point on the average cost curve. After this point the marginal cost curve is above the average cost curve and is pulling it up. Thus after the marginal cost curve has cut the average cost curve (from below) the average cost curve will be rising.

5.6   The long run

When short run costs are analysed a distinction is made between total fixed costs and total variable costs, in the long run this distinction is no longer necessary. In the long run all inputs are variable thus there is no fixed cost. Long-run costs are total costs.

The long run average cost curve

Every firm operates in the short-run, but plans and varies output capacity in the long-run. Over a period of time a firm can establish a number of different production possibilities. Each time a new production possibility is embraced, it will be with the objective of producing greater levels of output at lower cost. (This is the same as saying 'production function'. Different possible output levels and sizes of operation will depend upon the state of technology and the relative costs of the various factors.) It is possible, therefore, to imagine four or five different levels and sizes of operation each of them with their own short-run costs. As each level of operation becomes the current production there will be an average cost (AC) and marginal cost (MC) corresponding to that operation. The situation described might be represented graphically as in Figure 5.9.

Each of the short-run average cost curves in Figure 5.9 represents a particular production configuration. It would be possible to produce 40 units of output either by using the production process with AC1 or with the production process with AC2. By using the second process (AC2) the 40 units can be produced at a much reduced cost *per unit* (AC). The same is true for 60 units and for 90 units. The firm will obviously

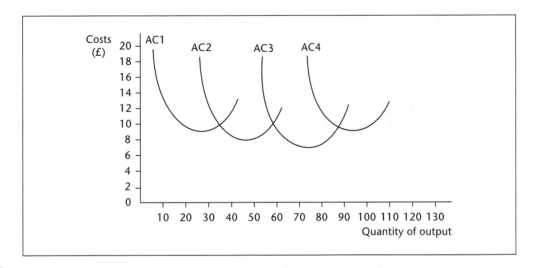

Figure 5.9

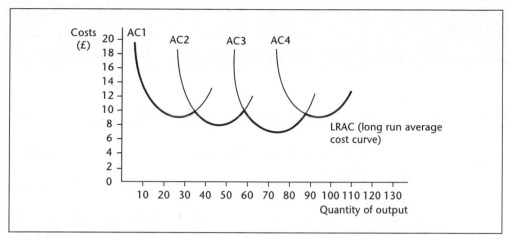

Figure 5.10 **The long run average cost curve**

choose the production process with the lowest AC for any level of output. The **long run average cost curve** shows the lowest average cost of production for any level of output, over the period of time which has allowed these four different processes to be developed. This curve is shown in Figure 5.10.

Economies and diseconomies of scale

When long-run average costs are decreasing there are **increasing returns to scale** or economies of scale. When long run average costs are increasing then there are **decreasing returns to scale** or diseconomies of scale. These two situations will occur either side of the lowest point on the LRAC. Figure 5.11 illustrates this point.

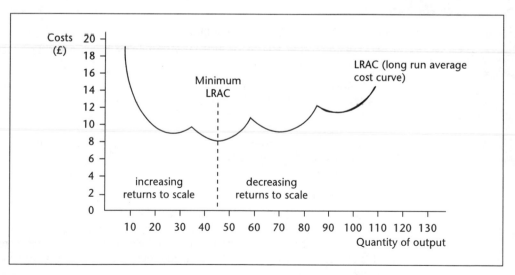

Figure 5.11 **Returns to scale**

5.7 Summary

Production theory and practice has been the sole subject of many texts, and the purpose of this chapter has been to introduce a number of the basic – but very important – ideas.

- Physical production is a technical matter. How any product can be produced will depend upon technical limitations. The possible combinations of the factors of production can be specified, for all technically possible processes.
- The various technically possible processes can be costed and a preferred production process undertaken.
- The various costs of production can be examined, and of particular importance are the average costs and the marginal costs.
- The idea of time periods is of great importance. Each preferred production process will operate in the short term, but be part of the long-term strategy.
- Firms operate in the short term and plan for the long term.
- Economies of scale are of great importance to manufacturers as they represent a possible competitive advantage over other competitors.

These basic ideas, together with the ideas of previous chapters, will allow the student to undertake some analysis of firm's behaviour within their product markets.

Further reading

BEGG, D., FISCHER, S. and DORNBUSCH, R. *Economics*, McGraw-Hill.
HARDWICK, P., KHAN, B. and LANGMEAD, J. *An Introduction to Modern Economics*, Longman.
SLOMAN, J. and SUTCLIFFE, M. *Economics for Business*, Prentice Hall.

Test your understanding

(Answers are provided at the back of the book.)

1. If a firm experiences an increase in its fixed costs, what will be the effect on average variable cost and marginal cost?

	Average variable cost	Marginal cost
A	rise	rise
B	rise	no change
C	fall	rise
D	no change	no change
E	no change	fall

2. Which statement about the long-run average cost curve of a firm is correct?

    A It falls continuously because of economies of scale
    B It traces out the costs appropriate to operating a given plant.
    C It assumes that factor input proportions are held constant as output increases
    D It is tangential at all points to the minimum points of U-shaped short run average cost curves.
    E It indicates the minimum average cost at which each level of output could be produced

3. In a given production process labour and capital are substitutable.
   What will be the effect on the quantities of labour and capital employed if the government announces a subsidy on capital investment?

	Quantity of labour	Quantity of capital
A	less	less
B	less	uncertain
C	uncertain	more
D	more	less
E	more	more

4. List the factors of production showing the rewards to each.

5. Within 100 words or less distinguish between the *long run* and the *short run*.

6. Complete the following table.

Total units of output	Total cost	Total fixed cost	Total variable cost	Average cost	Marginal cost
0	300				
42	656				
100	1050				
138	1390				
152	1684				
160	1932				

7. Complete the following table:

Total units of output	TC	TFC	TVC	AC	AFC	AVC	MC
0	75						
25			250				
50			400				
75			900				
100			1400				
125			2125				

8. What is the 'law of diminishing returns'? Using the figures in the table for question (7) describe how it works. (Maximum number of words 150)

9. Which of the following is correct?
   A When average fixed cost is falling average total cost is falling.
   B When average variable cost is rising average total cost is rising.
   C When total fixed cost is falling total variable cost is rising.
   D When average variable cost is rising faster than average fixed cost is falling, average total cost must be rising.

Theory of the firm I

Learning objectives

This is a chapter which seeks to lay the foundation for the next two more analytical chapters. The learning objectives therefore relate to an appreciation of the issues outlined.

There are many different types of businesses supplying the various markets. It is important therefore to recognise the different limitations and advantages of the various forms of ownership.

- To recognise the business situations where ownership and control are separate.

- To understand the benefits and disadvantages of separation of ownership and control, and to appreciate the potential complexities of managing large business organisations.

- To understand that firms have many objectives, one of which might be to maximise revenue.

- To appreciate that the term 'competition' needs to be carefully defined if its meaning is to be clear.

- To recognise that the idea of the public interest has a shifting focus and sounds more precise than in fact it is.

6.1   Introduction

Chapters 6 to 8 are mainly concerned with the behaviour of firms within different types of markets. There are three main themes which will continually be referred to: profit maximisation; competition; the public interest. These ideas are part of everyday language yet have a wide range of meanings and implications which are taken to be obvious or self explanatory – and this they most certainly are not. Thus the objective of this chapter is to clear the way for the analysis and comment which follows in the next two chapters.

The objectives of the firm – profit maximisation

It is frequently assumed that the principal objective of any firm is to maximise profits. It is a gross oversimplification to assume that the principal objective of any firm is to maximise profits. It is true that firms have to make profits, in order to survive; as was shown in Chapter 5 the entrepreneur will need a certain level of profit in order to continue organising the business. However firms are organised in a variety of shapes and sizes, and very often the structure of a firm will have a big influence upon how its objectives are shaped. Thus the four main forms of business organisation are briefly considered.

Sole trader

This is the easiest form of business to set up. The sole trader receives all the profits and is responsible for all the costs and losses. It is often difficult to obtain finance for capital, at normal market rates. The 'one man' business is typical of many street traders and service firms such as accountants, solicitors, consultants, etc. The proprietor will decide from day-to-day what the priorities are. In order to get new business he/she may sell goods at a large discount, or perform a service at cost. In this sense it is obvious that the firm has not 'profit maximised' *on every transaction*. The overall objective may well be to obtain the highest possible profit, but in order to do this certain short term objectives; such as market penetration and developing good customers; are necessary. It is up to the proprietor to decide upon objectives, and there will be many who are interested in a variety of objectives other than maximising profit – once they have a basic and continuing level of profit.

Partnership

This form of business is, in many respects, similar to the sole trader. The principal difference is size. A number of partners organise the business, and they receive all the profits and are responsible for the costs and losses. In most cases, they are jointly and severally liable for the business. This means that whilst they may have access to better lines of finance, they each individually run similar risks to those of the sole trader. Some partnerships have developed into huge multi-national businesses, such as the major accountancy firms; Price Waterhouse, Arthur Andersen, etc. Others have developed into large businesses within certain geographic areas, such as many firms of solicitors.

When a partnership becomes very large it is necessary to have management arrangements similar to those in large companies. Thus there will often be an 'executive committee' and a 'remunerations committee' together with various grades of partnership. In this way all the partners agree to be bound by the decisions of these various committees, and the objectives of the business are developed within this sort of structure. It is doubtful that there is a specific intention to maximise profits (i.e. make as much profit as is physically possible) as it is more likely that the executive partners will want to establish a reputation in the marketplace, a presence and reputation within their professional sphere of operations and a basis upon which their future earnings are protected. Provided that most of the partners are satisfied with their share of profits, there may be no major influence for change.

Private limited company (Ltd)

This form of business organisation has *limited liability* which means that, in contrast to the sole trader and the partnership, the company has a separate legal identity from those who own it. There are shareholders who own the business and they may receive dividends from time to time, as a distribution of the profits. The shareholders are only liable for debts of the company to the extent of the value of their shareholding; their private assets are safe.

This is a very common form of business organisation in the UK. Many companies are very small and the shareholders are the directors and managers. In these cases the legal form of organisation may be different from the sole trader, but the effective management of the business is the same. Thus the question of objectives for the small limited company may be similar to those of the sole trader. As a company gets bigger the question of separating the various management functions becomes more important. In large private companies the shareholders, directors and day-to-day management may all be separate people. There is an obvious potential for conflict as the various groups may have different priorities and conflicting objectives. The potential for conflict of interests is greater the larger the company, and the main points will therefore be made under the fourth heading, the public limited company.

Public limited company (plc)

This business organisation differs from the private limited company in two main respects.

- The shareholders are members of the public as well as other firms and institutions, and the shares are traded on the Stock Exchange. The shareholders have certain rights, among which are the rights to attend the Annual General Meeting of the company and the right to elect the board of directors.
- The business is usually very large, and in many cases having a market presence both nationally and internationally.

Within the context of the large company (Ltd., or plc) the question of 'objectives' or more specifically the main 'objective', becomes very confused. There are four main interest groups.

The shareholders may take a short term view of their investments and may put pressure on the directors (whom they elect) to pay high dividends. These dividends can only be delivered consistently through increasing company profits. Other shareholders, such as the institutional investors, may want long-term growth of the share price and the dividend, and be prepared to forego the short-term higher dividends. To achieve long term share price growth any company will need to develop its markets, its products and its internal efficiency. As there may be a conflict of interests among the shareholders it is unlikely that there will be an unequivocal message to management.

The directors, once elected, will decide as a body how to run and direct the company. They will formulate the strategic plans for the short and long term development of the company. They will have a number of pressures upon them. They will be aware of the interests of the major shareholders, whose support they will need for re-election at some future point. They may be paid a large element of their fees in 'profit related bonuses'. There will inevitably be a lot of negotiation between directors as they arrive at the various 'board' decisions, which they will all support. Again, it is unlikely that the various statements on strategy and objectives will be clear and unequivocal. The various executive directors will direct their departments.

The company managers are responsible for the day-to-day implementation of the board's strategy. They, led by their directors, will attempt to turn the short and long term elements of the strategy into daily and weekly work procedures. How much output, at what quality and at what cost will all be issues decided by the planning of the management. Their various areas of expertise and their own departmental aspirations will have influence upon the final market position of the company.

The workers will be implementing what they understand their managers want them to do. The workers will have interests of their own. They will want regular and steady work; not to have their work conditions varied continually so that the company can flexibly adjust its output to the market. They will undoubtedly want job satisfaction, but they may also want rising wages to combat inflation or to maintain their differentials with other groups of workers. Many workers will have ambitions to progress within the company and will have their own ideas as to how they might achieve this progression. All of these influences *might* come together to focus upon one or two principal market forces, but it is most unlikely.

The question of the company's objective(s), in a strategic sense, are the province of the principal shareholders and the board of directors. It is unlikely that a directive to 'maximise profits' – i.e. make as much profit as you possibly can – would be possible, as it would be difficult to turn such a directive into daily or weekly management tasks. It is much more likely that strategies will be couched in terms such as, 'to be a world class company', or 'to be a market leader', or 'to maintain a % market share'. In all these cases there is the unspoken underlying assumption **and to do it at a profit.** The question will arise as to whether the profit can be improved, over time. This is a very different issue from the simplified directive . . . maximise profit.

In conclusion to this topic, it is important for the student to understand that there is a gap between the way in which firms actually behave, and the way in which economic analysis predicts that they will behave. It is equally important to understand that there are options other than profit maximisation open to the firm – even within the theory. This will be clearly demonstrated in the following chapters. A final point is, that, where the theory assumes profit maximisation then the validity of the analysis *given that assumption* is what counts. Unrealistic theories often point towards the mechanics underlying more realistic economic situations.

6.2 The concept of competition

Competition as a concept, has two main elements. The first element concerns the number of firms operating within any particular market. The more firms there are, the greater the level of competition, *it is assumed*. This way of looking at competition is often used to construct an index to measure the degree of control that a small number of firms have over the market. The measure is known as a **concentration ratio.** There are different ways in which concentration ratios have been constructed, but the most commonly used method is called the **five-firm concentration ratio.** This measures the value of sales, of the five largest firms in a market or industry, as a percentage of the total sales in that market. Clearly if there was only one firm operating within a market, the concentration ratio would be 100 per cent. Thus the more firms there are in a market the more likely it is that the biggest five firms will only have a small fraction of the total market sales. The printing and publishing market is an example where the concentration ratio is low, i.e. below 20 per cent. Tobacco, Iron & Steel and Man-made fibres are examples of markets where the concentration ratios are high, i.e. over 85 per cent.

The use of the concentration ratio is to provide information about the competitiveness of a market. The question arises as to how useful is this information? There are problems in constructing the ratios. A principle problem is that every firm is allocated to a market or industry according to the Standard Industrial Classification (SIC) and many of the larger firms are diversified over many markets. However, for present purposes, there is a much more important issue when using concentration ratios to indicate levels of competition within any market. This focuses upon the second element of competition.

It is all very well knowing how many firms there are in a market, or how much of the total sales is controlled by the biggest five firms; but a far more important question is, 'how do they compete with each other'? To make the point consider the following two extreme hypothetical examples.

Example 1

There is a market characterised by one large firm, which controls 60 per cent of the market sales, and 1500 small firms which between them deliver the remaining 40 per cent of sales. The way in which the market seems to work is that the small firms ignore the presence of the main firm and sell to their own small niche markets. The small firms separate themselves geographically, within pockets of population, so there is no direct competition between them. The small firms take no notice of the prices charged by other small firms, as the cost to consumers in going from one area to another is greater than any small price differences. The small firms cannot compete with the main firm and therefore do not try to.

Example 2

There is a market characterised by four or five firms with approximately equal market shares. They give the appearance of great rivalry. There are many TV advertising campaigns, special offers, and customer loyalty programmes. However, the prices of the products vary only within very narrow bands and the four firms all seem to charge the same price. The profit levels of the firms all seem to be similar.

In the first example the market would be assumed to be competitive: yet there is no realistic competition. In the second example the market would be classified as highly concentrated, i.e. non-competitive: yet there is great non-price competition. From these two examples it is possible to see that there is no natural urge for firms to try and underprice the opposition. There appears to be more of a drive to distinguish each firm's products, service, quality or even geographical territory. There may even be, on the part of many small firms, a bespoke service or product for a few well known customers, which provides an adequate profit for the sole trader or small limited company.

The point of this section has been to introduce the concept of competition, together with some of the issues which surround it. It is necessary to appreciate that in the analytical chapters which follow, the word competition and the idea of competitiveness will be used extensively. Sometimes the word will refer to the market structures, and at other times to the behaviour of firms within a market. The emphasis on the idea of competition, following the section on profit maximisation, is not accidental. Competition is presumably the means by which profits are maximised, yet competition does not necessarily focus on money (or price) but on other factors. It will be of particular interest in the analytical sections that follow, to see how non-price competition might lead to profit maximisation.

6.3 The public interest explored

This is an interesting concept often referred to by politicians, and consumer groups. In terms of the market, 'the public interest' comes down to two issues: firstly is there adequate supply of the product or service and secondly, is the price charged within the ability of most consumers, to pay?

The question of whether or not a marketing strategy is in the public interest does not become a major issue for many products and services. In a market economy it is accepted that some consumers will be better off than others; and some consumers will be prepared to pay more than others for certain goods and services, for example foreign holidays, hotels, cars, etc. The question of a wider consumer access to products and services is most important when the product or service is central to the quality of life. Thus it would be politically unacceptable if most people could not afford, education, health services, necessary drugs, basic foods, water, electricity, heating, shelter, etc. These are mainly the groups of products and services known as public goods and merit goods. However, increasingly the call for more products and services to be more widely accessible, is the focus of attention from many consumer groups and 'watchdogs'.

There are a number of issues all mixed up in the idea of the 'public interest' and the purpose of this section is to lay bare some of these, not to debate the merits, or otherwise, at length.

- The concept of the public interest points to the issue of economic equality. There is an underlying moral position, which supports normative statements such as: 'all people ought to have access to (education or heath services or electricity, etc.).' This is marking out the boundary between market forces and those goods and services which all people ought to be able to enjoy *because all people are important as human beings*.
- It is assumed that firms will wish to maximise profits. In adopting market strategies to maximise profits firms will not price their products and services to be widely available to the public. Thus some consumers, perhaps even most consumers, will be barred from the marketplace on financial grounds.
- It is assumed that the markets in which firms are more likely to adopt high prices are those where there is little competition. Thus the more firms there are in a market the more likelihood there is that prices will be forced down by competition. The fewer the firms in a market the higher the prices will be.

6.4 Summary

It is important, even in an introductory text, to mark out areas where common assumptions are made.

The term 'the public interest' is one frequently used by politicians and other people representing various groups within the population. It is a sort of an appeal to higher authority.

From the points outlined above it is clear that the normative concept of 'public interest' is interpreted in terms of firm's strategies and how firms compete in their markets. The complexities of these questions are often ignored and the issue of public interest is reduced to:

the more firms there are in a market, the more competitive it will be . . . the more competitive a market the lower will be the prices and the greater will be the supply of goods and services . . . therefore competition equates with the public interest.

7 Theory of the firm II

Learning objectives

Analysis of a firm's behaviour brings together most of the theory introduced so far in this textbook. The learning objectives are separated into three sections: analytical, comparative and policy implications.

Analytical objectives

- To recognise the different forms of market structure.
- To be able to compare and contrast the different forms of market structure.
- To understand the defining assumptions for perfect competition
- To understand the defining characteristics of pure monopoly.
- To understand the defining characteristics of contestable markets.
- To be able to demonstrate the following, in graphical terms, for perfect competition and monopoly.
  - The profit maximising output
  - The price at which to sell
  - The level of any supernormal profit, or the level of any losses.
  - The firm and the market in equilibrium.
- To understand the circumstances under which a monopolist can practice price discrimination.

Comparative objectives

- To be able to describe the differences between perfect competition and monopoly.
- To understand that the more contestable a market is, the closer the market structure will be to perfect competition.
- To understand that monopolies have a choice of output and pricing options.

Policy implications objectives

- To appreciate the concept of the public interest in terms of the price and output decisions of firms.
- To appreciate the various policies adopted by governments to try and reduce the potential for abuse of monopoly power.
- To understand that the concept of the public interest may have been defined over a period of years by the provisions of different Acts of parliament.

7.1 Introduction

This chapter brings together much of what has been learned from previous chapters. The focus is upon two questions for any firm.

a. What quantity will be supplied to the market?
b. What price can be charged?

These questions lead to two further questions.

c. What total revenue will be generated?
d. Will the total revenue cover the total costs?

These questions will be asked in the context of two separate market situations, perfect competition and then pure monopoly.

Market descriptions

Markets are described here in terms of how competitive they are. They can be shown on a scale of 'competitiveness'.

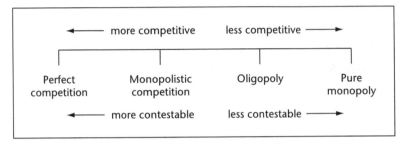

Figure 7.1 **Scale of market competitiveness**

Each of the four market structures can be further described in terms of four comparative characteristics.

COMPARATIVE MARKET CHARACTERISTICS

Market characteristics	Perfect competition	Monopolistic competition	Oligopoly	Pure monopoly
Number of firms	Many	Many	Few	One
Price control by the firm	None	Some	High degree	High degree (or regulated)
Barriers to entry	None	Some	Scale economies	Scale economies or legal (patents, etc.)
Product	Homogenous	Differentiated	Homogenous or differentiated	No close substitutes available

7.2 Perfect competition

The model of perfect competition depends upon the following assumptions.

- There are many firms in the market, such that no single firm or group of firms can influence market price by varying their supply.
- Each firm produces an identical product (homogenous).
- There is freedom of entry to the market by new firms wishing to set up: there is also freedom of exit from the market if firms wish to leave. (Freedom means that there is no 'cost' or barriers.)
- There is the assumption of perfect knowledge on the behalf of producers and consumers. (Thus suppliers will all be aware of the prices of the various factors of production, and the various production technologies available. Consumers will all be aware of any variations in the price of the product. Given that it is a homogenous product, any price reductions would result in that supplier's stock being quickly bought. Why should a supplier lower price when he can sell all he produces at the higher market price being charged by all other suppliers? Any price increases would mean no sales at all for that supplier, as the same product is widely available at the lower market price.)

The firm in perfect competition can be illustrated by the diagrams in Figure 7.2.

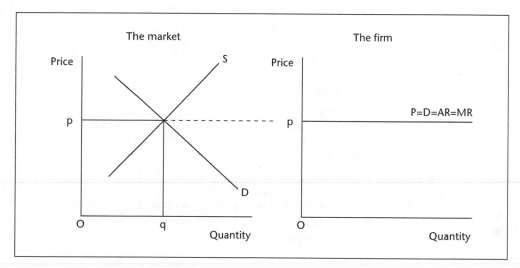

Figure 7.2 **The firm in perfect competition**

In Figure 7.2 the price of the product is determined by demand and supply in the marketplace. Each of the many small firms contributes to the market supply. The demand curve (D) represents the various quantities that consumers are willing to buy at the different prices. Thus the market price of Op will sell the market quantity of Oq.

The market quantity of Oq is very much greater than any single firm's output (or even a group of firm's outputs). Thus each firm producing in the market can contribute as much as they like towards the market quantity Oq and they will receive the price Op for all they can produce.

Each firm in the market will face identical conditions, therefore it is only necessary to describe one firm in the above diagram – that firm represents the situation facing all firms. The firm faces the market price, and this is drawn as a horizontal line. The horizontal line shows that at every level of the firm's output it will receive the same price. It is therefore the same as the demand curve for the firm. It is also the average revenue curve for the firm (AR) and the marginal revenue curve for the firm (MR). The brief numerical example below will show why this is the case.

Average revenue equals marginal revenue - an illustration

Assume that a firm is in perfect competition and the market price is 50p per unit. The following table shows the figures for five levels of demand.

Units demanded	Price	Total revenue	Average revenue	Marginal revenue
5	50p	250p	50p	
10	50p	500p	50p	50p
15	50p	750p	50p	50p
20	50p	1000p	50p	50p
25	50p	1250p	50p	50p

Marginal revenue calculation

Marginal revenue is the difference in total revenue from selling the extra level of output. Thus the difference in total revenue from selling 10 units instead of 5units. This is $500 - 250 = 250$. This extra revenue is for 5 extra units, thus $250/5 = 50p$ the extra revenue per extra unit.

The numerical example makes it clear that price is constant at 50p for all levels of demand. Average revenue is equal to the price and so is marginal revenue. Thus **demand, price, average revenue and marginal revenue** can all be represented by the same horizontal straight line, in any graph illustrating the firm in perfect competition.

Concentrating on the firm, it is now necessary to draw the firm's cost curves in order to ask the questions posed at the beginning of this chapter.

The questions to be answered in the context of Figure 7.3 are:

- What quantity will be supplied to the market?
- What price can be charged?
- What total revenue will be generated?
- Will the total revenue cover the total costs?

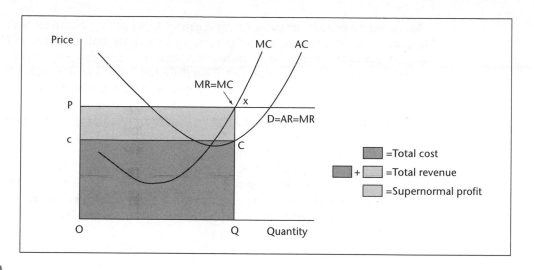

What quantity will be supplied to the market?

In the graph in Figure 7.3 quantity OQ is supplied. There is a rule for determining the profit maximising output of any firm. The rule is:

> The firm will produce the output where marginal revenue (MR) equals marginal cost (MC).

This is an important rule, where profit maximisation is assumed to be the main objective of the firm, therefore the reasoning behind the rule will now be made clear. Once again, this is most easily done by means of a numerical example.

Table 7.1 shows the various costs and revenue for an imaginary firm.

Profit is defined as Total Revenue (TR) minus Total Costs (TC). It follows therefore that the greatest distance between these two is the maximum profit.

Table 7.1　Costs and revenues

Quantity output (Q)	Total revenue (TR)	Total cost (TC)	Profit (TR − TC)	Marginal revenue (MR)	Marginal cost (MC)
5	250	225	25	50	28
6	300	257	43	50	32
7	350	296	54	50	39
8	400	346	54	50	50
9	450	410	40	50	64
10	500	489	11	50	79

Marginal revenue is the extra revenue gained from selling one more unit of output. Marginal cost is the extra cost of producing one more unit of output. Therefore if marginal revenue is greater than marginal cost, it is adding more to total revenue than marginal cost is adding to total cost. Therefore total revenue is growing by a greater amount than total cost, and the distance between them is getting bigger. That is, profit is getting bigger. When marginal cost is greater than marginal revenue, it is adding more to total cost than marginal revenue is adding to total revenue. Therefore total cost is growing by a greater amount than total revenue, and the distance between them is getting smaller. Thus profit is reducing.

MC usually starts off below MR and then continues to rise. (Check the shapes of the curves in Chapter 5 and make sure that you know why MC is below MR and rising before it cuts the MR curve). The above case is only different in that MR is constant to represent perfect competition, but MC still starts off below MR and rises to end up above MR. The conclusion is:

> even if MC is rising, all the time that MR is greater than MC profit is increasing. When MC is greater than MR profit is reducing. So produce that output where MR = MC.

The point where MR = MC is shown in Figure 7.3. At this point a line is dropped to the quantity axis, and that is the profit maximising output of the firm. In this case OQ. This is the output which, when produced and sold, will generate the maximum profit.

What price can be charged?

In the case of perfect competition the only price that can be charged is the given market price; OP in Figure 7.3. This horizontal straight line indicates that the price OP will be paid by consumers for any quantity the firm wishes to place on the market.

How to find the prices at which different levels of output can be sold

The way to find the price consumers will pay, for any given level of output is as follows. Draw a line from the quantity of output (Q) upwards until the line touches the demand curve (D); which is the same as the average revenue curve (AR). From the point at which it touches draw a line to the price axis. That is the price at which the given level of output can be sold. The following diagrams show this process with both a horizontal AR curve and a sloping AR curve.

Remember, it is only in perfect competition that the horizontal demand curve, or AR curve, is encountered.

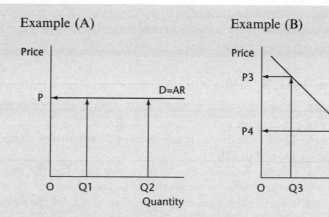

Example (A)

Example (B)

In example (A) there is perfect competition. Thus at output Q1 the line is drawn up to the AR curve (in this case a horizontal line) and then along the AR curve to the price at OP. At output Q2 a line is also drawn up to the AR curve and then along the AR curve to the price at OP. This confirms the fact that all output is sold at the same price – in perfect competition.

In example (B) there is a downward sloping AR curve. At output Q3 the line is drawn up to the AR curve and at the point where it touches, another line is drawn towards the price axis at P3. At output Q4 the line is drawn up to the AR curve and at the point where it touches, another line is drawn towards the price axis at P4. This confirms the fact that any firm facing a downward sloping demand curve, will have to lower the price in order to sell a greater output.

This is how to determine the price at which any output can be sold, NO MATTER HOW MANY OTHER CURVES THERE ARE ON A DIA- GRAM. Ignore the other curves and concentrate upon the AR curve, and then on to the price axis.

What total revenue will be generated?

In Figure 7.3 the output OQ is sold at price OP. Therefore the total revenue received is represented by the rectangle OPxQ, which is total cost plus supernormal profit.

Will the total revenue cover the total costs?

The average cost of producing output OQ is found in a similar way to finding price, illustrated above. A line is drawn from the output OQ up until it touches the AC curve. From the point at which it touches, a new line is then drawn towards the price axis. This is then the average cost, or the *cost per unit,* of producing output OQ. In Figure 7.3 this average cost is Oc.

If the average cost, or cost per unit, is Oc then the total cost of producing the whole output OQ must be represented by the rectangle OcCQ.

It is clear that the total revenue is greater than total costs, represented by the rectangle PxCc.

The questions have been answered, and as total revenue is greater than total cost there is a profit. This is the maximum profit the firm can make, given its current costs, and needs to be further explained.

Profit – further analysed

In Chapter 5, when the costs of a business were examined, it was stated that the costs of all factors of production were included – including the normal profit required by the entrepreneur. Thus, included in total costs, and therefore included in the AC curve is an amount of **normal profit**.

If the total revenue received, by the firm, was equal to the total costs of producing the output sold, then the normal profit for the entrepreneur would be covered. If the total revenue is greater than the total costs then a greater than normal profit has been made, this is called **supernormal profit.**

The firm in Figure 7.3 is making a supernormal profit. This will be seen by other firms outside the market (perfect knowledge assumption) who will see an opportunity to make more than a normal profit by joining this market. The firms wishing to join will have access to the technology for production (freedom of entry assumption) and will know about the prices and availability of the necessary factors of production. Firms will therefore enter the market to compete for the supernormal profits available. When additional firms enter the market they will demand factors of production. The demand for factors of production will increase but the supply is fixed – at least in the short run. This means that the prices of the factors of production will rise **to all firms.** The costs of production will therefore go up for all firms, and this will be represented in a graph by the AC curve being higher up the graph. The situation now faced by all firms in this market is shown in Figure 7.4.

Note that the market conditions remain the same, it is just the firms that are competing to supply this market – at the current market price.

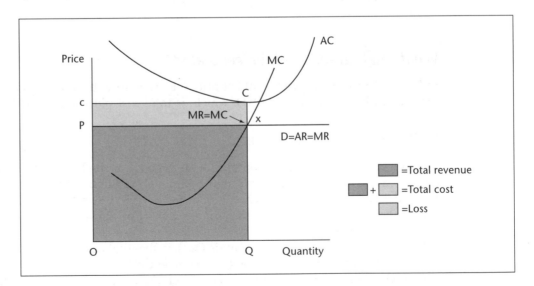

Figure 7.4

In Figure 7.4 the firm's AC curve has moved up between the axes to represent the increased costs of production as the result of competition from other firms entering the market. The situation is again analysed, by asking the same four questions.

What quantity will be supplied to the market?
OQ will be supplied (where MR = MC).

What price can be charged?
OP is the market price at which all the output available can be sold. (Go from point x where MR = MC towards the price axis to establish the price at OP.)

What total revenue will be generated?
The price per unit of output multiplied by the total units sold is Op times OQ, represented by the rectangle OQxP.

Will the total revenue cover the total costs?
Average costs are found by going from the output OQ up to the AC curve and then across to the price axis. The cost per unit multiplied by the number of units sold is total cost, which is OcCQ. Total costs are greater than total revenue therefore the firm is making a loss.

Firms in this market situation will see opportunities in other markets and will leave the market. As firms leave the market they no longer need to demand the factors of production necessary to produce this particular product. This means that demand will decrease while supply remains the same, therefore in the factor markets the prices of the factors of production will fall. This fall in the price of factors will affect the total costs of the remaining firms: they will fall. If total costs fall then the AC curve of the firm will be lower between the axes of a graph. This sort of rise and fall of the AC curve of firms, associated with firms entering and leaving the market is seen as the hallmark of the competitive process. The position in Figure 7.5, will be reached eventually.

In Figure 7.5 the firm's AC curve has moved down between the axes to represent the decrease in costs of production as the result of firms leaving the market. The situation is again analysed, by asking the same four questions.

What quantity will be supplied to the market?
OQ will be supplied (where MR = MC).

What price can be charged?
OP is the market price at which all the output available can be sold.

What total revenue will be generated?
Total revenue is represented by the rectangle OQxP.

Will the total revenue cover the total costs?
Average costs are found by going from the output OQ up to the AC curve and then across to the price axis. The cost per unit multiplied by the number of units sold is total cost, which is represented by rectangle OQxP. Total revenue is the same as total cost, therefore the firm is neither making a profit nor making a loss. The firm has covered all of its costs and is therefore making a **normal profit**.

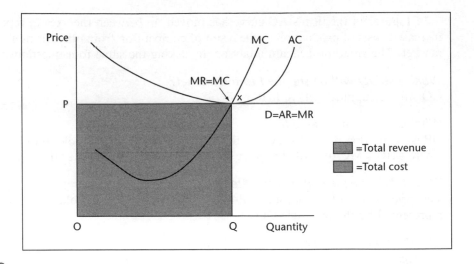

Figure 7.5

As firms are now making a normal profit – that profit required by the entrepreneur to keep the productive factors in their current use – there is no incentive for other firms to enter the market, nor for any of the existing firms to leave the market. Firms will not enter the market because they are, presumably, already earning their normal profits elsewhere and they do not see an added opportunity to earn supernormal profits. Firms will not leave the market as they are earning those normal profits which are the reward to the entrepreneur. **The firm is said to be in EQUILIBRIUM**, i.e. there is a balance where no further adjustment is necessary.

At this point both the market and the firm are said to be in equilibrium. The market is in equilibrium when demand equals supply at a particular price. The firm is in equilibrium when normal profits are being made. This situation of dual equilibrium is shown in Figure 7.6.

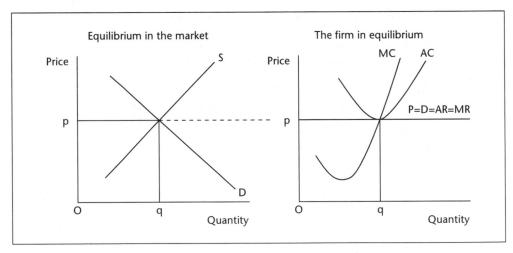

Figure 7.6   **Dual equilibrium**

7.3 Monopoly (pure monopoly)

The pure monopolist is the only firm supplying the market. Thus the monopolist is the market, and for the purpose of analysis there is no distinction between market and firm. The same four questions will be addressed as were addressed in perfect competition, namely:

a. What quantity will be supplied to the market?
b. What price can be charged?
c. What total revenue will be generated?
d. Will the total revenue cover the total costs?

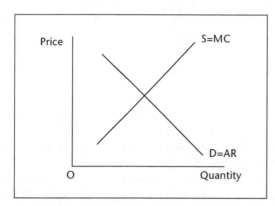

Figure 7.7   **The market**

A starting point is the market. Figure 7.7 shows the graphical representation of the market with demand and supply curves. As the monopolist is the market, the point here is to show the links graphically.

The market demand curve is the same as the monopolist's average revenue curve (AR). The market supply curve is the monopolist's marginal cost curve (MC). In order to answer the four questions, the marginal revenue (MR) and average cost (AC) curves of the monopolist need to be drawn. This is done in Figure 7.8.

The marginal revenue curve (MR) is below the average revenue curve (AR). This is because the AR curve is the demand curve which slopes down from left to right. Therefore with a downward sloping AR curve, in order to sell more the price for all units has to fall. The price gained from each extra unit is less than the price gained from the previous unit. The following numerical example shows the relationship.

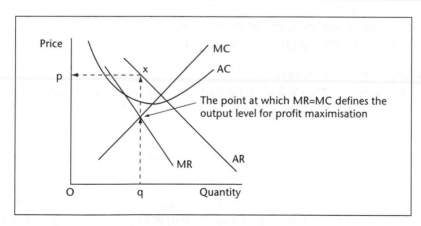

Figure 7.8   **Marginal revenue and average costs of the monopolist**

Marginal revenue is below average revenue – an illustration

The following table shows the demand for a product. In order to encourage consumers to buy more of the product the supplier has to reduce the price.

Units demanded	Price	Total revenue	Average revenue	Marginal revenue
5	50p	250p	50p	
10	45p	450p	45p	40p
15	40p	600p	40p	30p
20	35p	700p	35p	20p
25	30p	750p	30p	10p

Marginal revenue calculation

Marginal revenue is the difference in total revenue from selling the extra level of output. Thus the difference in total revenue from selling 10 units instead of 5 units. This is $450 - 250 = 200$. This extra revenue is for 5 extra units, thus $200/5 = 40p$ the extra revenue per extra unit.

Notice that average revenue (AR) is the same as price (P). The relationship between AR and MR is clearly shown in this example. Although TR is rising all the time, it is rising more slowly as more units are sold. Marginal revenue (MR) measures the **extra** total revenue generated from selling the **extra units** of output.

- To sell 15 units the price must fall to 40p, **for all 15 units.** The first 5 are not sold at 50p and the second 5 at 45p, and only the third 5 at 40p. All 15 are sold at 40p. Thus to encourage even more sales the price of **all units** must be lowered. It is this mechanism that means **MR must be below AR** at all times.

What quantity will be supplied to the market?
The profit maximising output is where $MR = MC$. This is Oq in Figure 7.8.

What price can be charged?
From output Oq draw a line vertically to the AR curve (the demand curve), and then from the AR curve to the price axis. This is price Op in Figure 7.8.

What total revenue will be generated?
Total revenue is Op times Oq which is the rectangle Opxq in Figure 7.8.

Will the total revenue cover the total costs?
Figure 7.8 is redrawn as Figure 7.9. The average cost of producing output Oq (i.e. how much it costs to produce each unit of the output Oq, *on average.*) is found by moving from Oq up to the AC curve, and then across to the price axis. In Figure 7.9, Oc is the

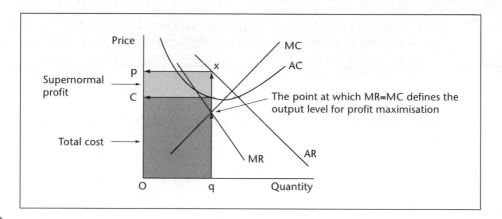

average cost per unit of output. The total cost is therefore Oc times Oq which is the rectangle Ocyq. Total revenue is clearly greater than total cost. Rectangle Opxq is greater than rectangle Ocyq. The difference is rectangle cpxy, and this measures the **supernormal profit** of this monopolist.

The final question has been answered, and the monopolist is making a supernormal profit. Unlike in perfect competition there are no outside firms waiting to compete and so there are no market forces acting to reduce the supernormal profit. This in essence is the case against the monopolist. A firm in this position could reduce output to the profit maximising level and sell this output at the price which only the richest consumers can afford to pay.

The monopolist is making a product with no close substitutes, thus the consumer has no choice other than not to buy the product at all. It may be that the monopolist has refined the production process to the limits of technology and efficiency, and that the AC curve is as low as it can go, given the existing technology and scale. Less efficient production processes would have AC curves higher between the axes of the graph and the supernormal profit would vanish. This is illustrated in Figure 7.10, so that the student is aware of this mechanism. In (A) the AC is low between the axes indicating

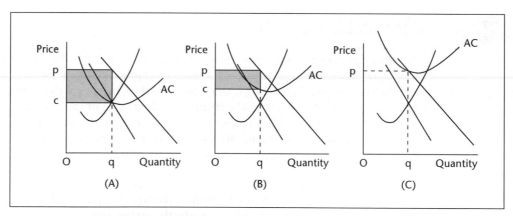

Figure 7.10 The effect of less efficient production processes

low costs per unit of output. In (B) the AC curve has moved higher, and the higher costs per unit of output have eaten into the supernormal profit. In (C) the AC curve is higher still and the supernormal profits have disappeared.

No-one would argue that the monopolist should become less efficient so as to eradicate supernormal profit. The argument is that more consumers should be able to enjoy the benefits of the monopolist's efficiency, by way of greater market supply at a lower price. It is the restriction of output which creates the supernormal profit, by keeping prices high. If output was expanded then prices would fall and the supernormal profit would be reduced. This situation is illustrated in Figure 7.11.

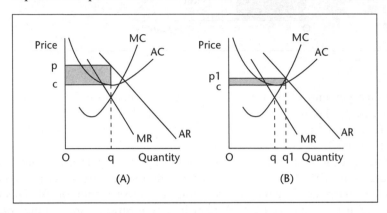

Figure 7.11 **The effect of output expansion**

In Figure 7.11(A) the monopolist supplies the profit maximising output Oq (MR = MC). This output sells at price Op per unit and costs Oc per unit to make. This gives rise to a large supernormal profit shown in the shaded box. In Figure 7.11(B) output is expanded from Oq to Oq1. This is no longer the profit maximising output and sells at a lower price per unit of Op1. The costs remain the same at Oc and the supernormal profit is reduced. The critical decision for the monopolist is the level of output; restriction of output pushes up the price and reduces overall consumer utility.

7.4   Contestable markets

The theory of contestable markets is a theory which challenges the traditional theory of monopoly. This theory asserts that a market characterised as monopolistic, having perhaps one or two large firms, may be a market in which those firms have little control over output and price. The theory highlights one of the assumptions of perfect competition, namely *freedom of entry into or exit from the market*. If entry into the market is **potentially** easy then, although the firms are monopolists, they will behave more like firms in perfect competition where P = MC.

> If the costs of entry into or exit from a market, for potential competitors, are **zero** then the market is said to be **perfectly contestable**.

The analysis is similar to that of perfect competition. If supernormal profits are being made then competitors will see a more profitable use for their factors of production, and will enter the market. The increased competition should compete away the supernormal profits and return all firms to a normal profit. The theory is couched in terms of *barriers to entry and exit,* but there are underlying implications to this which should be made clear.

Implications of the assumption of 'freedom of entry and exit'

1. Although the impractical assumption of perfect competition, **perfect knowledge**, has not been imported into the theory of contestable markets – it is still implied. The ease with which competitors can enter a market will depend to a large extent on their knowledge of the required technology and production techniques. If they do not have this knowledge, can it be easily and cheaply acquired?
2. If firms are to have *freedom of exit* from a market then they must have low **sunk costs**. If a firm wishes to leave one market and enter another then a major issue is whether the existing capital is transferable. If the capital is specialised and not really usable outside the current application then this presents a considerable barrier to entry and exit from the market.

Thus a market can be described as more or less contestable. If there are no barriers to entry and exit (i.e. perfect knowledge and no sunk costs) then the market is perfectly contestable (perfect competition, as the assumptions are effectively the same). If there are very high barriers to entry and exit then the market is not contestable (monopoly or oligopoly exists). For entry and exit conditions between these two extremes markets are more or less contestable.

In reality many monopolies and oligopolies are firmly entrenched behind very high entry barriers. An example would be the pharmaceutical companies which are very large multi-national companies with huge research budgets (sunk costs) and sheltering their pricing and profits structures behind patents (restriction of knowledge).

Contestable markets

This theory is important because it focuses upon the central issue which determines the competitiveness of a market. **Barriers to entry and exit.** The fact that there are only a few firms in a market does not automatically mean they can exercise unrestrained market power – the market may be contestable.

7.5 Comparing monopoly with perfect competition

The table at the beginning of this chapter shows a comparison in terms of market features, but a much more focused question must be answered. How do the quantities produced, prices charged and profits compare for these two types of firm?

These questions can be answered, and the comparison made on one diagram.

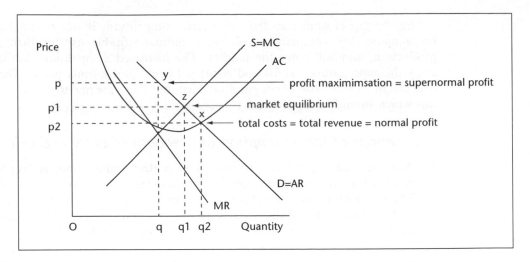

Figure 7.12

In Figure 7.12, the amount of output that would be sold in a competitive market (under perfect competition) would be Oq1. The price at which this output would be sold is Op1. The dangers of monopoly, we are told, is that the monopolist can restrict output and therefore force up the price. This possibility is clearly seen on the above graph, where the monopolist can restrict output to the profit maximising level (MR = MC) at Oq. There are consumers who are prepared to pay Op for this level of output. (The demand curve (AR) shows what consumers are prepared to pay for the different levels of output.)

A third possibility exists, given the cost circumstances of the monopolist in Figure 7.12. The monopolist could choose not to profit maximise, but to maximise the market output. In this case he could produce output Oq2 and receive price Op2. At this price level he would be just covering all his costs (AC = AR) and therefore no longer making a supernormal profit, but instead a normal profit. The reason that this possibility exists is because the monopolist can take advantage of scale economies and therefore his AC curve is likely to be lower between the axes than the individual firm in perfect competition.

Whilst a monopolist may not wish to erode all the supernormal profit, it may also be the case that his strategy is not profit maximisation. In the short term a monopolist may aim for maximum market penetration, and therefore increase out put beyond Oq, even up to point Oq2. The example shown in Figure 7.12 indicates that it is not necessarily the case that monopoly is 'bad', that is, against the public interest. The example does show the inherent ability of the monopolist to restrict output and therefore behave against 'the public interest'.

The monopolist, because the product has no close substitutes and there is a wide range of outputs available, has another strategy for maximising revenue (and in this case profit). If the monopolist can discriminate between different groups of consumers then the different groups could be charged different prices. This practice would enable some consumers to pay above price Op in Figure 7.12 at the same time as others paid prices between Op and Op2.

Price discrimination

The way in which price discrimination works, can be shown in the following example.

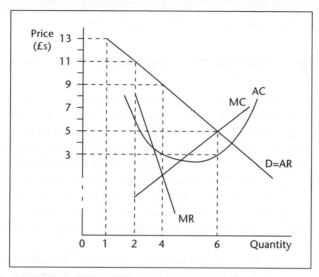

Figure 7.13 **Price discrimination**

Profit maximising output = 4000 units
Price consumers will pay to clear 4000 units is £9 each
Profit maximising revenue = £36 000
Total cost of 4000 units is £12 000 (cost per unit is £3, as indicated by the AC curve)
Profit is £36 000 less £12 000 = £24 000   **Supernormal profit is £24 000**

Calculation under price discrimination.

First 1000 units can be sold for £13 each	revenue = £13 000
Second 1000 units can be sold for £11 each	revenue = £11 000
Next 2000 units can be sold at £9 each	revenue = £18 000
Next 2000 units can be sold at £5 each	revenue = £10 000
	Total revenue £52 000

Total cost of the first 4000 units is £12 000
Cost of the last 2000 units is £6000   Total cost   £18 000

Profit is £52 000 less £18 000 = £34 000   **Supernormal profit is £34 000**

Price discrimination is profitable, but can take place only under two specific conditions.

- The product must not be able to be resold. If the product could be resold then some consumers could buy at a low price and sell to others willing to pay higher prices. This happens with tickets for pop concerts, Wimbledon and other events where a few consumers are willing to pay far higher prices than the prevailing price.

- **There must be clearly identifiable groups of consumers each with different price elasticities of demand for the product.** The different groups must be identified (i.e. described) within the law. If a manufacturer of a particular rug discovered that this rug was a prescribed article for prayer for certain religious groups, he would not be able to sell to Muslims at one price and the general public at another. This form of discrimination is illegal.

There are many good examples of price discrimination in the various transport markets.

- On the British railway systems there are a variety of prices, for the same journey, depending on what time of day the consumer travels, and how far in advance the ticket is purchased. It is generally recognised that commuters have to use the railway system within certain well defined times. Their price elasticity of demand for rail travel is therefore low – inelastic. They will pay a higher price for the tickets they want, and the rail companies take advantage by setting peak fares at a very high level. Those consumers travelling out of peak times have a range of options from cheap day returns, to apex fares booked in advance of travel. There are also discount cards available to various groups such as the young, the old, and the off peak traveller.
- Air travel is characterised by different passenger groups. First class for those who can afford it, such as the rich and senior business executives. Club class and business class for those who cannot afford first but do not want to travel economy. Economy for those who wish to travel as cheaply as possible. In many cases the decision to travel first or club or business class is to do with status within a person's business: the travel plans are not variable. Those travelling as tourists have a greater choice as to when they wish to travel, and therefore the cost of their seats is very much lower than the other classes. Even tourists can be trapped into displaying their inelastic demand, when they wish to travel during school holidays when there is peak demand for seats. Thus the prices of economy fares, during these periods are as high as demand will allow.

The public interest re-examined

The government has never defined the 'public interest', even though the idea is invoked frequently whenever the market behaviour of businesses are in the spotlight. This is often as the result of consumer complaints, and the activities of consumer organisations. The government could try and restrain private firms from restricting output and therefore engineering high prices. However, privately owned companies with a strong incentive to behave in a particular way will spend a great deal of time and effort in trying to legally oppose any restrictions imposed on them. The costs of enforcement could possibly exceed any savings or any increased efficiency. Another approach to the problem is one of trying to preserve competition, in the belief that the consumer is best served in competitive markets. There seem in practice to have been three aspects to UK competition policy:

- The control of existing monopolies.
- The control of markets likely to be monopolised through mergers.
- The prevention of restrictive trade practices.

In order to gauge more accurately how the idea of the public interest has been developed over the last few decades, it is necessary to look at the actions of various governments since 1948, with respect to the above three headings.

7.6 Monopoly and the state since 1945

The Monopolies and Restrictive Practices Act of 1948

This Act set up the Monopolies and Restrictive Practices Commission. The Commission had between four and ten members but this was increased to 25 in 1953. It was charged with inquiring into any firm which supplied more than one-third of the UK market for a particular good, or where there was evidence to suggest that some firms were colluding in a manner detrimental to competition. It was up to the appropriate minister, rather than up to the firms concerned, to initiate any inquiry. Furthermore, it was for the Commission to show that any practice was, on balance, against the public interest: the onus of proof was on the accuser rather than the firm accused. The Commission made recommendations to the appropriate minister who decided whether the restrictive practice should be allowed or not.

A problem inherent in this procedure is that monopolies and mergers are open to public inspection, but many restrictive practices are not. How could the minister reasonably be expected to identify cases of collusion for reference to the Commission?

> Monopoly defined by this Act:
> 'any firm which supplied more than one-third of the UK market for a particular good.'

The 1956 Restrictive Trades Practices Act

This Act made it the responsibility of colluding firms to register their restrictive practices. The Act also reversed the burden of proof, established in the 1948 Act, so that it was up to the firms, rather than the minister, to show that these practices were not against the public interest. The Restrictive Practices Court, consisting of five judges and ten lay members with the status of a High Court, was set up to hear cases. Restrictive agreements were considered to be **against the public interest** unless they could satisfy at least one of seven 'gateways'. These gateways are as follows:

1. That the restrictive agreement protects the public against injury in connection with the installation, use, or consumption of goods.
2. That the restrictive agreement makes available other 'specific and substantial' benefits to the consumer.
3. That the restrictive agreement counters existing restrictive measures taken by other firms.
4. That the restrictive agreement assists the negotiation of fair trading terms for the purchase or sale of goods with buyers and sellers.

5. That the restrictive agreement prevents the occurrence of serious and persistent unemployment in an area.
6. That the restrictive agreement maintains the volume of earnings of the export trade.
7. That the restrictive agreement supports some other restriction which the Court holds to be justified.

Even if a firm could satisfy one of these gateways it was still required of the firm to show that the benefits accruing from the restriction outweigh the costs. In 1968 an eighth gateway was added.

8. That the restrictive agreement neither restricts nor deters competition.

The 1964 Resale Prices Act

Resale price maintenance was not just an issue of collusion between several suppliers to restrict competition by charging the same price for their products. It also concerned the practice of some suppliers insisting that all retail outlets sold their products at pre-determined prices. This meant that retailers did not have the choice of reducing profit margins, in order to compete, by lowering prices. The 1964 Act presumed that resale price maintenance was **against the public interest**. Firms could appeal to the Restrictive Practices Court on the following grounds that abolishing price maintenance would:

1. Reduce the quality or variety of goods available.
2. Reduce the number of shops.
3. Lead to higher prices in the long run.
4. Create a danger to health.
5. Interfere with pre-sales or after sales services.

Even if a firm successfully argued its case on one of the above grounds, it was still required to show that the benefits accruing from the price agreement outweigh the costs to the consumer.

The 1965 Monopolies and Mergers Act

This Act provided for the investigation of mergers or acquisitions which might produce, or strengthen, a monopoly. The Act charges the Monopolies Commission to investigate proposed and completed mergers in which more than £5m worth of gross assets are involved. The Commission would only rule against a merger if it was deemed to be **against the public interest**.

Many mergers were abandoned before they got off the ground simply because it was felt that the Commission would not approve them. Even if approval had been certain, there remained the question of whether it was worthwhile undertaking such time-consuming argument. Some 50 major proposed mergers were abandoned between 1965 and 1975 following informal advice from the Commission. The effect of the 1965 Act was to slow down the trend towards greater market concentration, rather than to prevent the growth of larger firms.

The 1973 Fair Trading Act

- The Monopolies and Restrictive Practices Commission was renamed the Monopolies and Mergers Commission.
- The unitary monopoly definition is extended to situations where 25 per cent or more of the market is controlled by a single buyer or seller.
- Mergers could be investigated when the merging firms together would control 25 per cent of a market, or where the merger involved gross assets of over £30m.
- This Act set up the Office of the Director General of Fair Trading (DGFT).

> Monopoly re-defined by this Act:
> 'any firm which controls more than one-quarter of the UK market for a particular good.'

There was an attempt, in 1973, to focus upon the issue of the **public interest.** It was not defined, as such, but a number of pointers were given towards what might be major features of the public interest.

Section 84 of the 1973 Fair Trading Act states:

When considering whether any particular matter operates against the public interest the Commission shall take into account among other things, the desirability of:

(1) maintaining and promoting effective competition between persons supplying goods and services in the UK;

(2) promoting the interests of consumers, purchasers and other users of goods and services in the UK in respect of prices charged for them and in respect of their quality and the variety of goods and services supplied;

(3) promoting, through competition, the reduction of costs and the development and use of new techniques and new products and of facilitating the entry of new competitors into existing markets.

(4) maintaining and promoting the balanced distribution of industry and employment in the UK.

(5) maintaining and promoting competitive activity in markets outside the UK on the part of producers of goods, and suppliers of goods and services in the UK.

The findings of the Commission, for each referral, are published in a *Command Paper*. In order to see how these guidelines are applied the student can refer to the various *Command Papers* published since 1984.

The Competition Act of 1980

This Act extended the power of the Director General of Fair Trading to apply to the nationalised industries the same control as operates for the private sector.

7.7 Summary

Prices and output under the unrealistic model of perfect competition have been compared to the more realistic conditions of monopoly. The monopolist does not have to restrict output and focus upon supernormal profits. He has room to manouevre. If the barriers to entry and exit are not too high then the motive to keep prices low and output high may be found in the fact that the market is contestable. There does not appear to be any automatic market strategy that is against the public interest. Firms need profits but the extent to which their sole motive is maximum profit, is questionable.

Another thread throughout this section has been to try and deduce what the various governments, since 1945, have taken to be in the public interest. There appears to be an underlying belief, probably from the influence of theory, that the more small firms there are in a market the cheaper the product will be, and the better served will be the customer. This influence pervades the legislation since 1948. The clearest indication of the public interest being in the 1973 legislation where price and quantity were prominent landmarks alongside frequent mentions of competition.

Further reading

ANDERTON, A., *Economics*, Causeway Press.

BEGG, D., FISCHER, S. and DORNBUSCH, R. *Economics*, McGraw-Hill.

CLARKE, R. *Industrial Organisation*, Basil Blackwell.

COOK, M. and FARQUHARSON, C. *Business Economics*, Pearson Education Limited [especially pages 364–402].

GRIFFITHS, A. and WALL, S. *Applied Economics*, Longman.

HARDWICK, P., KHAN, B. and LANGMEAD, J. *An Introduction to Modern Economics*, Longman.

PORTER, M. *Competitive Advantage: creating and sustaining superior performance*, Macmillan/Free Press: New York.

SLOMAN, J. and SUTCLIFFE, M. *Economics for Business*, Prentice Hall.

Test your understanding

(Answers are provided at the back of the book.)

1. A firm that is practising price discrimination will be

   A charging different prices for different product qualities
   B buying in the cheapest market and selling in the dearest market
   C charging different prices in different markets for the same product
   D charging a uniform price in different markets for the same product

2. If a firm wished to maximise its profits from a market it would set a price where

   A marginal revenue is zero
   B marginal revenue equals marginal cost
   C average revenue equals average cost
   D marginal revenue equals average cost

3. If a firm wished to maximise its share of the market without making a loss it would set a price where

   A marginal revenue is zero
   B marginal revenue equals marginal cost
   C average revenue equals average cost
   D marginal revenue equals average cost

4. A supernormal profit is

   A Where a firm is earning above the industry average
   B Where a firm is earning higher profits than in the last accounts
   C Where the firm is earning more revenue than is needed to cover total costs
   D Where the firm is earning sufficient revenue to cover its marginal costs.

5. Monopoly is considered to be against the public interest, compared to perfect competition, because

   A The monopolist restricts output and forces up price
   B The monopolist reduces competition by producing where MC=price
   C The monopolist does not consider the welfare benefits of consumers
   D The monopolist has higher costs and therefore forces up prices

6. From the information given in the following diagram calculate the maximum profit a monopolist could make if able to price discriminate in four separate markets.

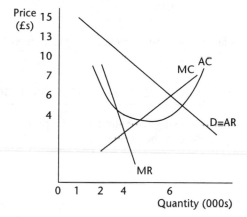

7. A profit maximising monopolist will seek to produce at a level of output where

   A average costs are lowest
   B there is the greatest difference between marginal revenue and marginal cost
   C the highest price can be obtained
   D there is the greatest difference between total revenue and total costs

8. In which of the following market situations is the firm identical to the industry?

   A Oligopoly
   B Monopoly
   C Perfect competition
   D Imperfect competition

9. A perfectly competitive industry producing a product X, experiences an increase in demand for the product. Which of the following diagrams illustrates the effect of this increase in demand on the industry in the short term?

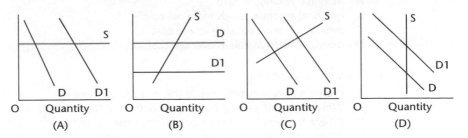

(A)	(B)	(C)	(D)

10. From the following data, calculate the 5 firm concentration ratio.

European Chocolate Confectionery Manufacturers
(Market Shares, %, 1992)

Nestlé	20
Mars	16
Suchard	18
Cadbury	10
Ferrero	10
Lindt	4
Imhoff	4
Others	18

11. The following table shows a firm's total costs corresponding to different levels of output.

Units of output	1	2	3	4	5	6	7	8	9	10
Total cost (£)	6	11	15	18	21	25	30	36	43	51

If the market price is £5, within which range of output would a profit maximising firm in a perfectly competitive industry produce in the short run?

A   1–2 units
B   3–5 units
C   6–7 units
D   8–10 units

12. The following table shows a firm's total costs corresponding to different levels of output.

Units of output	1	2	3	4	5	6	7	8	9	10
Total cost (£)	6	11	15	18	21	25	30	36	43	51

If the market price is £6 within which range of output would a profit maximising firm in a perfectly competitive market produce in the short run?

A   1 to 2 units
B   3 to 5 units
C   6 to 7 units
D   7 to 8 units

13. A perfectly competitive market becomes a profit maximising monopoly. The marginal cost curve of the monopolist is identical to the supply curve of the perfectly competitive market. How will output and price be affected?

	Output	Price
A	higher	higher
B	higher	unchanged
C	lower	higher
D	lower	unchanged

14. Outline the main issues involved in distinguishing between different meanings of the idea of 'competition'. (350 words maximum)

15. How does the way in which a firm is organised affect its strategic objectives? (750 words maximum)

16. Describe the market for petrol and assess the nature of 'competition' within that market.

Theory of the firm III

Learning objectives

Monopolistic competition and Oligopoly are examined in this section. As these forms of market structure can lead to some very detailed and complex analysis the learning objectives are confined to introductory analytical objectives.

- To understand the defining characteristics of monopolistic competition.
- To understand the defining characteristics of Oligopoly.
- To be able to demonstrate the following, in graphical terms, for monopolistic competition.
  - The profit maximising output
  - The price at which to sell
- To understand and be able to demonstrate the reasons for non-price competition in oligopoly.

8.1 Introduction

The extreme cases of perfect competition and pure monopoly give a valuable insight into the limits of *competition* and the competitive behaviour of firms. However, most of the activities of firms in the UK take place in market conditions which lie between these extremes. The case of monopolistic competition lies closer to the perfect competition extreme, whilst the case of oligopoly lies closer to the pure monopoly extreme (see page 90). Each will be considered in this chapter.

8.2 Monopolistic competition

Monopolistic competition incorporates elements found in both perfect competition and monopoly. There are three defining characteristics of monopolistic competition.

- There is freedom of exit and entry to the market (as in perfect competition).
- There are a large number of firms in the market (as in perfect competition).
- Each of the firms faces a downward sloping demand curve (as in monopoly).

As there are a large number of firms in the market no single firm can have a significant influence on the market price and quantity, or on the strategies of other firms. This also means that there is a competitive market in the sense that the *concentration ratio* is low.

Freedom of entry, and exit, means that there will be no long-term supernormal profits. The analysis is similar to that of perfect competition, where in the presence of supernormal profits firms will enter the market to try and share in the supernormal profits being made. Competition for factors of production and raw materials will raise the costs to all firms in the market. Although costs have risen, the new firms entering the market will take some of the demand away from existing firms, and prices will fall. With rising costs and falling prices losses will be incurred, and some firms will leave the market. This exit of firms means that factors of production and raw materials are in less demand, and therefore their prices will fall, leading to falling costs. The remaining firms will see increased demand higher prices and higher profits. The whole process will come to rest when each firm is making a normal profit – in long run equilibrium.

Each firm, in monopolistic competition, produces a differentiated product. Thus consumers have the choice of a variety of products each fulfilling similar functions. Each firm will face a normal demand curve for its products; a downward sloping demand curve. Unlike the pure monopolist, these firms are aware that there are substitutes for their products, i.e. all other firms in the market are producing products which can perform the same *function*.

In Figure 8.1(A) the firm chooses to supply the profit maximising output Oq. At this output consumers are prepared to pay Op. The cost of this output to the firm is Oc. Therefore a supernormal profit is being made equal to the rectangle cpxw.

This supernormal profit encourages other firms to enter the market. These firms make a product similar, but slightly different, to existing products in the market. The product is similar enough to be a substitute in the eyes of consumers, and demand will transfer from the existing firms to the new firms. Demand will decrease for existing firms, and their demand curves (AR) will shift to the left. This shift to the left is shown in Figure 8.1 (B). Notice that when the AR curve shifts to the left so does the MR curve. The hypothetical new position is reached in Figure 8.1 (B).

In Figure 8.1 (B) the firm chooses to supply the profit maximising output Oq. At this output consumers are prepared to pay Op. The cost of this output to the firm is Oc. Therefore as costs exceed revenue a loss is being made equal to the rectangle yczp. The AR curve has shifted too far to the left causing this loss to be made. This implies that too many former customers have transferred to competing firms.

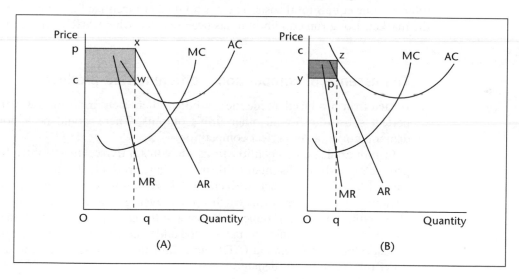

Figure 8.1

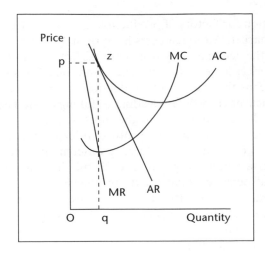

Figure 8.2

The losses for some firms means that they will leave this market and look for other products, in other markets, where they can compete profitably. As firms leave the market the demand for their products will be transferred to the other remaining firms. The demand curves of these firms will shift to the right as demand increases. There may be a number of adjustment periods in the short run, as firms enter the market and others leave. Supernormal profits may turn into losses, and losses back into supernormal profits. This market adjustment will reach an equilibrium position in the long run. This is shown in Figure 8.2.

In Figure 8.2 some customers have returned to this firm. The AR curve has moved a little to the right until it is just tangential to the AC curve. The firm chooses to supply the profit maximising output Oq. At this output consumers are prepared to pay Op. The cost of this output to the firm is Op. Therefore a normal profit is being made as total revenue equals total costs. There is no further incentive for firms to enter or leave the market. Long run equilibrium has been reached where MR = MC and AR = AC.

The essence of competition – differentiated products

If each firm produced an identical product, then each firm's output would be a perfect substitute for all other firm's outputs. There would be a horizontal demand curve, as in perfect competition.

In monopolistic competition firms are constantly seeking to introduce new products, and to distinguish their existing products from those of their competitors. New products with enhanced features may give a brief competitive advantage, until other firms catch up and even go ahead. The more a firm is able to differentiate a product **in the eyes of the consumer** then the higher prices consumers may be willing to pay for the added consumer value. Thus the more inelastic the firm's demand (AR) curve, and the less susceptible the firm is to short run decreases in demand.

Differentiation is the key to competitive survival. Firms attempt to differentiate the consumer's perception of the product in a variety of ways, but advertising is the principal method. Advertising is expensive, and therefore consumes resources. To the extent that advertising provides product information and market comparisons for the consumer, the expense is probably justifiable in terms of providing consumers with wider choice. Advertising often seeks to persuade the consumer that a particular product is not similar to another product, but far superior and in fact different. To the extent that advertising is successful a firm will be able to secure customer loyalty – **which means demand is less price elastic.**

8.3 Oligopoly (competition among the few)

Oligopoly is where a small number of firms in a market, compete with each other. The number of firms is not specified but there is a special case of oligopoly where two firms are competing, called duopoly. If a market had four equal sized firms then officially each would be a monopolist (25 per cent of the market); but the theory by which we try to make sense of their competitive strategies is oligopoly theory. The key feature of oligopoly is that each of the firms in the market has to take account of the behaviour of the other firms.

Key feature of oligopoly

Each firm has to take into account the effect of its own actions on the behaviour of the other firms. Each firm will also take account of the actions of other firms and the potential effect of these actions on its profit. **All firms are interdependent.**

In order to understand the problems facing the oligopolist it is best to start with an example. In choosing a hypothetical example it is important that features of the real economy are recognised.

Assume that there are four petrol stations in a small geographical area. Each of the stations wants to sell as much petrol as possible, so as to maximise revenue. Although none of the stations is aware of the exact cost of the other station's petrol, they each assume that the costs will be similar. What to do? If one station cuts the price of petrol, it is certain that it will increase its total revenue. As petrol is price elastic, between local petrol stations, this means that a cut in price will bring a greater than proportionate increase in total revenue. However, the extra revenue can only be at the cost of falling revenue for the other three stations. They also will wish to maximise revenue, and they will have no choice but to retaliate, and reduce their prices. The question for each of the firms is how far do they reduce price? There must come a time when they all realise that to engage in a price war will eventually reduce the profit for each of them. They will wish to seek other ways to tempt customers away from their competitors, leaving price at a common level. If one petrol station could show that it was selling a qualitatively better petrol, then consumers might be prepared to pay a little more for a superior product. The essence of the problem is that each firm's product is a substitute for the other's. Even if the products are not identical they are not sufficiently differentiated that the consumer will view them as 'unique'.

A variety of models have been developed to explain firm's behaviour under conditions of oligopoly. None are totally satisfactory in explaining how these market situations can be resolved. The models fall into two categories: traditional models and game theory.

Traditional models of oligopoly

The Sweezy model (the kinked demand curve)

The Sweezy model is based upon a single assumption: **each firm will make the most pessimistic assumption about its market demand.** This is not an unrealistic assumption to make as most managers might consider this gives them a 'bottom line' position. This pessimistic assumption means for each firm:

- If I drop my price I will be facing an inelastic demand curve
- If I raise my price I will be facing an elastic demand curve.

These are the most pessimistic assumptions possible. It means that if a firm lowers price, and the demand is inelastic then it will decrease total revenue. If it raises price and demand is elastic then it will also decrease total revenue. **If price is altered, at all, under these assumptions then total revenue will fall.** The firm faces the demand curve in Figure 8.3.

In Figure 8.3, the demand curve is kinked. The portion above the kink is elastic whilst the portion below the kink is inelastic. The price Op stays in the kink because to move is to invite a reduction in revenue. The marginal revenue curve is an odd shape because it is really two different marginal revenue curves with a discontinuous section in the middle. So long as marginal cost passes through the MR curve in the discontinuous section the firm can continue to maximise profits by producing quantity Oq and charging price Op.

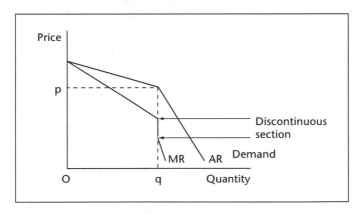

Figure 8.3 The kinked demand curve

This model explains why, under the specified condition, prices will tend to be **sticky**. The model works best where all firms are of roughly equal size and structure. There are a number of problems with this explanation, the two most important of which are:

- The model does not explain how price is arrived at in the first place
- The model does not explain what happens if beliefs change or are modified.

Dominant firm oligopoly

In this case there is a large firm which supplies the majority of the market, and a number of small firms each of which supplies a small part of the market *at the price established by the dominant firm*. The analysis is as follows.

Assume that there is one large firm, within a geographical area, and 15 small firms each selling gas in bottles. The large firm supplies 55 per cent of the market sales and each of the small firms supplies 3 per cent of the market sales. The price of gas and quantity of gas sold is determined as follows.

Fifteen small firms and market demand

Figure 8.4 shows the aggregate supply curve of the 15 small firms and the demand curve for the whole market.

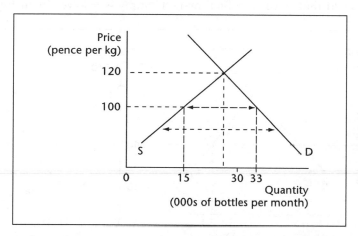

Figure 8.4 **Supply curve of the 15 small firms against the whole market demand**

The demand curve (D) shows the total amount consumers will demand at each level of price. Thus at a price of 120p per kg, the total quantity demanded in the market will be supplied by the small firms. However at any price below 120p more is demanded than can be supplied by the small firms together. For example at 100p per kg, the market demand is 33 000 bottles but the small firms together can only supply 15 000 bottles. Thus there is an additional 18 000 bottles required and the large firm has this part of the demand curve all to itself. If we plot all the differences between what the small firms can supply and the total market demand we arrive at the demand curve for the large firm. This is shown in Figure 8.5.

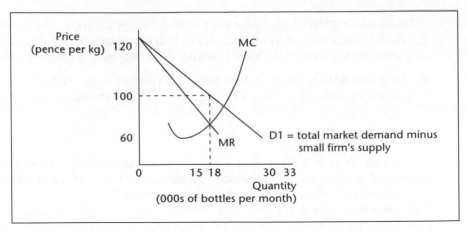

Figure 8.5 **Demand curve for the large firm**

Figure 8.5 shows that there is no demand at 120p per kg but at lower prices there is demand above what can be supplied by the small firms. Thus this large firm will maximise profits by producing that output where MR = MC. The profit maximising output is 18 000 bottles and the price for this output in the market is 100p per kg.

As the large firm is the market leader (dominant firm) the small firms will follow the lead and supply at that price. The final market supply is resolved as in Figure 8.6.

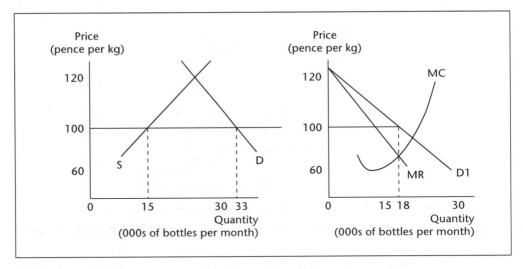

Figure 8.6 **Final market supply**

In Figure 8.6 the large firm is prepared to supply 18 000 bottles per month at the price of 100p per kg. This is the output that gives the large firm a maximum profit. The total market demand at this price of 100p is 33 000 bottles, which leaves 15 000 bottles short of market demand at this price. The 15 small firms each supply 1000 bottles at 100p. The small firms are price takers in this situation whilst the large firm is the price maker.

Game theory

In a situation where it is not possible to be certain about the behaviour of competitors, a firm can only envisage certain scenarios and try to work out a suitable response. Thus if that scenario ever arose the firm would have some idea as to how it might behave in response. There are many possible scenarios, and the statement of the scenario in the form of a problem, together with the solution, is the methodology of game theory.

Game theory seeks to understand oligopoly (as well as many political scenarios, and interpersonal relationships, etc.) by using a method of analysis particularly suited to understanding games of all types. Most games are governed by a set of rules and the object is to form a game plan to win the game. In oligopoly the rules are, 'a small number of players (firms)' and 'each firm is interdependent of all the others'. The object or strategy is to use any method available, such as pricing, product differentiation, etc., in order to maximise profits. Winning is in terms of profit or loss. It is not a function of a text, at this level, to enter into a detailed account of the various games in the economic literature, however a simple example of a game with a solution will illustrate the technique.

To understand how an oligopoly game works it is best to use an example using only two players (duopoly). The prisoners' dilemma is the usual game used in most introductory texts and will also be used here.

The prisoners' dilemma

Two criminals have been caught in the act and are held in custody. They are interviewed and during the interview the police officer in charge suspects that they are responsible for another crime that he is investigating. The police officer has no evidence and realises that without their confession he can do nothing. He therefore comes up with the following strategy. He places both the criminals in separate cells, so that there is no possibility of communication between them. He informs them that each of them is facing 2 years in prison for the crime that he can prove against them. He then tells each of them in turn that he suspects them of the second, more serious crime and proposes a deal. If one confesses to the second crime and his accomplice does not, then the one confessing will get only 1 year for both crimes whilst the accomplice will get 2 years plus 8 years a total of 10 years. If however both confess separately to the second crime then both will serve a total of 3 years. Each of the prisoners knows that if neither of them confess to the second crime they will only serve 2 years for the current offence. What should they do?

Solution

Each of the prisoners has two possible options.

1. Confess to the second crime
2. Say nothing

As there are two players, each with two options, there are four possible outcomes.

1. Both confess
2. Neither confesses
3. Prisoner A confesses and prisoner B does not
4. Prisoner B confesses and prisoner A does not

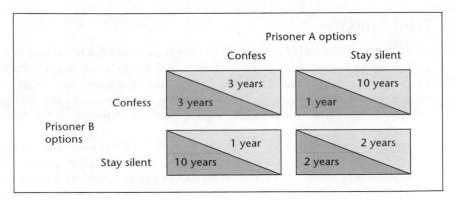

All possible options

It is possible to work out the best solution for each prisoner. This is done diagrammatically in Figure 8.7.

Each square shows the result of the various options for the two prisoners. If prisoner A confesses and so does prisoner B then each gets 3 years. If prisoner A stays silent but prisoner B confesses the prisoner A gets 10 years and prisoner B gets 1 year. If both prisoners stay silent then they both get 2 years (bottom right box). Prisoner A reasons as follows.

> If prisoner B confesses then it pays me to confess as I get 3 years rather than 10.
> If prisoner B stays silent then it pays me to confess as I get 1 year instead of 2.
> Thus no matter what prisoner B does **it pays me to confess.**

Prisoner B reasons as follows.

> If prisoner A confesses then it pays me to confess as I get 3 years rather than 10.
> If prisoner A stays silent then it pays me to confess as I get 1 year instead of 2.
> Thus no matter what prisoner A does **it pays me to confess.**

The solution is that both confess and both get 3 years. In economic terms this would be considered an equilibrium point, that is the point where one firm takes the best possible action given the possible options of the other firm(s). Notice that this equilibrium point is sub-optimal. The optimum position for **both** is 2 years. But the inter-dependent nature of the relationship leads to this sub-optimal conclusion. Economic commentators would point out the waste of resources that is implied by oligopoly.

8.4 Summary

The theme of this chapter has been intense competition.

Under monopolistic competition firms are trying to differentiate their products and services. They are competing within market structures where there are many possible alternatives open to consumers.

Under oligopoly firms realise their interdependence and therefore also compete fiercely to distinguish their products from all others in the marketplace.

The unifying feature is that all firms are trying to avoid price competition. If price competition takes place the firms lose and the consumer gains.

Further reading

BEGG, D., FISCHER, S. and DORNBUSCH, R. *Economics*, McGraw-Hill.
HARDWICK, P., KHAN, B. and LANGMEAD, J. *An Introduction to Modern Economics*, Longman.
SLOMAN, J. and SUTCLIFFE, M. *Economics for Business*, Prentice Hall.

Test your understanding

(Answers are provided at the back of the book.)

1. Firm X sells its product in an oligopolistic market in which there are many competing brands, and Firm Z sells its product in a market characterised by monopolistic competition. Which of the following descriptions of these products is correct?

    Products supplied by:

	Firm X	Firm Z
A	Differentiated	Differentiated
B	Unique	Differentiated
C	Identical	Differentiated
D	Differentiated	Unique

2. It is reported that there is a potential new entrant into an oligopolistic market. Which of the following measures seems likely to increase the possibility of the new firm entering the industry?

    A   The existing firms advertise their products more heavily.
    B   Existing firms lower their prices.
    C   Patent rights on a process vital to the industry continue to exist for ten years.
    D   Existing firms raise their prices.
    E   The government imposes tight environmental regulations on the industry.

3. Insert the AC curve, price and quantity in the diagram to show a firm in long run equilibrium.

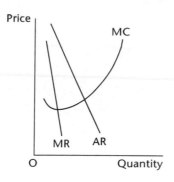

123

4. **European Chocolate Confectionery Manufacturers**
   (Market Shares, %, 1992)

Nestlé	20
Mars	16
Suchard	18
Cadbury	10
Ferrero	10
Lindt	4
Imhoff	4
Others	18

Which of the following best describes the market for chocolate?

A Monopoly
B Oligopoly
C Monopolistic competition
D Perfect competition

5. Assume a market with 16 small firms and one large dominant firm. The small firms can between them sell 32 000 tons per month. Draw a demand curve to show the difference between what is offered for sale, in the diagram below, and the total market demand for the product.

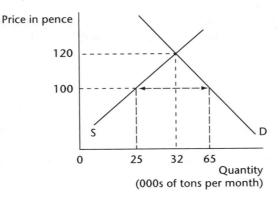

PART II

Macroeconomics

9 Macroeconomics

Learning objectives

- To understand the way in which money circulates within an economy.
- To understand that national income = national expenditure = the value of national output.
- To understand and be able to demonstrate the effects of injections and withdrawals on the circular flow of income.
- To be able to demonstrate the following, within a simple model of the economy.
  - The relationship between falling aggregate demand and unemployment.
  - The relationship between an increase in money supply and inflation.
  - The effects of international trade upon the circular flow of income.

9.1 Introduction

Macroeconomics deals with the economy as a whole and not individuals or firms or even markets. Thus, for example, when we talk about income we do not mean the income for a group of workers, or the income for an industry but all income for everyone in the economy. We are dealing with totals.

It is within macroeconomics that topics such as inflation, employment and international trade are introduced, and with them the closely related areas of government policy. These topics will be dealt with in detail in future chapters, but the starting point is to build up a simple model of the economy so as to understand how the different parts are related.

9.2 The circular flow of income

A very simple model of an imaginary economy is shown in Figure 9.1. There are only three elements, factories, shops and some people who live on a single housing estate.

The people who live on the estate will wish to buy various goods, but they have no money. They go to the factories to work, producing the goods which they will later wish to buy, and in return they earn wages. The factories, at the end of each week, send the goods which have been produced to factory owned shops. The workers go to the shops to buy the goods, with the wages they have received. The shops sell the goods to the workers and pass the money on to the factories in payment for the goods. Let us follow this process concentrating on the money.

The flow of money

In Figure 9.1 the flow of money is traced by the arrows. The money starts in the factories and passes to the workers in their homes. It is spent by the workers and

127

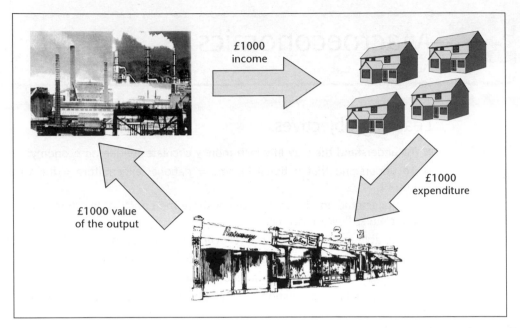

Figure 9.1 **Circular flow of income**

therefore passes from them to the shops. The shops have to pay for the goods which the factories sent them, and so the money passes back to the factories. At the end of this first cycle (call it one week for the purposes of this example) the money is back in the factories. It is now available for payment to the workers so that they can produce more goods, which will be sold through the shops, and the whole process starts over again and continues week in week out. The money flows in a circle from factories to workers to shops to factories. In this very simple model there is nothing to stop the money circulating forever, creating goods for sale and employment for the workers. A number of points can be made.

National income

The amount of income which the workers receive is £1000. Each time the £1000 circulates it provides more income, so that if it is circulating 52 times in one year, the total national income generated will be £52 000.

National expenditure

The workers spend the money they earn in the shops, buying the goods made in the factories. They spend £1000 in the shops. The total amount spent each week is £1000 (assuming at this stage that all income is spent each week). Each time the £1000 circulates it provides more expenditure, so that if it is circulating 52 times in one year, the total national expenditure generated will be £52 000. Another way of looking at national expenditure is to think of it as total (or aggregate) demand. Demand is a want backed by the ability to pay, thus when money is spent on goods in the economy it is effective aggregate demand.

National output

The goods made by the workers in the factories are sent to the factory owned shops to be sold. The value of the goods sent to the shops is £1000 each production cycle. Assuming that all the goods are sold each week the value of the national output in 52 weeks will be £52 000.

National Income = National Expenditure = National Output

This model can be built up to reveal further insights into the real complex economy. For the next stage assume that 1000 products have been made by the workers for their £1000 wages. The following assumptions are made in three separate time periods.

Assumptions
Week 1   The 1000 products are all sold.
Week 2   One of the workers receives some money from abroad, say £1000, and he spends it.
Week 3   Some of the workers send money to relations overseas, say £1000.

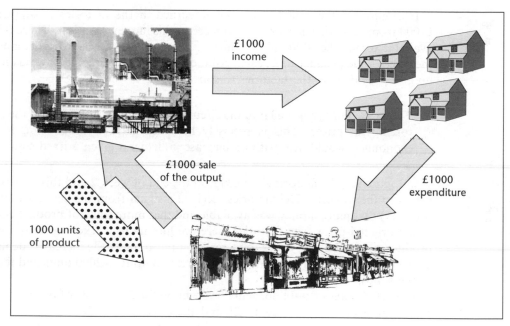

Figure 9.2   **Week 1**

In Figure 9.2 the £1000 income received from employment in the factories, is spent in the shops. The 1000 products sell at £1 each, and the £1000 returns to the factories to begin week 2.

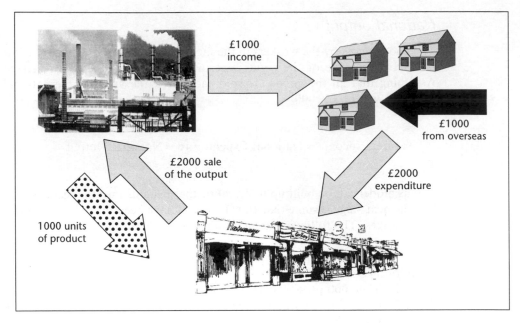

Figure 9.3 Week 2

In Figure 9.3 the £1000 total income earned in the factories is supplemented by £1000 from abroad. The worker who receives this money spends it. There is now £2000 available to buy the 1000 units of output. The pressure of this extra demand forces up the price of the product to £2 each. All the money in the circular flow has been soaked up and passed on to the factories to start week 3.

> The extra money **injected** into the circular flow is spent and has had the effect of forcing up prices. This is precisely how the market mechanism, in micro-economics, would deal with an increase in demand given a fixed supply.

In Figure 9.4, the factories had £2000 at the end of week 2 and this they passed on in wages to the workers. The factories received a signal from the economy (the shops in this case) that more money was available and that more units of product could be sold at the original price. The factories therefore hire more workers or look for increased productivity, or both in order to increase output to meet the increased demand. In the above example the factories manage to increase output to 2000 units and these are sent to the shops.

The £2000 wages would normally be spent on the 2000 units of product and the unit price would normally return to £1 and there would be £2000 circulating. However according to the assumptions some workers do not spend all their wages but send some to relatives overseas, in this example £1000. Thus there is only £1000 of income left to spend in the shops and the shops have 2000 units of product to sell. The lack of demand will cause the market clearing price per unit to fall to 50p. £1000 will now be passed to the factories, who will note the decreased demand and make less output on the next round of production.

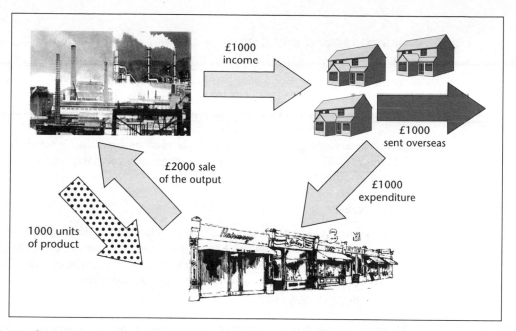

Figure 9.4 Week 3

Note

You should make sure that you can follow the above example and that you can work out why on week 4 the circular flow of income will be £1000 and the price per unit of output will be back to £1.

Do not read on if this is not clear, go back and follow the examples.

9.3 The circular flow and the effect of injections and withdrawals

In the last two examples (Figures 9.3 and 9.4) there was a marked effect when extra money was **injected** into the circular flow of income, and when money was **withdrawn** from the circular flow of income. In the first case the extra money had the effect of increasing the circular flow of income (and therefore increasing national expenditure and the value of national product). This increase in national income created a pressure of demand which forced up the prices of goods in the shops. In the second case the withdrawal of money from the circular flow had the effect of reducing the circular flow of income (and therefore reducing national expenditure and the value of national product). This decrease in national income created a situation of low demand which led to price reductions of goods in the shops.

It is the level of the national income (the circular flow) which is of critical importance. As shown in Figures 9.3 and 9.4, the level of national income can rise or fall depending on whether there are injections (causes national income to rise) or withdrawals (causes national income to fall). Two points need to be made.

Injections and withdrawals – the net effect

It is possible to imagine that there will be many injections of money not earned within the system, and many withdrawals of money from the system. It is the net effect of these injections and withdrawals that is important. **If injections are greater than withdrawals then national income will rise** and so therefore will national expenditure (aggregate demand) and the value of national output. **If withdrawals are greater than injections then national income will fall** and so therefore will national expenditure (aggregate demand) and the value of national output.

Time periods

A very important issue is the idea that the effects of injections and withdrawals are not immediate. In Figures 9.3 and 9.4 it took a complete cycle for the effects to work through the system. It was not until week 4 that the circular flow settled down after the initial injection followed by the withdrawal.

There are a number of withdrawals and injections in an advanced economy. The examples so far have not made any allowances for people's desire to save money, or to borrow money. They have not considered the actions of the government and they have not considered overseas trade. The example of workers, factories and shops will be extended systematically to cover all these points but the main injections and withdrawals are summarised below.

Injections	Withdrawals
Investment	Savings
Government expenditure	Taxation
Exports	Imports

9.4 The circular flow and the effect of government

The government has a number of important influences upon the national income. These will be explored using the simple example of factories, shops and houses. In the following diagram there is a government and it has decided to build a hospital and a school for the people who live in the houses. The workers now have extra work opportunities, they can work on the government sponsored building as well as in the factories. There is extra work for those who might not have a job. The workers are taxed on their earnings.

In Figure 9.5 it is possible to see the effects of both the injection and the withdrawal. The factories had £1000 pay to workers as income, but this was added to by the government financing a building project, and the wages of people working on this

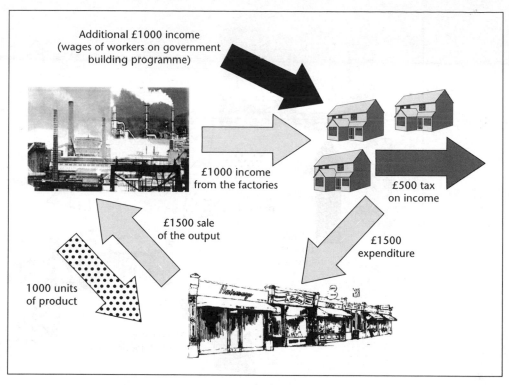

Additional £1000 income
(wages of workers on government
building programme)

£1000 income
from the factories

£500 tax
on income

£1500 sale
of the output

£1500
expenditure

1000 units
of product

Figure 9.5 **The effect of government on the circular flow**

building are added to the wages from the factories. In the above example the extra
money **injected** into the system is £1000. The workers have to pay tax on their income
and this is £500 in the example. The tax is a **withdrawal** from the system (as it cannot be
spent, and goes back to the government). The workers therefore take home £1500
which they can spend.

> **Note** The effect of the injection into the circular flow of income (government
> spending) is to raise the level of the circular flow. The effect of the withdrawal
> from the circular flow of income (government taxation) is to lower the level of
> the circular flow.
>
> The net effect is that the injection (£1000) was greater than the withdrawal
> (£500) and therefore the circular flow increased by the difference.

9.5 The circular flow and the effect of overseas trade

Overseas trade affects the circular flow of income in two ways. Exports are injections
and imports are withdrawals. These will be explored using the simple example of
factories, shops and houses. In Figure 9.6 the factories send 1000 units of output

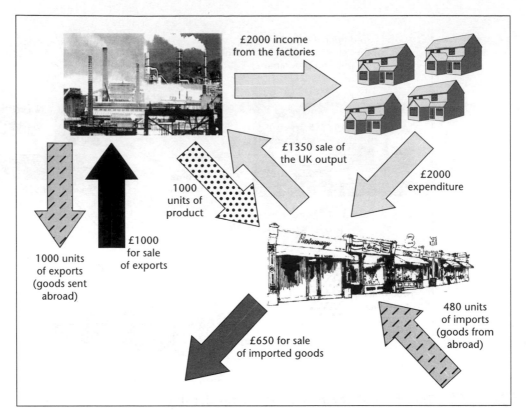

Figure 9.6 The effect of overseas trade on the circular flow

abroad (export). At the same time overseas factories send 480 units of their output to this country (imports).

In Figure 9.6 it is possible to see the effects of both the injection and the withdrawal. The factories had £2000 pay to workers as income. The workers produced 2000 units of output, but only half of this output was sent to the shops, the other half was sent abroad to another country's circular flow (exported). To satisfy some of the demand in the shops for goods (the workers have £2000 to spend and are therefore creating a pressure of demand) the shops import some goods from abroad. To see the effect that imports and exports have on the circular flow of **income it is important to follow the money, not the goods.**

In Figure 9.6 the payment for the exported goods is money **injected** into the circular flow – in this case £1000. The payment for imported goods is money **withdrawn** from the circular flow – in this case £650.

In Figure 9.6 only £1350 of the workers' £2000 is passed on to the factories, because £650 had to be sent abroad in payment for the 480 units of product which were imported. This £1350 was added to by the £1000 which was received from abroad for the 1000 units of product which were exported. To start the next cycle the factories have £2350 to produce more goods. (Note: There were 1480 units of output available in the shops to soak up £2000. This means a price of £1.35 each. $480 \times £1.35 = £650$ and $1000 \times £1.35 = £1350$)

Note. The effect of the injection into the circular flow of income (payment for exports) is to raise the level of the circular flow. The effect of the withdrawal from the circular flow of income (payment for imports) is to lower the level of the circular flow.

REMEMBER. Follow the money NOT the goods.

The net effect is that the injection (£1000) was greater than the withdrawal (£650) and therefore the circular flow increased by the difference.

A lot of different ideas have been introduced, and these ideas and the topics they represent will be examined in detail in the following chapters. For present purposes the ideas can be summarised in Figure 9.7.

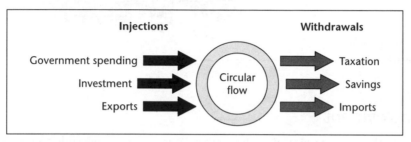

Figure 9.7   **Macroeconomic model**

The income within the circular flow represents a changing circulation of money. This flow of national income can be increased by the various forms of injection and decreased by the various forms of withdrawal. When the injections are equal to the withdrawals the circular flow is neither rising nor falling and is in a state of *balance*. In this state of balance it is said to be in **equilibrium.**

The equilibrium condition in symbols is $G + I + X = T + S + M$

Government spending (G) + Investment (I) + Exports (X) = Taxation (T) + Savings (S) + Imports (M)

9.6   Some further ideas introduced in the model

Within the basic models explored so far, a number of issues have arisen but have not been focused upon. Some of these issues will be introduced now so that the student can see where they fit into the idea of the circular flow. The topics to be introduced include, employment, production and productivity, inflation and overseas trade.

In order to start upon the explanation of these issues the basic model introduced in Figure 9.2 is reproduced as Figure 9.8.

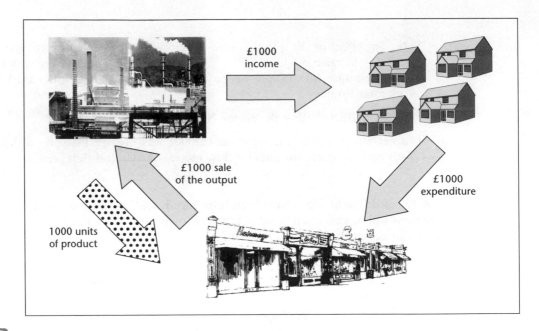

£1000
income

£1000 sale
of the output

£1000
expenditure

1000 units
of product

Figure 9.8

Employment

The workers are employed in the factory. It may not be possible to give every person, who would like to work, a job. The number of jobs available will depend upon technology (see the chapter on production in the microeconomics section) and upon how much demand there is for the goods. The demand for the goods will be reflected in the amount of money flowing into the factories from the shops. Thus if national income rises there will be more money to spend (creates greater demand) and more money available in the factories to hire more workers. If national income falls there will be less money to spend (demand falls) and less money available in the factories to pay for wages. Thus workers will be made redundant.

Employment depends upon demand for goods and services in the economy. In Figure 9.8 the expenditure in the shops, which is passed on to the factories, is supporting the workers in employment. Therefore any injection into the circular flow has the effect of raising the national income, which leads to raised national expenditure (which is aggregate demand), which leads to pressure on the factories to produce more goods, which leads to the factories wishing to employ more workers. Any withdrawal from the circular flow has the effect of reducing the national income, which leads to lower national expenditure (which is aggregate demand), which leads to the factories wishing to produce less goods, which leads to the factories wishing to employ less workers.

INJECTIONS – investment (I), government spending (G), exports (X)
These all have the effect of creating pressure for greater demand within the economy and therefore increased employment.

> **WITHDRAWALS – savings (S), taxation (T), imports (M)**
> These all have the effect of reducing demand within the economy and therefore less employment (or unemployment).

Production and productivity

When there is increased demand for goods in the shops (as in Figures 9.3, 9.5 and 9.6) the factories become aware of that demand and seek to produce more goods to meet it. They have a choice of how to increase their output, in the short term.

a.   They can ask the present workers to work harder, perhaps do overtime.
b.   They can employ more workers

The first option is about productivity. If there is spare capacity in the factories and the workers can produce a greater output for a small increase in costs, then the factory management may take this option until they are confident that the increased aggregate demand will continue.

The second option is about increased employment. This option assumes that there is the physical capacity for extra workers to produce more goods. For example, it is not just a case of working the existing capital more intensely, but of having extra capital for the extra workers to use. This option is seldom a short-term measure, and the factory managers would have to be confident that the increased aggregate demand was not a temporary feature.

There is a third option in the short term – do nothing, because the factories are working at full capacity and it will take time (long term) to increase the factory's capacities. This last option can lead to inflationary pressure within the economy.

Inflation

When there is greater demand for goods than there are goods to satisfy that demand, the shopkeepers cannot immediately meet demand. They therefore soak up the extra money circulating in the circular flow, by raising their prices (Figure 9.3). If more goods can be produced then there may be no further pressure within the circular flow for prices to continue rising. However if no more goods can be produced, or if productivity falls, then the increase in prices is likely to remain. This is a case of too much money (same as aggregate demand) chasing too few goods. To import goods is one way in which this situation may be relieved, but the relief will prove only temporary.

Overseas trade

Factories producing similar goods overseas will see the high prices being paid in the UK and will export their goods to the UK. The UK is not in a position to export any goods abroad as all the capacities of the factories are used to produce for the home market. It is this full capacity situation which caused the problem in the first place. Thus the shops will receive imports to sell. This will relieve the pressure of demand in the first circulation of the circular flow. The money for the imports will go abroad i.e. leave the UK circular flow – thus causing less money to be available in the factories for the next circulation. Less money in the factories means less income for the workers and perhaps less jobs, less income for the workers means less expenditure in the shops, less expenditure in the shops means less demand for the goods from the factories.

9.7 Summary

The purpose of this introductory section has been to introduce some of the relationships between various elements of the macro economy. It will prove useful to the student in determining likely outcomes from a variety of government policies and other economic events.

If in doubt as to the effect of a variable upon the level of national income, use this basic model to think through the sequences. It is always helpful to know the outcome.

Test your understanding

(Answers are given at the back of the book)

1. Which of the following are injections into the circular flow of income?

    1. A government sponsored road building program
    2. British citizens send money to overseas relations
    3. A firm builds a new factory
    4. The level of National Savings has risen

        A   1 and 2
        B   1, 2 and 3
        C   1 and 3
        D   2, 3 and 4

2. Which of the following statements is true?

    A $I + G = S + X$
    B $S + G = T + M$
    C $G + X = T + M$
    D $I + M = G + X$

3. Explain why national income equals national output and national expenditure.

4. Starting with a circular flow of £5000 explain in detail how each of the following will affect the level of national income. (You should explain the mechanisms and give the new level of national income, if it has changed).

    A   There is a new government building started costing £2000
    B   The factories sell £1500s worth of goods overseas
    C   The factories receive £3000 to build new factories and the government announces all earnings are to be taxed at 50%.
    D   The government encourages people to save, and it is estimated that new savings are £1000.

5. How does inflation arise in the economy? Explain using the circular flow diagram introduced in this chapter.

6. How does unemployment arise in the economy? Explain using the circular flow diagram introduced in this chapter.

7. What do you understand by the term **equilibrium level of national income**?

10 Aggregate demand

Learning objectives

To understand the basic Keynesian model of aggregate demand.

- To understand and to be able to demonstrate the consumption function graphically.
- To understand the components of aggregate expenditure.
- To be able to demonstrate the components of aggregate demand graphically.
- To understand and be able to calculate from given data.
  - The average propensities to consume and save.
  - The marginal propensities to consume and save.
  - The propensity to withdraw.
- To understand the concept of the multiplier. Also to be able to calculate the value of the multiplier from relevant data.

10.1 Introduction

In 1936 J. M. Keynes published his ideas on relationships within the economy in *The General Theory of Employment, Interest and Money*. In the Keynesian view of the economy both employment and output are determined by the level of aggregate demand. Thus if policy makers wish to prevent output and employment from falling to unacceptable levels they must initiate corrective monetary or fiscal action. It is important to understand the fundamental links in the Keynesian argument.

10.2 Aggregate demand

Aggregate demand is the **total planned expenditure on goods and services** within the economy. The components of aggregate demand are: consumer spending (C), expenditure by firms on investment goods (I), government demand for goods and services (G) and net exports (exports minus imports: X − M).

> **Note** As it is the aggregate demand for UK goods and services that is being considered, the demand by foreigners for UK goods and services (exports) is part of UK aggregate demand. Whereas demand in the UK for foreign goods and services is part of the demand for another country's goods and services (imports) and therefore has to be deducted from the exports so that only net exports are counted as part of aggregate demand.

Thus aggregate demand can be written as: $AD = C + I + G + (X - M)$

By far the largest element in aggregate demand is consumer spending.

10.3 The consumption function

Keynes argued that 'the fundamental psychological law . . . is that men are disposed, as a rule and on the average, to increase their consumption as their income increases, but not by as much as the increase in their income' (Keynes, 1936, p. 96). From this statement a number of propositions can be derived.

Consumption is a function of income	$C = f(Y)$	Remember Y is the symbol in economics for income
Consumption will increase by a fraction of increasing income	$C = b(Y)$	b stands for some fraction i.e. 0.5 or 0.3 of Y
The fraction of income not spent is assumed to be saved	$C + S = Y$	Consumption + saving = income

It is clear that at low levels of income, or no income at all, people still have to eat, clothe themselves and keep warm. This means that they will have to spend income they do not have. Thus they either spend their savings or rely on welfare support, or both. This aspect of general consumption is added into the consumption function by adding a positive constant.

The consumption function: $C = a + b(Y)$

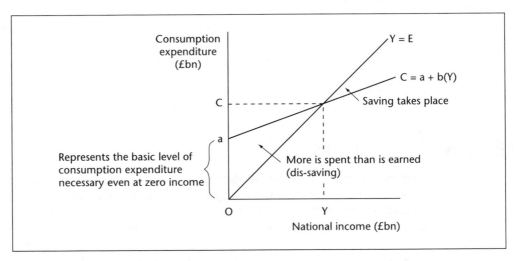

Figure 10.1 **The consumption function in diagrammatic form**

In Figure 10.1 the consumption function $[C = a + b(Y)]$ starts at point a on the expenditure axis to show that even at zero income some level of expenditure is necessary. The line then rises constantly at the rate of $b(Y)$ to indicate that at all levels of national income the fraction (b) will be spent on consumption. The 45° line ($Y = E$) is a line which joins all points where national income equals consumption expenditure. Thus at every point along this line $Y = E$. This line is useful because the consumption function can be compared with it.

Up to the level of national income OY consumption expenditure is greater than national income. After the OY level of national income consumption expenditure is less than national income, indicating that saving is taking place. Only at OY level of national income is consumption equal to national income. The relationship between national income (Y), consumption (C) and saving (S) can be shown in a table of hypothetical figures (Table 10.1) and Figure 10.2.

Table 10.1 Relationship between national income, consumption and saving

National income (Y) (£bn)	Consumption (C) (£bn)	Saving (S) (£bn)
0	30	−30
50	70	−20
100	110	−10
150	150	0
200	190	10

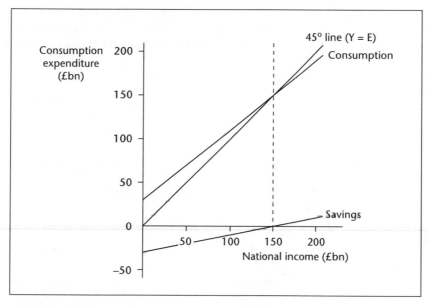

Figure 10.2 Graphical representation of data in Table 10.1

In Figure 10.2 it can clearly be seen that up to £150bn level of national income there is more spent on consumption than is earned. The savings function shows negative savings up to the £150bn level of national income. At £150bn level of national income consumption expenditure equals £150bn. (at this level it crosses the 45° line where Y = E.) Also at this level of national income savings is zero (the savings function cuts the 0 line at £150bn). Above the £150bn level of national income savings are positive and therefore total consumption expenditure is less than national income. The consumption line is below the 45° line at all levels of national income over £150bn.

Table 10.2 Aggregate planned expenditure in £bn

National income (Y)	Consumption (C)	Investment (I)	Government expenditure (G)	Exports (X)	Imports (M)	Aggregate planned expenditure (C + I + G + (X – M))
0	30	25	25	40	0	120
50	70	25	25	40	15	145
100	110	25	25	40	30	170
150	150	25	25	40	45	195
200	190	25	25	40	60	220
250	230	25	25	40	75	245

Having considered the main component of aggregate expenditure the other components can now be added. The aggregate expenditure curve can be derived from the data in Table 10.2, which adds to the consumption data in Table 10.1.

In Figure 10.3 the data has been put into the diagram separately. The investment spending is the amount of investment that is *planned* in order to support the planned levels of output. Added to this planned investment is the planned expenditure of the government. The government will plan to buy various goods and services, and the £25bn is added to the investment £25bn and the I + G line represents the expenditure level of both. Added to this £50bn is the £40bn of exports as this represents the planned

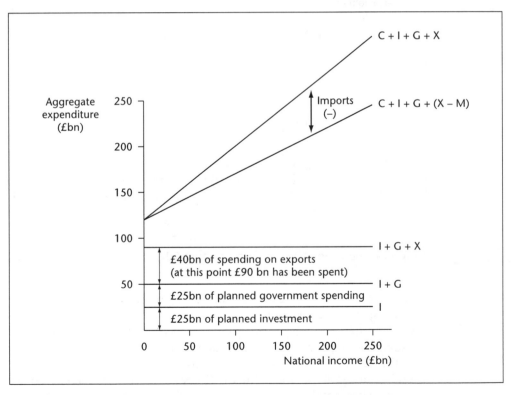

Figure 10.3 Aggregate expenditure curve

expenditure of foreigners on UK output. Thus I + G + X equals £90bn. If the levels of planned consumption expenditure are added to this base line of £90bn the C + I + G + X line is generated. This will be above the final aggregate expenditure curve because expenditure on imports has to be deducted from the planned UK expenditure, as this represents UK expenditure on foreign countries outputs. The final aggregate expenditure curve represents C + I + G + (X − M).

10.4 The propensities to consume and save

The word **propensity** merely means *a tendency or an inclination*. Thus the propensity to consume refers to the nation's collective tendency to spend on consumption. The propensity to save refers to the nation's collective tendency to save rather than spend on consumption.

Total consumption and saving

As was shown on page 140 total income can either be spent or saved. Thus Y = C + S and if consumption does not equal income then the balance must be saving. As was shown in diagrams of the consumption function, at low levels of national income more is spent on consumption than is earned and there is therefore a dis-saving. As income rises there will come a point when the average family will save some money, and the higher that incomes rise the greater will be the savings. This household behaviour is reflected in the trends for the national income.

The average propensity to consume and save

The average propensity to consume (APC) is calculated by dividing consumption expenditure by income. This calculation can be shown by using the figures from Table 10.1, which are reproduced here.

Table 10.1 **Relationship between national income, consumption and saving**

National income (Y) (£bn)	Consumption (C) (£bn)	Saving (S) (£bn)
0	30	−30
50	70	−20
100	110	−10
150	150	0
200	190	10

When the national income is £50bn the APC is 1.4. This is calculated by dividing the consumption expenditure by the national income level. Thus 70 ÷ 50 = 1.4.

> Calculate the rest of the APCs in Table 10.1.

The average propensity to save (APS) is calculated by dividing savings by income. This calculation can be shown by using the figures from the table above. When the national income is £50bn the APS is −0.4. This is calculated by dividing the savings by the national income level. Thus $-20 \div 50 = -0.4$

Calculate the rest of the APSs in Table 10.1.

You will notice that the two average propensities add up to ONE. This must always be the case as $C + S = Y$. If we divide all three elements in this equation by income the answer will confirm that $APC + APS = 1$.

At the 200 level of Y in Table 10.1:

$$APC + APS = 1 \equiv \frac{C}{200} + \frac{S}{200} = \frac{Y}{200} \equiv 0.95 + 0.05 = 1$$

Table 10.1 is now reproduced as Table 10.3 with the APCs and APSs attached.

Table 10.3

National income (Y) (£bn)	Consumption (C) (£bn)	Saving (S) (£bn)	APC	APS
0	30	−30	−	−
50	70	−20	1.4	−0.4
100	110	−10	1.1	−0.1
150	150	0	1	0
200	190	10	0.95	0.05

The marginal propensity to consume and save

The marginal propensity to consume (MPC) is calculated by dividing the change in each successive level of consumption expenditure by the change in each successive level of income.

The **MARGINAL** propensity to consume is no different in concept than any other marginal calculation. The **MARGIN** concerns **differences in totals.** The **difference** between one level of national income and the next level of national income is the **marginal level of national income.** The **difference** between one level of consumption expenditure and the next level of consumption expenditure is the **marginal level of consumption expenditure.**

IT IS THESE MARGINAL VALUES WHICH ARE USED TO CALCULATE THE MARGINAL PROPENSITY TO CONSUME.

This calculation can be shown by using the figures from Table 10.1.

Table 10.1 **Relationship between national income, consumption and saving**

National income (Y) (£bn)	Consumption (C) (£bn)	Saving (S) (£bn)
0	30	−30
50	70	−20
100	110	−10
150	150	0
200	190	10

When the national income is £50bn the MPC is 0.8. This is calculated by dividing the marginal consumption expenditure by the marginal level of national income. Thus $\Delta C \div \Delta Y = MPC$ with $\Delta C = 40$ (70 − 30) and $\Delta Y = 50$ (50 − 0). The calculation is therefore $40 \div 50 = 0.8$.

Calculate the rest of the MPCs in Table 10.1.

The marginal propensity to save (MPS) is calculated by dividing the change in each successive level of savings by the change in each successive level of income.

The **MARGINAL** propensity to save is no different in concept than any other marginal calculation. The **MARGIN** concerns **differences in totals.** The **difference** between one level of national income and the next level of national income is the **marginal level of national income.** The **difference** between one level of savings and the next level of savings is the **marginal level of savings.**

IT IS THESE MARGINAL VALUES WHICH ARE USED TO CALCULATE THE MARGINAL PROPENSITY TO SAVE.

This calculation can be shown by using the figures from Table 10.1. When the national income is £50bn the MPS is 0.2. This is calculated by dividing the marginal savings by the marginal level of national income. Thus $\Delta S \div \Delta Y = MPS$. $\Delta S = 10$ (−20 − −30) and $\Delta Y = 50$ (50 − 0). The calculation is therefore $10 \div 50 = 0.2$.

Calculate the rest of the MPSs in Table 10.1.

You will notice that the two marginal propensities add up to ONE. This must always be the case as each additional pound of income must either be spent or saved. Thus $\Delta C + \Delta S = \Delta Y$. If we divide all three elements in this equation by the change in income the answer will confirm that $MPC + MPS = 1$.

At the 200 level of Y in Table 10.1:

$$MPC + MPS = 1 \equiv \frac{\Delta C}{50} + \frac{\Delta S}{50} = \frac{\Delta Y}{50} \equiv 0.8 + 0.2 = 1$$

Table 10.3 is now reproduced as Table 10.4 with the MPCs and MPSs attached.

Table 10.4

National income (Y) (£bn)	Consumption (C) (£bn)	Saving (S) (£bn)	APC	APS	MPC	MPS
0	30	−30	–	–	–	00
50	70	−20	1.4	−0.4	0.8	0.2
100	110	−10	1.1	−0.1	0.8	0.2
150	150	0	1	0	0.8	0.2
200	190	10	0.95	0.05	0.8	0.2

From Table 10.4 it is clear that unlike the average propensities, which change as income increases, the marginal propensities are constant.

The propensity to withdraw

The purpose of distinguishing between consumption and saving is to quantify the proportion of national income which is used as expenditure to create aggregate demand, and the proportion of national income which is not spent – or which is withdrawn from the circular flow of income. Savings are not the only withdrawals from the circular flow of income.

As Keynes pointed out consumption is the most important element of aggregate demand but not the only element. Aggregate demand (aggregate expenditure) consists of government spending, investment spending and exports as well as consumption spending. The withdrawals from the circular flow of income i.e. that income not passed on in expenditure, are taxation (T) and imports (M) as well as saving (S). Thus aggregate demand plus all withdrawals equals the level of national income.

Thus from C + S = Y in a realistic economy it can be written:

$$[C + I + G + X] + [S + T + M] = Y$$

Just as there is a marginal propensity to save, there is a marginal propensity to taxation, and a marginal propensity to spend money on imported goods. Consumers decide upon the levels of savings they wish to make at various levels of national income. They also decide upon the products they wish to buy, including purchasing goods made overseas (imports). The government and local authorities decide upon the levels of taxation at the different levels of national income.

10.5 The multiplier

The concept of the multiplier is central to Keynesian analysis. Because Keynes was concerned with aggregate demand he was interested in any mechanism which would have a major effect upon this aggregate. Aggregate demand is directly related to the circular flow of income and the multiplier has a direct major effect upon national income.

The concept is that if there is an injection into the circular flow of income, then the national income will rise, but the greater the proportion of the extra income that is spent, and therefore passed on to someone else, the greater will be the eventual rise in national income. In money terms, it is possible that extra investment of say £25m will lead to national income rising by £50m. This process will now be explained.

A basic example of the multiplication process

Assume that there are 10 self employed people and each person spends money with one of the other self employed people. Thus No. 1 spends money with No. 2 and No. 2 with No. 3 and so on. The following two examples illustrate the idea of the multiplier.

Example 1

Each of the self employed people will spend 90% of any extra income (i.e. for each their MPC is 0.9). The first self employed person has received an unexpected extra income of £1000.

No. 1 receives extra income of £1000	£1000
No. 1 spends 90% (or 0.9) of the extra £1000 with No. 2	
No. 2 receives extra income of £900	£900
No. 2 spends 90% (or 0.9) of the extra £900 with No. 3	
No. 3 receives extra income of £810	£810
No. 3 spends 90% (or 0.9) of the extra £810 with No. 4	
No. 4 receives extra income of £729	£729
No. 4 spends 90% (or 0.9) of the extra £729 with No. 5	
No. 5 receives extra income of £656	£656
No. 5 spends 90% (or 0.9) of the extra £656 with No. 6	
No. 6 receives extra income of £590	£590
No. 6 spends 90% (or 0.9) of the extra £590 with No. 7	
No. 7 receives extra income of £531	£531
No. 7 spends 90% (or 0.9) of the extra £531 with No. 8	
No. 8 receives extra income of £478	£478
No. 8 spends 90% (or 0.9) of the extra £478 with No. 9	
No. 9 receives extra income of £430	£430
No. 9 spends 90% (or 0.9) of the extra £430 with No. 10	
No. 10 receives extra income of £387	£387
Total income generated ⟶	£6511

Because each of the people spent 0.9 of their extra income, the original £1000 has generated an extra £5511 as it was passed from person to person creating new income every time it was passed on.

147

Example 2

Each of the self employed people will spend 25% of any extra income (i.e. for each their MPC is 0.25).

The first self-employed person has received an unexpected extra income of £1000.

No. 1 receives extra income of £1000   £1000
No. 1 spends 25% (or 0.25) of the extra £1000 with No. 2
No. 2 receives extra income of £250   £250
No. 2 spends 25% (or 0.25) of the extra £250 with No. 3
No. 3 receives extra income of £63   £63
No. 3 spends 25% (or 0.25) of the extra £63 with No. 4
No. 4 receives extra income of £16   £16
No. 4 spends 25% (or 0.25) of the extra £16 with No. 5
No. 5 receives extra income of £4   £4
No. 5 spends 25% (or 0.25) of the extra £4 with No. 6
No. 6 receives extra income of £1   £1
No. 6 spends 25% (or 0.25) of the extra £1 with No. 7
No. 7 receives extra income of 25p   £0.25
No. 7 spends 25% (or 0.25) of the extra 25p with No. 8
No. 8 receives extra income of 6p   £0.06
No. 8 spends 25% (or 0.25) of the extra 6p with No. 9
No. 9 receives extra income of 2p   £0.02
No. 9 spends 25% (or 0.25) of the extra 2p with No. 10
No. 10 receives extra income of 0.5p   £0.005

Total income generated   ——————————→   £1334.33p

Because each of the people spent 0.25 of their extra income, the original £1000 has generated an extra £334.33p as it was passed from person to person creating new income every time it was passed on.

One fact is obvious from the above examples. The more people spend of their extra income the more others receive in extra income, and the greater the eventual total of all extra income.

The greater the fraction of extra income that is passed on in expenditure, the greater will be the eventual increase in the national income.

The fraction of extra income passed on (or spent) is called the **MARGINAL PROPENSITY TO CONSUME (MPC)**.

The higher the MPC the greater will be the total increase in national income, when there are extra injections into the circular flow of income.

Calculating the multiplier

In an economy where there are millions of people spending money it would be impossible to go through the process of the above examples. There is a formula which will calculate a value for the multiplier. Once this value is known then the extra injection(s) into the circular flow can be multiplied by the value of the multiplier so that the final increase in national income will be known.

The formula

The multiplier can be referred to in some texts as K, for present purposes the full title will always be used.

$$\text{Multiplier} = \frac{1}{1 - \text{MPC}}$$

As MPC + MPS = 1 it follows that 1 − MPC must equal MPS

$$\text{Therefore the multiplier} = \frac{1}{\text{MPS}}$$

Examples

We can now recalculate the two examples on pages 147 and 148. The number of people do not need to be restricted as with the formula we can calculate the total increase in national income when all the extra fractions have been passed on and there is nothing left to pass on.

The first example showed an injection of £1000 and a MPC of 0.9

A MPC of 0.9 means that the MPS is 0.1 and applying this to the formula we get:

$$\frac{1}{\text{MPS}} = \frac{1}{0.1} \quad \text{The multiplier is 10}$$

Therefore we multiply the original injection of £1000 by the multiplier to discover the extra amount of national income that will be generated by that particular injection. The answer is £10 000.

The second example showed an injection of £1000 and a MPC of 0.25

A MPC of 0.25 means that the MPS is 0.75 and applying this to the formula we get:

$$\frac{1}{\text{MPS}} = \frac{1}{0.75} \quad \text{The multiplier is 1.333}$$

Therefore we multiply the original injection of £1000 by the multiplier to discover the extra amount of national income that will be generated by that particular injection. The answer is £1333.

The multiplier within the international economy

As was shown on page 146 savings are not the only withdrawals from the circular flow of income. Any withdrawals which prevent income from being spent, so as to create more income, must be included in the calculation of the multiplier. When tax is deducted from income that amount of money taken away cannot be spent. When we buy imports we are spending our income on another country's goods and the money has to leave the UK and go to that other country – it is not therefore passed on as income to other UK people. To account for the effect of these withdrawals on the national income the multiplier formula has to be modified.

The basic formula is the same

$$\text{Multiplier} = \frac{1}{1 - \text{MPC}}$$

That income which is not spent (consumed) is withdrawn. Savings are one type of withdrawal as are various taxes and spending on imports. Therefore to make the multiplier more realistic it should be stated that $\text{MPC} + \text{MPW} = 1$ where the $\text{MPW} = \text{MPS} + \text{MPT} + \text{MPM}$

MPW = The marginal propensity to withdraw
MPS = The marginal propensity to save
MPT = The marginal propensity to suffer taxation
MPM = The marginal propensity to spend on imports

$$\text{Therefore Multiplier} = \frac{1}{\text{MPS} + \text{MPT} + \text{MPM}} \text{ or } \frac{1}{\text{MPW}}$$

Autonomous changes in spending

The word **autonomous** means from *outside the system*. Thus in the above chapter all references to extra spending, increased investment, etc., are referring to autonomous changes.

The multiplier will come into effect as the result of any autonomous change in spending.

An example of the multiplier

We are frequently told by politicians that the government is to spend certain sums of money on various projects. For this example let us assume that the government is to institute a national road improvement project for £50m. Further assume that people save about 20% of their income, that taxation is about 40% of income (including VAT and other indirect taxes) and that people in the UK spend about 25% of total income on imported goods.

MPS = 20% which is 0.2
MPT = 40% which is 0.4
MPM = 25% which is 0.25

Therefore the MPW = MPS + MPT + MPM or MPW = 0.2 + 0.4 + 0.25 or MPW = 0.85

The multiplier $= \dfrac{1}{0.85} = 1.18$

The amount that national income would rise by, is £59m, given the £50m extra spending by the government (£50m multiplied by 1.18 = £59m).

10.6 The paradox of thrift

The paradox may be concisely stated. An increase in savings by all people in an economy may lead to a fall in savings.

Successive governments have frequently urged the population to save, whether for a pension or other purpose. From all that has been stated in the preceding two chapters it is clear that savings are a withdrawal from the circular flow of income. Withdrawals lead to decreased expenditure, decreased output, decreased employment, and decreased national income. If people are receiving less income and are unemployed then they are likely to use their savings to maintain their standards of living. Thus savings lead to a decrease in savings.

10.7 Summary

The purpose of this chapter has been to introduce the student to basic Keynesian analysis. Aggregate demand is the main determinant of national output and employment, says Keynes, so a close look at the structure of aggregate demand, and its effect on national income are important ideas.

Consumption spending is the main ingredient of aggregate demand. Thus the consumption function is introduced. The propensity to consume is an idea which is central to this analysis. It leads to the introduction of the APC and the MPC. These ideas are building blocks towards an understanding of the multiplier.

The multiplier effect will arise from any autonomous change in spending. Thus autonomous changes in investment, government spending, exports and consumption will all have the same multiplier effect upon the level of national income.

Note   In more advanced texts the student will be introduced to other multiplier processes such as the tax multiplier or the balanced budget multiplier)

Further reading

ANDERTON, A., *Economics*, Causeway Press.
BEGG, D., FISCHER, S. and DORNBUSCH, R. *Economics*, McGraw-Hill.
GRIFFITHS, A. and WALL, S. *Applied Economics*, Longman.
HARDWICK, P., KHAN, B. and LANGMEAD, J. *An Introduction to Modern Economics*, Longman.
SLOMAN, J. and SUTCLIFFE, M. *Economics for Business*, Prentice Hall.

Test your understanding

(Answers are given at the back of the book)

1. What is the level of national income given the following?

   Exports £4000, Investment £2000, Imports £2500, Consumption £8000 and Government expenditure £2500

2. What is the level of imports given the following?

   Exports £2500, Investment £2750, National income £13000, Consumption £9500 and Government expenditure £1750

3. Complete the following table

Aggregate planned expenditure	Consumption	Investment	Government expenditure	Exports	Imports
8 000	4 000	2 000	1 500	3 000	
	8 000	4 000	2 750	1 000	3 250
8 500	3 000		2 500	750	1 250
14 250	6 000	1 500	3 000		750

4. Complete the following table by filling in the *average propensity to consume* values (APCs).

National income (Y) (£bn)	APC	Saving (S) (£bn)
150		60
300		90
500		130
750		180

5. Complete the table in question 4 by filling in the *marginal propensity to consume* values (MPCs).

National income (Y) (£bn)	MPC	Saving (S) (£bn)
150		60
300		90
500		130
750		180

6. Assume that the government is to institute a hospital building program for £50m. Further assume that people save about 10 per cent of their income, that taxation is about 60 per cent of income (including VAT and other indirect taxes) and that people in the UK spend about 25 per cent of total income on imported goods. If the level of national income was £350m before the government building program, what will it be after the government has built the hospitals.

7. From the following information calculate:
   i. the value of the multiplier
   ii. the increase in national income

   'The chancellor announced that the government had authorised an extra £40m spending for road building and a further £30m to renovate school buildings, which were likely to deteriorate further without this support. Thus the government was addressing two of the most pressing concerns of motorists and parents. He went on to point out that it was necessary to increase the level of indirect taxation to 20 per cent on average, but that direct taxation would remain at an average of 35 per cent. This adjustment to the levels of taxation was necessary, according to the Chancellor, because people were spending an even greater proportion of their income, about 80 per cent, and this might lead to an inflationary level of demand. An additional problem was that consumers were reported to be spending 25 per cent of their income on overseas produced goods, rather than home produced goods.'

8. Assess the validity of the following comments, made in relation to the Chancellor's statement in question 8.

   'Commentators claimed that the Chancellor was giving with one hand and taking away with the other. They further claimed that the spin off effect of the government spending plans would be minimal.'

Aggregate demand and aggregate supply

Learning objectives

- To understand the use of demand and supply analysis applied in an aggregate sense to the whole economy.
- To understand that aggregate demand and supply are related to real GDP and the price level.
- To be able to understand and to demonstrate the following, in graphical terms.
    - Aggregate demand and supply conditions that lead to increased output and employment without increased prices.
    - Aggregate demand and supply conditions that lead to increased prices with no increased output.

11.1 Introduction

In Keynesian terms aggregate demand is the same as aggregate expenditure $(C + I + G + (X - M))$, and is directly related to national income. In this chapter the idea of aggregate demand and aggregate supply is introduced.

The analysis here is very different from the Keynesian analysis. The aggregate demand schedule is not the same as the aggregate expenditure function of Chapter 10. The Keynesian analysis is not able to focus upon price levels, and the following analysis shows aggregate demand as the amount of goods and services required at any given price level. An aggregate demand curve therefore relates the level of aggregate demand at various levels of price.

Before Keynes published his *General Theory* economists (often referred to as Classical economists) believed that the whole economy worked in a similar way to a large product market. That there would be equilibrium where demand equalled supply. If there was excess of supply or demand in the economy then general prices would adjust so as to return the economy to a state of equilibrium. Keynes showed that this model of the economy was unrealistic and had no answer to the fact that prices tended not to fall as readily as they rose. Having warned the student that aggregate demand and aggregate supply are very different concepts from demand and supply in the product markets, we now continue to the construction of aggregate demand and supply curves.

11.2　Aggregate demand

> Aggregate demand is the total amount of goods and services, which households, firms, overseas buyers and the government plan to purchase at different values of the general price level.

The aggregate demand curve in Figure 11.1 is downward sloping, similar to the demand curve for a product. However there are a number of important differences.
The elements of Figure 11.1 are explained below.

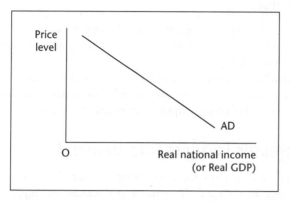

Figure 11.1 **Aggregate demand curve**

Price level

This is an average of all the prices in the economy. This axis is often measured by means of index numbers which stand for various price levels.

Real national income (Real GDP)

The word real refers to a constant purchasing power. Thus it could be the value of 1998 national output [or Gross Domestic Product (GDP)] at 1980 prices; or any other constant price level. It is the national income without varying levels of inflation.

> The national income is the same as the value of the national product or output. Thus there is no difference in the labels **real national income** and **real GDP**.

Contractions and expansions of aggregate demand

A movement along the demand curve will be the result of a change in the average price level – **and nothing else.** If the price level rises there will be a contraction in aggregate demand and if the price level falls there will be an expansion in aggregate demand.

Price rises

There will be three main effects.

a. A decrease in real income therefore less purchasing power.
b. An increase in the current cost of goods and services, leading to a postponing of current expenditure in the hope that future costs will be lower.
c. The cost of domestically produced goods increases relative to foreign goods, leading to a tendency to buy more imported goods.

Price falls

There will be three main effects.

d. An increase in real income therefore greater purchasing power.
e. A decrease in the current cost of goods and services, leading to a tendency to spend now as future costs might be higher.
f. The cost of domestically produced goods decreases relative to foreign goods, leading to a tendency to buy more home produced goods: also the sale of exports may increase as they are relatively cheaper in overseas markets.

Increases and decreases in aggregate demand

When the whole demand curve moves then something other than the average price level has caused the change in demand. The main influences on aggregate demand which cause the demand curve to shift are:

i.   Expectations
ii. Fiscal policy
iii. Monetary policy
iv. Overseas or international influences.

Expectations

People tend to tailor their current consumption behaviour to their view of the economy in the future, the so called 'consumer confidence'. There are three areas of expectation which are of considerable importance to people.

Expected inflation

If people feel generally that inflation is going to increase, they will tend to increase current demand, therefore aggregate demand will increase. As inflation increases future prices are rising, and the value of future income is falling in real terms (i.e. what it will buy). It therefore makes sense to spend 'now' whilst purchasing power is high.

Expected future incomes

If people expect their future incomes to increase they will tend to increase their current demand patterns in anticipation of the increased future income streams. Households planned spending on consumer durables, cars and holidays are a few of the items which may attract extra demand in anticipation of higher future incomes. If, however, people expect their future incomes to decrease or they perceive their employment prospects to be less than safe, they will tend to decrease their current demand patterns in anticipation of the decreased future income streams.

Expected future profits

Firms tend to renew their capital, and structure new investment, according to their view of the future prosperity of the industry, and their firm in particular. Prosperity may mean many things but it certainly includes profitability. If there is confidence that future profits will be maintained or improved then investment projects will go ahead and these constitute demand for capital equipment – a major constituent of aggregate demand. If, conversely, there is a lack of confidence that future profitability will be maintained, the investment projects may be postponed or cancelled. Demand for capital goods will decrease and aggregate demand will decrease.

Fiscal policy

When the government attempts to influence factors within the economy it does so by either spending money on various projects, or by imposing taxes. Government action whether by spending or by claiming taxes is called *fiscal policy*.

Government spending

Whether the government spends money by directly giving it to consumers; such as pensions, welfare payments, health and social security support; or by indirectly feeding it into the economy; such as road building, hospital building; it creates increased demand for goods and services and therefore has the effect of increasing aggregate demand.

Government taxes

If direct taxes increase then there is less for consumers to spend as these are taken directly from wages and salaries. If indirect taxes such as VAT increase then this has the effect of raising prices and also reducing spending. Thus increased taxes means a decrease in aggregate demand. If taxes are lowered then the opposite effect, of increased aggregate demand, will be achieved.

Monetary policy

The influence on the economy of variations in money supply and interest rates is known as **monetary policy.** The subject of the money supply is vast and complex and will be dealt with at length in Chapter 12, but for present purposes the simple examples shown in Chapter 9 are sufficient. The greater the amount of money circulating in the economy the more aggregate demand that is possible. Any action which increases the money supply also increases aggregate demand, and any action which reduces the money supply decreases aggregate demand. Interest rates in the UK are the responsibility of the Bank of England. Increases in interest rates have the effect of damping down demand for many goods and services but principally houses. Increases in interest rates decrease aggregate demand, whilst decreases in interest rates have the effect of increasing aggregate demand.

International (overseas) influences

The main influence is the foreign exchange rate. The exchange rate for the pound sterling will govern what foreigners pay for UK goods and services abroad, also what UK consumers pay for imported goods from abroad. If the value of the pound rises then exports are more expensive for foreigners to buy and imports are relatively more cheap. So there will be a reduction in exports (**and therefore less money coming into the UK from abroad**) and an increase in aggregate demand for imports (**and therefore more money leaving the UK and going abroad**). If the value of the pound falls then exports become cheaper in foreign markets encouraging foreigners to buy more and imports become relatively more expensive in the UK. There will be an increased demand for exports (**and therefore more money coming into the UK from abroad**) and a decreased aggregate demand for imports (**and therefore less money leaving the UK and going abroad**).

Increases and decreases in aggregate demand are shown diagrammatically in Figure 11.2.

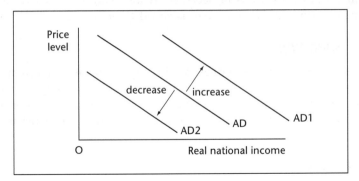

Figure 11.2 **Increases and decreases in aggregate demand**

11.3   Aggregate supply

The aggregate quantity of goods and services supplied is the total of all planned output from all firms and government departments in the economy. It is measured as real gross domestic product supplied.

> REMEMBER   Real gross domestic product is the same as real national income.

Aggregate supply occurs within two macroeconomic time frames: the short run and the long run.

Short run

The short run is a period during which the prices of goods and services change in response to changes in demand and conditions of supply, but the prices of some factors of production – wage rates and raw materials – do not change. Wage rates are often negotiated annually or periodically, and salaries are often enforced by labour contracts which frequently run for 3 to 5 years. Thus in these cases wage rates change more slowly than prices. Raw materials prices are frequently artificially maintained at a predetermined level by the action of international suppliers acting in concert; oil is a good example. There are also occasions when the prices can change by very large amounts.

Long run

The long run is a period during which the prices of all factors of production have adjusted to account for any market disturbances (national or international) so that aggregate demand and aggregate supply are equal in all factor markets. In the long run there is *full employment*.

Short run aggregate supply

The short run aggregate supply curve is not an upward sloping supply curve, as shown in Figure 3.6 page 39. It has three ranges and is shown graphically in Figure 11.3.

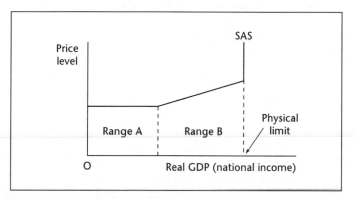

Figure 11.3 **Short run aggregate supply curve**

Range A – often referred to as the 'depression range'.

When the economy is in depression national income is at low levels, there is a lot of unemployment and firms have a lot of spare capacity. Firms are therefore very keen to sell whatever they can at the going price. Further, in order to try and utilise their spare capacity – which is expensive to maintain – they would like to sell more output without putting up the price. So each firm is effectively a 'price taker' and has a horizontal supply curve. As firms in the economy have a horizontal supply curve, so is the aggregate supply curve also horizontal.

Range B – an intermediate range

This part of the short run aggregate supply curve (SAS) is upward sloping. This implies that producers are anxious to sell more if prices increase, so as to capture the higher levels of revenue. As wage rates are constant, the aggregate quantity of goods and services will increase in response to increasing prices. To increase their output, in the short run, firms will take on extra labour and offer overtime to the existing labour force. So the higher the price level, the greater is the aggregate quantity of goods and services supplied, the higher is the level of employment and the lower is the level of unemployment.

It is this part of the short run SAS that is usually shown in textbooks, often without an explanation that it is one section of a complete curve.

The physical limit to real GDP or real national income

There is a physical limit to the output which the economy can produce. There is a limit to the number of hours workers are prepared to work. There is a limit to the physical production capabilities, as firms are unwilling to incur high maintenance and repair charges to keep machinery working harder than it was designed to do. There is a limit to the number of workers available who wish to work. Once these limits are reached there can be no more output produced **no matter how high prices rise.**

The diagram in Figure 11.3 can now be restated and interpreted in terms of the above explanations.

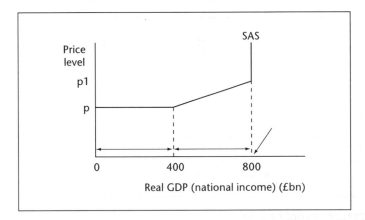

Figure 11.4

In Figure 11.4 the depression range of real GDP is up to £400bn. At levels of real GDP below £400bn there is no need for prices to rise in order to induce firms to produce more output. Thus the price level remains at p. Over the range of real GDP from £400bn to £800bn a rise in the average price level will encourage firms to produce more goods for sale. The physical limit to the extra amount of output that can be induced by increasing price levels is £800bn at a price level of p1. After this level of output no more can be produced so if the price levels rise then what has been produced is merely more expensive.

11.4 Macroeconomic equilibrium

This is where aggregate demand (AD) equals aggregate short run supply (SAS). Equilibrium does not necessarily occur at full employment. At **full employment** the economy is on its **long run aggregate supply curve** but macroeconomic equilibrium is where AD intersects the **short run** AS curve. This may be above, below or equal to full employment level of national income.

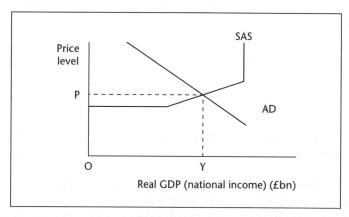

Figure 11.5 **Macroeconomic equilibrium**

In Figure 11.5 equilibrium level of real national income is OY at the average price level of OP.

The question of full employment

At full employment the economy is on its long run aggregate supply curve (LRAS). The LRAS curve shows the relationship between the quantity of real GDP supplied and the price level when there is full employment. As there is only one level of real GDP that can be produced when there is full employment, the LRAS curve is a vertical line. The LRAS is shown in Figure 11.6.

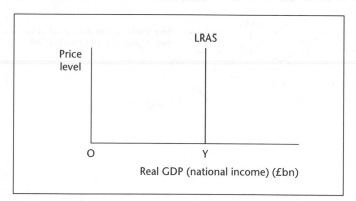

Figure 11.6 **Long run aggregate supply curve**

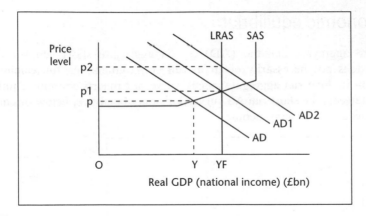

Figure 11.7

In Figure 11.6 OY level of real GDP is the full employment level, but this need not be where the economy is in equilibrium. There are three alternatives, illustrated in Figure 11.7.

In Figure 11.7 above the LRAS curve has been added to the SAS, showing a full employment level of real GDP of OYF. With a level of aggregate demand of AD the economy is in equilibrium at a real GDP level of OY. This is below the full employment level of GDP so output can increase. If aggregate demand increases to AD1 then the average price level will increase to p1 and real GDP to OYF – the full employment level of real GDP. If aggregate demand increases beyond AD1 to say AD2, real GDP may increase beyond OYF level in the very short term as firms work flat out, increasing worker's hours and delaying maintenance on machines. However it will not be long before workers ask for extra wages to compensate for the harder work and increased productivity, nor will firms be prepared to postpone maintenance indefinitely. Thus costs will rise and the SAS curve will shift to the left. The level of real GDP will fall back to OYF and the price level will rise to p2. This sequence is shown in Figure 11.8 using only the middle section of the SAS curve.

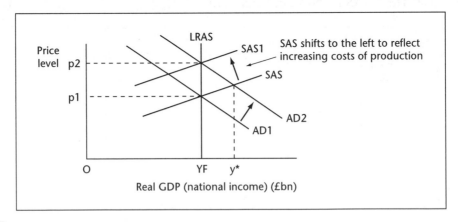

Figure 11.8

In Figure 11.8 aggregate demand (AD1) has increased beyond the full employment level of real GDP to AD2. At this level of demand and increased average prices, real GDP increases to y* in the very short term. As the result of increasing wage costs and material costs, and the need for machine down time, the SAS moves to the left to new position SAS1. The new equilibrium level of real GDP is OYF at an increased average price level of p2.

INFLATION

Notice how in Figure 11.8 the final position is one where the real GDP has not increased (in the long term) but the average price level has. Thus people are paying more money for the same amount of output. This raises a number of questions each of which begs a number of answers. These issues are dealt with in the chapter on inflation.

11.5 Summary

The tools of analysis used in this chapter have been demand and supply curves, and these relate to real GDP and the price level. The motivating force is usually changes in aggregate demand which then leads to various outcomes. The outcomes are usually couched in terms of inflation and unemployment.

At low levels of real GDP increasing aggregate demand can lead to increased output (and employment) without the penalty of increased prices. At the full employment level of GDP increased aggregate demand will lead to increased prices (inflation) and no long term increase in output and employment.

These concerns with inflation and levels of employment will be a continual thread throughout the rest of this textbook.

Further reading

BEGG, D., FISCHER, S. and DORNBUSCH, R. *Economics*, McGraw-Hill.
GRIFFITHS, A. and WALL, S. *Applied Economics*, Longman.
HARDWICK, P., KHAN, B. and LANGMEAD, J. *An Introduction to Modern Economics*, Longman.

Test your understanding

(Answers are given at the back of the book)

1. Explain briefly **three** effects on aggregate demand of a rise in prices.

2. Explain briefly **three** effects on aggregate demand of a fall in prices.

3. Explain in detail how **future expectations** can affect the level of aggregate demand.

4. Which of the following changes in an economy will cause both a rise in the price level and falling real output?

  A The aggregate demand curve shifting to the right
  B A significant fall in the exchange rate
  C The aggregate demand curve shifting to the left
  D The aggregate supply curve shifting to the left
  E The aggregate supply curve shifting to the right

5. The most likely cause of a leftward shift in the aggregate supply curve would be

  A a decrease in VAT
  B a decrease in consumer spending
  C an increase in the currency's exchange rate
  D an increase in labour costs per unit of output
  E a decrease in social security benefit payments

6. An economy is in equilibrium at point X as shown in the diagram. Which of the points labelled A–E indicates the new equilibrium if the government increases both capital expenditure and current expenditure on education and health?

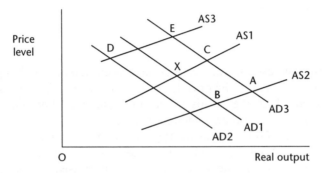

Money and banking

Learning objectives

The subject areas covered by money and banking have filled many volumes. This section is necessarily large but the learning objectives are considered minimal for a basic understanding of the topics, and as a basis for further reading.

Introductory ideas concerning money

- To understand the
  - Functions of money as distinct from the necessary attributes of money.
  - The definition of liquidity and to appreciate the importance of the concept.
  - The components of 'official money' in the UK.

Banking

- To be aware of how banks make money from deposits.
- To understand how the credit multiplier works.
- To appreciate the extent that modern banks can create credit and influence aggregate demand, and therefore inflation and employment. To understand therefore why various governments sought to find measures to control credit creation.

The Bank of England

- To have a detailed knowledge of.
  - The functions and objectives of the Bank.
  - The ways in which it carries out the functions.
  - The management of the Bank, particularly
    - The provisions of the Bank of England Act 1998
    - The functions of the Monetary Policy Committee
- To have a detailed understanding of selected technical mechanisms.
  - Open market operations.
  - The implied interest rate.
  - Bills that the Bank will buy.
  - The effects of interest rate changes within the economy.

Economic theory

- To understand the Keynesian theory of money.
- To understand the Fisher quantity theory of money.
- To understand Friedman's theory of the demand for money.
- To appreciate the differences between these theories and the implications for policy makers who wish to control inflation and unemployment.

12.1   Money

The functions of money

> **THE FOUR FUNCTIONS OF MONEY**
>
> MEDIUM OF EXCHANGE
> UNIT OF ACCOUNT
> STORE OF VALUE
> STANDARD OF DEFERRED PAYMENT

Medium of exchange

In earlier economic systems barter was a fundamental characteristic. This was mainly because the local communities were often isolated and had to try and be self-sufficient. Thus most people provide for the majority of their own needs and exchange any surplus goods for others which they may want. This system becomes very cumbersome as people specialise because it depends upon a *double coincidence of wants*. For example, a toolmaker who wants to exchange his tools for shoes must find, not only a person who wants tools, but a person who wants tools and has an excess of shoes for exchange. The alternative is to exchange his tools for other products and then to exchange these products for the shoes and other things he wants: a cumbersome process to say the least.

The use of money as a medium of exchange allows people to sell their labour for money, and with this money they are able to purchase a wide variety of goods and services.

Unit of account

Money acts as a measure of value. As each product or service is measured in units of money it is possible to compare the various products for value. The use of money as a unit of account leads directly to other economic principles such as the *equi-marginal principal* (Chapter 2).

It is an interesting feature of the various types of money in the different economies, dollars, yen, francs, etc., that they all have certain units or denominations of the currency. In the UK we have 1p, 2p, 5p, 10p, 20p, 50p, £1, £2, £5, £10, £20, £50. Any price, or number, that can be imagined can be paid by using this combination of currency values. In the USA the currency is divided into 1c, 5c, 10c, 25c, $1, $5, $10, $20, $50, $100, $500. Once again, any price, or number, that can be imagined can be paid by using this combination of currency values.

Store of value

Money need not be spent immediately, it can be saved or stored and exchanged at a future time for goods and services. The value referred to is the satisfaction derived from consuming goods and services, not from the money itself. Thus when money is saved, or stored, the satisfaction that will come from consumption is also stored. Thus there is a store of *future* value. The more stable an economy's money is, and the less inflation that is present, the better the money will act as a store of value.

Standard of deferred payment

Many debts and contractual commitments are settled in the future. Thus in order for there to be any point in relying on these future receipts or payments they must be in an acceptable currency – money. People know that one pound in ten years time will still be one pound, and therefore money is acting as a standard of deferred payment. Whilst one pound in ten years time is still one pound the question as to what it will buy in ten years time is of interest. This question is addressed by both borrowers and lenders when they try to anticipate inflation by means of the interest rate charged and received on their funds.

The necessary attributes of money

THE PROPERTIES OF MONEY

ACCEPTABILITY
DURABILITY
PORTABILITY
DIVISIBILITY
HOMOGENEITY

Acceptability

Every person using the money must be certain that all other people in the country will accept and use the money in the same way.

Many materials can be used as money. During world war II cigarettes were often used as money; gold and precious stones may still be used as money in some special circumstances. Anything may be used as money but the money will be acceptable only if it has the following properties.

Durability

Where the commodity to be used as money has an intrinsic value, such as gold, it is important that the coins or units are durable so as to maintain the intrinsic value. For example a gold coin weighing one ounce would lose value if it were to be worn away from constant use, so that it now only weighs 0.75 of an ounce. Most very valuable metals are soft and therefore are not able to maintain their intrinsic value. This is why modern money is made from mixtures of metals which are hard and durable though not intrinsically valuable. The value of the money derives from what it represents rather than from what it is intrinsically worth.

Portability

Money must be easily carried around. The problem with gold and other precious metals is that they are very heavy. Paper money is easy to carry around but it is not very durable, and therefore has to be constantly replaced. Lightweight metal alloys are durable and easily portable, which is why they are used to make money.

Divisibility

This property refers to the need for money to be divided into small units with each piece retaining its share of the original value. This can be seen in a few examples. If diamonds were to be used as money, there would soon become a problem of how to pay for goods which were very low in value. To cut a diamond into very small pieces is to reduce the value of all the pieces, because it is more valuable the larger is the whole diamond. A similar problem would occur with gold. Although gold will retain its intrinsic value, even in small quantities, it becomes a problem to mint a coin small enough to have a very small intrinsic value. The problem is overcome when the commodity to be used as money has no intrinsic value, and can be divided into arbitrary units, each small unit of value retaining its share of the value of the larger units.

In the UK we have 1p, 2p, 5p, 10p, 20p, 50p, £1, £2, £5, £10, £20, £50. The 1p unit is half the value of the 2p unit and one-tenth the value of the 10p unit. Thus it retains its share of the value of the larger units. The same is true of all the other units.

Homogeneity

If the commodity to be used as money was not homogenous then there would be differences in the money stock. People might come to prefer one quality of commodity to another. This means that one quality would be more acceptable than another as money. We would not have a medium of exchange but a variety of media of exchange, which would defeat the object of having money. Money must therefore be homogenous. In the UK the homogeneity refers to the value placed on each unit of money rather than to the look or shape of the actual coin. Thus some 50p pieces are new and shiny, others scuffed and tarnished, and yet others of slightly different design, but none of this matters because they are all identical (homogenous) in that they all are worth 50p.

12.2 Liquidity

The idea of liquidity is closely related to the medium of exchange function of money. Cash is perfectly liquid as it can always be used immediately to purchase goods and services. Other assets are less liquid because they cannot be used **immediately** to purchase goods and services, but may take time before they can be turned into cash. Thus liquidity is a measure of how **quickly** an asset can be turned into cash. Some assets are considered to be illiquid because of the long time it may take to turn them into cash, and the fact that in trying to turn them into cash, they may lose capital value and incur transaction costs. A house, for example, may have to be sold when market prices are falling, and there are considerable costs attached to selling a house. A liquid asset is defined.

LIQUID ASSET

One which can be turned into cash quickly and without capital loss or interest loss.

There is therefore a scale of liquidity which runs from liquid to illiquid. At the one end is cash and at the other are assets such as land and buildings, and specialist assets which have few alternative uses. Financial assets rest on the scale between these two extremes, depending upon how quickly their full monetary value may be realised. The following financial instruments are examples of varying liquidity.

i. **Current Accounts**   These are considered to be near perfect liquidity.
ii. **Time Deposit Accounts**   These accounts with banks and building societies are considered be very liquid. However there may be a 'notice period' before money can be obtained free of any interest penalty. This notice period would measure the liquidity of the particular deposit.
iii. **Treasury Bills**   These can be issued with 63-day maturity, 91-day maturity or 182-day maturity. The shorter the maturity period the more liquid the Treasury Bill. Those bills approaching their maturity date, regardless of when they were sold, are more liquid than those with more time to run. The fact that Treasury Bills can be traded and turned into cash immediately is of little relevance for the strict definition of liquidity, they would lose interest in so doing and that contravenes the strict definition.
iv. **Gilt-edged securities**   These usually have original maturity periods from 5 years upwards, with some of the longer dated securities being over 20 years. For most of the lives of these securities they are considered illiquid. But as their maturity date approaches they become more liquid. Thus a 20 year security with only 30 days to maturity would be as liquid as a Treasury Bond with the same period to go to maturity. As with Treasury Bills the Gilt-edged securities are tradeable, but at different times during their lifetimes there is the risk of serious capital loss, when interest rates are rising.
v. **Certificates of Deposit**   These normally have original maturity periods ranging from 28 days to 5 years, and for liquidity purposes will cover the issues raised under (iii) and (iv) above.

12.3   Money in the modern economy

Given the issues raised under the concept of liquidity, there is some ambiguity as to the precise components of the money supply. This uncertainty as to which assets to include in the money supply, for policy purposes, has led to the evolution of a range of different definitions.

Cash and current accounts

Cash in circulation with the private sector is clearly a part of spending power (aggregate demand). Most people would include the money balances held in current accounts, at banks and building societies, also as part of the money supply. These funds may be transferred by cheque in settlement of transactions. However, it is important to understand that cheques are not cash but merely documents to transfer balances from one account to another. The fact that cheques may be refused or unpaid, makes them slightly less liquid than cash but the difference in practice is negligible. For practical purposes cash and current account balances represent immediate purchasing power (aggregate demand).

Deposit accounts

Although some deposit accounts require a period of notice for withdrawals, it is frequently the case that banks and building societies will transfer funds from deposit to cheque accounts, even if there is a minimal loss of interest. Thus deposit accounts represent almost immediate spending power.

There is no clear boundary between liquid assets which are classified as money and other assets which are fairly liquid but not classified as money. Thus the monetary authorities have considered it necessary to define the money supply in order that they may monitor aggregate demand and perhaps intervene to support the growth of the money supply or to reduce it. This is because the growth of the money supply is thought to have important influences upon certain critical economic variables. It is thought to be a major determinant of the rate of inflation, the level of unemployment and the rate of economic growth.

The definition of the money supply

THE BANK OF ENGLAND'S OFFICIAL MONETARY AGGREGATES

M0   Notes and coin in circulation outside the Bank of England + the commercial banks' operational balances at the Bank of England.

M2   Private sector holdings of notes and coin + private sector holdings of sterling retail deposits with UK banks + private sector holdings of sterling retail deposits and shares with UK building societies.

M4   M2 + private sector holdings of all other sterling deposits (including sterling certificates of deposit) with UK banks and all other sterling shares and deposits (including sterling certificates of deposit) with UK building societies.

M3H   M4 + private sector holdings of foreign currency deposits with UK banks and building societies + sterling and foreign currency deposits held by UK public corporations with UK banks and building societies.

Note   The term M3H is used to describe an aggregate which is wider than M4 because the bank of England wishes to maintain consistency of terminology with that used for comparable aggregates measured in other EC countries.

These different measures of the money supply shown above may be grouped under two headings.

Narrow measures of money

These are assets which may be used as immediate purchasing power. Narrow money is held for *medium of exchange* purposes. This is usually measured by M2. (M0 may sometimes be included, but this measures the base level of money and does not necessarily relate to purchasing power.)

Broad measures of money

These include the narrow measures plus assets which are held partly for their *store of value* purposes, and which are relatively liquid. These additional measures include M4 and M3H.

12.4 Banking

The purpose of this section is not to go into detail about how the banks and the banking system works, but to review one particular aspect of banking. The banks earn the majority of their income by lending, and it is consumers and firms ability to borrow which fuels much of the aggregate demand within the economy. This section therefore concentrates upon the process by which banks can create credit, and the ways in which control may be exercised over them.

The process is illustrated by an hypothetical historical example.

The development of banking – an hypothetical example

In 17th- and early-18th-century England there were not the communications facilities and transport networks which we enjoy today. Merchants went from town to town on horseback and had to carry their money and trading goods with them. The towns were far apart and the whole process was very hazardous due to the existence of thieves and other wandering criminals. Thus often when a merchant arrived in a town he would search out a local goldsmith, or other town based merchant, who had a secure vault in which to temporarily store his gold. The local goldsmith or town merchant might not make any charge if he was doing business with the travelling merchant.

The local goldsmiths found that they had large amounts of gold in their vaults belonging to other merchants. They also found that they were handing out gold to one merchant only to receive it back from another merchant. This was an inefficient use of their time and energy. They therefore introduced a record system.

Instead of dealing in physical gold, they recorded each merchant's deposit with them. Thus the gold could be kept in one heap, and not in designated heaps belonging to each owner. When a merchant wished to pay another person, so long as both were depositors or willing to be so, he issued a letter authorising the goldsmith to transfer ownership of a certain value to the other person. The goldsmith recorded this transfer in his record book, and the gold remained in his vault. Only when someone was not a depositor, or did not wish to be one, or specifically wanted cash (gold) was there a need to go to the vault and get the gold. This system worked very well so long as the goldsmith was trusted to keep the gold safe and to record ownership accurately.

Over time the goldsmiths realised that the majority of the gold remained in their vaults all the time. Some merchants left town and took their gold with them, but others arrived and deposited their gold. Similarly some depositors withdrew gold to pay non-depositors but others deposited gold received from non-depositors. All these transactions involving the physical movement of gold had the tendency to cancel each other out, and the net effect was that value of the gold in the vault remained fairly static. They realised that so long as they kept enough of the gold to pay out to merchants leaving town, and for day-to-day local transactions, they could lend some to the many traders who wanted to borrow for short periods of time. They could therefore earn interest on other people's money.

There were two critical issues of judgement which would govern the success or otherwise of the operation.

a. The amount of gold remaining in the vault had to be sufficient, at all times, to pay people who demanded their money. **Confidence** that the goldsmith would be able to pay out, all depositors at any time, was paramount. Thus the amount of gold to be held in reserve had to be **a conservative proportion** of the total deposits. This **reserve ratio** was a matter of judgement to be assessed over time.

b. When lending out depositor's funds the goldsmith had to be as sure as possible that the borrower was trustworthy and a good risk. Any bad debts would have to be covered by the goldsmith and would seriously affect his reputation if his customers became aware of the problem.

From these early beginnings and throughout the 19th century, many banking operations failed. The principle cause of failure was lack of confidence. There were often 'runs on banks' when the depositors would hear a rumour (whether true or not) and all go to the bank to demand their money. If the bank could not pay them it was finished as a bank. The early 20th century saw banks getting larger as the result of merger and confidence grew in their ability to provide necessary services and to pay all those who wished to withdraw their funds. Later in the 20th century the banks became even larger as they merged and developed their products and customer bases, and this led to the need for regulation of their activities.

12.5 The deposits (or credit) multiplier

Before leaving the hypothetical example of the goldsmith, it will be useful to give an example of how they were able to create extra deposits (credit) with the gold they held. This example will introduce the concept of the **credit multiplier.**

Example

The following assumptions are made:

a. The goldsmith banker has decided to hold 10 per cent of the total deposits at all times so that he can pay day-to-day demands for cash.

b. The goldsmith banker operates a book-keeping system to record the deposits of his customers.

Assume he has £1000 in cash on deposit.

Table 12.1 The goldsmith's book-keeping system – stage one

Total deposits (£)	Reserve ratio (10%)	Amount that can be lent (£)	Total deposits = cash + credit (£)
1000	100	900	1900

In Table 12.1 £1000 in cash has been deposited. The goldsmith has to keep 10 per cent or £100 in reserve. This leaves £900 which he can lend to suitable customers. He does not give them the money but opens an account for them and credits this account with the £900. He has given credit. The effect of this is that they can spend the money but they have to pay it back with interest. Thus the goldsmith has created both an extra liability and an extra asset. The liability is created because he is liable to pay the customer the money on demand (just like any other depositor) and therefore the customer is a creditor. (Current liability on the balance sheet). However the customer owes the goldsmith the money lent plus interest and is therefore a debtor to the goldsmith. (Current asset on the balance sheet).

The total deposits are now £1900 but of this £1900 there is still £1000 in cash. Only 10 per cent of the cash is needed for reserve ratio purposes so he can still lend out money so long as 10 per cent of the total deposits is held in cash. The situation develops as in Table 12.2.

Table 12.2 The goldsmith's book-keeping system – stage two

Total deposits (£)	Reserve ratio (10%)	Amount that can be lent (£)	Total deposits = cash + credit (£)
1000	100	900	1900
1900	190	1710	3610

The total deposits have again been increased by the creation of the extra deposits (credit). This situation will continue, as shown in Table 12.3, until the £1000 in cash is all used as the reserve ratio.

Table 12.3 The goldsmith's book-keeping system – stage three

Total deposits (£)	Reserve ratio (10%)	Amount that can be lent (£)	Total deposits = cash + credit (£)
1000	100	900	1900
1900	190	1710	3610
3610	361	3249	6859
6859	686	6173 (but only 3141)	10000
10000	1000	0	10000

The reason that only £3141 of the total deposits of £6859 could be lent out, is that if more had been lent the reserve ratio would have been greater than £1000, and £1000 is all the **cash** available to pay to those who want cash.

> The limit to how much credit can be created is the **amount of cash held**, and what the **reserve ratio** needs to be.

Instead of working through lengthy calculations, such as shown above, the **credit multiplier** can be used to calculate the total deposits which can be created with any particular reserve ratio. The credit multiplier is calculated as follows.

Credit multiplier

$$\frac{100\%}{\text{Reserve ratio }\%}$$

For example $\quad \dfrac{100}{10\%} = 10 \text{ or } \dfrac{100}{25\%} = 4$

In the first example above the credit multiplier was 10.

Once the credit multiplier is known then the total deposits that can be created from any cash deposit are calculated by multiplying the cash deposits by the credit multiplier. In the first example above total deposits are 10 (credit multiplier) multiplied by £1000. Thus £10 000 total deposits can be created with £1000 cash.

> The credit multiplier critically depends on the size of the reserve ratio. The higher the reserve ratio the *lower* the credit multiplier. The lower the reserve ratio the *higher* the credit multiplier.

The following example shows the same figures as above but with a reserve ratio of 25 per cent. Notice how the increased reserve ratio reduces the amount that can be lent at each stage. The credit multiplier is only 4 compared with a multiplier of 10 in the previous example.

Table 12.4   **The effect of an increased reserve ratio (25%)**

Total deposits (£)	Reserve ratio (25%)	Amount that can be lent (£)	Total deposits = cash + credit (£)
1000	250	750	1750
1750	437	1313	3063
3063	766	2297 (but only 937)	4000
4000	1000	0	4000

12.6 Modern banking
The reserve asset ratio

The process of credit creation within modern banking is restricted in exactly the same way as the 18th century merchants. Banks know that a proportion of their total deposits are likely to be withdrawn, *in cash,* at some stage. Therefore it is necessary for all banks to hold cash or other liquid assets readily available to meet withdrawals by their customers. The ratio of reserve assets to total deposits which any bank will wish to hold will depend upon the past experience of that institution. It will also depend upon the level of risk the bank wishes to be exposed to when developing its interest bearing deposits (loans).

In the past, during the 1970s, the Bank of England was able to restrict the commercial banks' ability to create credit by requiring them to hold a prescribed level of eligible reserve assets, and by being able to call for *special deposits.* The idea behind this sort of central control was that the banks had little incentive to hold liquid assets as the larger profits were to be made on long term (illiquid) assets and loans. It was thought that by controlling the level of liquid assets held by the banks, and by defining what those liquid assets should be, the government could control the money supply and therefore inflation. Also by demanding special deposits of liquid assets the Bank of England could withdraw money directly from the banking sector, and therefore prevent the creation of additional deposits. However experience has shown the government that it is very difficult to police these sort of controls on banks, and they have therefore been discontinued. The banks are now self-regulating and special deposits have not been called for since 1979.

In general the commercial banks do not have an unrestricted ability to create credit. Banks may have liquid funds available to support loans but they may have difficulty in finding the quality of borrower they wish to attract. Reducing lending criteria increases the risk associated with lending money and the banks, whilst wishing to make as much profit as possible, do not want to be exposed to high levels of risk. This issue is well illustrated by the slump in house prices during the early 1990s. Many banks had relaxed their lending criteria in the drive for higher profit levels. As the prices of houses rose ever higher, with no end to the boom in sight, banks lent increasing multiples of money secured on property. Thus where prudence indicated that banks should only lend 3 to 3.5 times a person's salary, they were lending 4 and 5 times salary. They reasoned that the prices of houses had not fallen, in living memory, and if the loan was secured against a property their loan was safe. Then came the crash in the housing market which coincided with a world economic depression. The banks lost considerable sums on many of their loans with forced sales of property, the value of which had fallen below the level of the outstanding debt.

12.7 The Bank of England (the Bank)
The main objectives

- To maintain the integrity and value of the nation's currency. (This effectively means the fight against inflation.)
- To ensure the stability of the financial system.
- To promote the efficiency and competitiveness of the financial system.

The Bank's customers

The Bank's services are specialised and therefore it does not undertake commercial banking business. There are a small number of private account holders who are staff and pensioners of the Bank itself. The three main customer groups, and the Banks specialised services to them, are as follows.

(a) The commercial banks

All the clearing banks keep accounts at the Bank of England. During the day-to-day business of the banks large numbers of cheques and credits are written by their customers. For example, cheques drawn on the Midland Bank may be paid into accounts at Barclays, Lloyds and other banks. Thus at the end of each day each bank has to pay the money owed to the other banks. They do this using their accounts at the Bank of England. The commercial banks are obliged to keep *operational* balances large enough to cover the payments to other banks **and are not expected to overdraw.**

All banks and building societies operating in the UK must keep 0.15 per cent of their sterling deposits on deposit with the Bank of England. These deposits are non-interest bearing, and are therefore a free loan. They provide the main source of income for the Bank of England to carry out its functions.

(b) Other central banks

These banks keep accounts with the Bank of England and they also keep gold at the Bank. They are therefore enabled to conduct foreign exchange and bullion business, in London, through the Bank of England.

(c) The Government

The main government accounts are kept at the Bank of England. Thus receipts from taxes and duties, etc., are collected in these accounts and all payments made by the government go out from these accounts. The government accounts are managed in such a way that any surplus funds are invested in the money markets or are used to reduce the government's short-term debt.

Note The management of the government's day-to-day cash will eventually become the responsibility of the newly created Debt Management Office, which was created on 1 April 1998 as an executive agency of the Treasury.

As banker to the government, the Bank manages the UK's reserves of gold and foreign exchange.

Note The responsibility for issuing gilt-edged debt and the management of the debt is no longer part of the Bank of England's responsibility. It is the responsibility of the newly created Debt Management Office.

12.8 Fighting inflation – maintaining the integrity and value of the nation's currency

The first objective of any central bank is to preserve the purchasing power of the currency. In the UK **monetary policy** is directed towards fighting inflation and preserving the external value of the pound. Monetary policy is concerned with the price of money, in other words **interest rates.** Deciding the level of short-term interest rates in the UK is the responsibility of the Bank of England. This has not always been the case.

The Bank of England Act 1946

This Act gave the Treasury power to issue directions to the Bank of England. The Treasury was therefore able to set and control interest rates. This was usually done by the Chancellor of the Exchequer after consulting with the Governor of the Bank of England.

May 1997

The government gave responsibility for setting interest rates to the Bank of England. The Bank discharges this responsibility through the Monetary Policy Committee. The government still retains the right 'in extreme circumstances' to give instructions to the Bank on interest rates, for a limited period of time.

The Bank of England Act 1998

This Act came into force on the 1st June 1998 and put onto a statutory basis the changes introduced in May 1997.

The management of the Bank of England

The Bank of England Act provides for the appointment, by the Crown, of the Governor, two Deputy Governors, and 16 non-executive Directors. These are collectively known as the **Court of Directors.** The Governor and the Deputy Governor are appointed for five years and the Directors for three years.

The Court is responsible for determining the objectives and strategy of the Bank, ensuring efficient use of the Bank's resources and ensuring that the Bank carries out its functions effectively. A sub-committee of the Court is formed by the 16 non-executive directors. The functions of this sub-committee are: to review the Bank's performance in relation to its objectives; reviewing internal financial controls; monitoring the financial management and determining the salary and pensions of the Governor and Deputy Governors. It is also responsible for reviewing the procedures of the **Monetary Policy Committee,** and in particular whether the committee has collected the regional, sectoral and other information necessary for formulating monetary policy.

Preserving the value of the currency is seen as being a central Government objective when the annual inflation target is set (currently 2.5%). Setting monetary policy and deciding upon the level of short-term interest rates necessary to meet the Government's inflation target, is the responsibility of the Bank. This responsibility is discharged through the Monetary Policy Committee.

The Monetary Policy Committee (MPC)

The MPC consists of the Governor, two Deputy Governors and six other members. They meet every month and their decision on interest rates is announced immediately after the meeting. The minutes of those meetings are published on the Wednesday following the subsequent meeting – approximately five weeks later. These minutes contain not only an account of the discussion of the MPC, and the issues which it thought important for its decisions, but also a record of the voting of each MPC member. The Bank also prepares a quarterly **inflation report**, which provides a detailed analysis of inflation and gives an assessment of prospects for inflation relative to the Government's published target. When preparing the *inflation report* and deciding on interest rates the MPC looks at a range of domestic and international economic and monetary factors. The factors chosen will be those thought to have an influence on inflation over the following two years, as it is thought that it takes about two years for the full effects of interest rates to work through the economy. The Bank's policy takes account of developments affecting industry and commerce throughout the UK. Information on such developments is supplied by the bank's agents in the regions. The Bank monitors the money markets, foreign exchange and the gilt markets very closely, as it is important that the Bank's policy takes account of financial market sentiment. Once monetary policy is decided the Bank implements it in three basic ways.

a. Operations in the domestic money market.
b. Operations in the foreign exchange market.
c. Operations in the government securities market.

Operations in the domestic money market

The main instrument of monetary policy is the short-term interest rate. The Bank of England has a variety of techniques for influencing interest rates but they are all designed, in one way or another, to affect the cost of money to the banking system. In general this is done by keeping the banking system short of money and then lending the banks the money they need at an interest rate which the Bank decides through daily operations in the money markets.

The way in which this works is as follows. The Bank of England is banker to the UK banking system. Each of the commercial banks has an account at the bank of England. Transactions between commercial banks are finally settled between the accounts held at the Bank of England. The commercial banks are expected to hold positive balances on their accounts at the Bank each day. The commercial banks' total funds are altered by transactions in a variety of ways.

a. Transactions between themselves and the Government accounts at the Bank.
b. Transactions between themselves and the Bank

(Note. Transactions between banks merely redistribute funds between themselves. Their total funds are left unaltered.)

Transactions between the commercial banks and government accounts at the Bank

The total payments from the private sector to the government are finally settled by a transfer of funds between the commercial banks' accounts at the Bank and the Government's accounts. When individuals and companies pay their tax bills, or buy car road tax, for example, the money will be paid by the bank on whom the cheque is drawn. All such payments are added together and the total, for each bank, is transferred to the appropriate government account at the Bank of England.

When the government pays unemployment benefit, social security or a range of other welfare payments the money flows from the Bank to the commercial banks. The people receiving their cheques deposit them at the various high street banks.

Transactions between the commercial banks and the Bank

The commercial banks will have customers who wish to buy and sell government securities. And there will be foreign exchange transactions which will result in flows of money between the Bank and the commercial banks.

The movement of money out of the commercial banks and the movement of money in to them will rarely be the same. It will often be the case that the commercial banks will pay out more than they receive, and will therefore be short of money. [*Remember: they have to keep a positive balance with the Bank, and they have to have funds to settle with all other banks each day.*] The Bank will be able to relieve this shortage and it will decide the price (interest rate) which it will charge for doing so. The Bank does not give the commercial banks the money directly but operates through the Money Markets by what are known as Open Market Operations.

OPEN MARKET OPERATIONS

Discount Houses borrow money from the commercial banks and invest this money in various financial assets, mainly Treasury Bills and Certificates of Deposit (CDs). The money which they borrow is very short term – usually 'overnight' or 'at call' and is secured on the financial assets purchased.

(**Overnight** money is where the commercial banks lend their surplus money each evening to the money market. It is repayable the next day. Money **at call** can be called for without notice at any time. Thus in both cases the commercial banks can get their money back very quickly if they need it.)

The money lent by the commercial banks attracts a rate of interest, thus their surplus funds are always working for them. However as the result of daily transactions the commercial banks will either have surplus funds or be short of funds. Their position will quickly be communicated to the money market (Discount Houses) as they either offer new deposits or call in existing deposits.

Money market is in surplus When there are new deposits being offered to the market the Bank of England will sell the Discount Houses Treasury Bills in order to mop up the surplus funds. The price at which the Bank sells the Treasury Bills establishes the interest rate that it is happy with. The interest earned by the Discount Houses must be greater than that which they pay the commercial banks for their funds.

Money market is short of funds When the commercial banks are calling in their short term loans the Discount Houses will be short of funds as they have already spent the money on Bills and CDs. In this case the Bank will announce its willingness to buy Bills from the Discount Houses, but will leave the Discount Houses to decide the price at which to sell the Bills. If the Bank is happy at the short-term interest rate implied by the price it will buy the Bills, and relieve the shortage of funds in the money market. If the Bank it is not happy with the implied short term interest rates it can refuse to buy. In this case the Discount Houses have to apply to the Bank for a 'lender-of-last-resort' loan. They will pay a penal rate of interest for this loan.

How much the Bank of England will sell a bill for will determine the effective interest rate.

By buying from, and selling to, the discount houses the Bank of England is establishing the interest rate that they have to pay, or will receive. The discount houses in turn will have to adjust the interest rates they give the commercial banks for their funds. The commercial banks will adjust the interest rates they pay for savings and they charge for loans.

The Bank of England does not instruct the commercial banks to alter their interest rate structure. However, by open market operations the Bank of England can influence general short-term interest rates, in accordance with what the monetary policy committee decides at its monthly meetings.

BILLS THAT THE BANK OF ENGLAND WILL BUY

Traditionally, in open market operations, the Bank has bought Treasury Bills, and other eligible local authority and bank bills. In addition the Bank will now buy '**gilt repo.**'.

A **gilt repo** is a sale and repurchase agreement. 'A' sells gilts to 'B', with a legally binding agreement to repurchase equivalent gilts from 'B' at a pre-determined price and date. In effect gilt repo is a cash loan with the gilts used as security.

THE PRICE OF A BILL AND THE IMPLIED INTEREST RATE

In general there are two types of financial instrument.

a. One paying a stated rate of interest (a coupon rate) with the capital value being repaid at a stated future date.
b. One paying no interest but the capital value being repaid at a stated future date.

The principle for calculating the implied interest rate is the same in both cases. We will take both cases in turn and illustrate the implied interest rate at different price levels.

Example 1
A Bill is for £100 and has a coupon rate (a stated rate of interest) of 10%

If a Discount House buys this bill for £100 it will get £10 interest which is 10%.
If a Discount House buys this bill for say £120 it will get £10 interest which is 8% on the £120 spent.
If a Discount House buys this bill for say £80 it will get £10 interest which is 12.5% on the £80 spent.

In this case whatever the price paid for the bill, the amount of interest paid is £10. This interest becomes a percentage of the money spent and THIS IS THE IMPLIED INTEREST RATE.

Example 2
A Bill has a face value of £100 but no coupon rate, and is repayable in full

If a Discount House buys this bill for £100 it will get no interest when the Bill is repaid.
If a Discount House buys this bill for say £80 it will get £100 when the Bill is repaid. Thus £20 will have been earned for an outlay of £80. This is the same as interest of 25% on the £80 spent.

In this case the price paid for the bill must be less than the amount which will be repaid at maturity. The difference between the price paid and the amount repaid at maturity is similar to interest. This difference (or interest) becomes a percentage of the money spent and THIS IS THE IMPLIED INTEREST RATE.

12.9 The effects of interest rates within the economy

A change in the cost of loans will affect both consumer and business spending decisions. A rise in interest rates will make savings more attractive for consumers and borrowing less so. The rise will affect the investment decisions of firms, as money now costs more and returns from any investment will have to be recalculated, especially if consumers are not spending so much as when the investment plans were first made.

A change in interest rates affects the cash flow of borrowers and creditors. A rise in interest rates will mean more cash for those with variable interest deposits at banks and building societies. But a rise will mean less cash for those on variable mortgages. A fall in interest rates will mean more cash for those with variable mortgages, but less cash for those who hold their cash in variable bank deposits. Cash flow is important as it influences day-to-day spending patterns, and therefore influences aggregate demand.

A change in interest rates affects the value of certain assets, notably housing and stocks and shares. Such a change in wealth may influence people's willingness to spend.

A rise in domestic interest rates relative to those overseas will tend to result in a net inflow of capital and an appreciation of the exchange rate. (This mechanism is fully explained in Chapter 16 on exchange rates.) A rising pound will mean that imports become cheaper and this will have the effect of encouraging UK producers to reduce their costs and prices. The drive to reduce costs and prices could mean unemployment, thus reducing inflation directly by lower prices and reducing still further aggregate demand because of the unemployment.

All of these influences on demand are likely to affect prices and inflation. A rise in short-term interest rates can be expected to reduce demand for UK output. That in turn is likely to put downward pressure on UK prices and the rate of inflation.

Operations in the foreign exchange market

In addition to their direct effects on the domestic economy, movements in interest rates influence the value of sterling in terms of other currencies. If interest rates on sterling assets rise in relation to rates on other currencies, then (other things remaining equal) money will flow into sterling (there will be increased demand for sterling) and sterling's exchange rate will rise. The exchange rate will also reflect market expectations about economic, financial and political developments here and abroad.

The Bank can attempt to influence the exchange rate through direct market intervention, using the country's foreign exchange reserves. When sterling is weak the Bank can enter the market and buy sterling in an attempt to support or increase the exchange rate. If sterling is thought to be too strong the Bank can enter the market and sell sterling. (This mechanism is fully explained in Chapter 16 on exchange rates.) The UK's exchange reserves used to be held solely in the Exchange Equalisation Account owned by the Treasury. This was operated by the Bank on behalf of the Government. As part of the changes introduced by the passing of the 1998 Bank of England Act, the Bank can now manage its own pool of foreign exchange reserves, separately from those managed on behalf of the Treasury. These reserves are now available for use in operations related to monetary policy, subject to limits authorised by the Bank's Court of Directors.

Operations in the Government securities market

Each week the Bank will invite applications for an amount of Treasury bills. The applications are to be at or above a minimum price. (*You should be sure that you understand the idea of the implied interest rate*). This process is known as the weekly tender and is used to help manage the money market as well as raising cash for the Government.

The Public Sector Net Cash Requirement (PSNCR) is, however, funded mainly through the sale of gilt-edged securities which are long term investments used to finance the shortfall between Government revenues and expenditure. Prior to 1 April 1998, the role of managing the Government's debt was undertaken by the Bank of England. On this date, however, the responsibility for the management of the Government's debt and the oversight of the gilt market passed to a new Debt Management Office (DMO) which is an executive agency of the Treasury. The DMO also provides policy advice to the Treasury on the annual gilt programme, makes decisions concerning the initiation of sales of gilts and liaises with market participants.

12.10 The demand for money

The question of the demand for money is a question about the factors which lead people to want to hold money. It is not the purpose of this book to attempt an in-depth account of monetary theory, the purpose rather is to outline and link various important topics so that the reader may, with this necessary background, read more advanced books. There are three reasons (motives) why people wish to hold money and these motives are related to the *functions of money* (explained on page 166):

1. **Transactions demand**   This is the demand for day-to-day money by firms and households, so that they can buy those goods and services which they want. *Motive:* medium of exchange.
2. **Precautionary demand**   This demand comes about by firms and households wishing to hold some money in case of the unexpected. *Motive:* medium of exchange.
3. **Speculative demand**   This is demand for money as a financial asset. *Motive*: Store of value.

12.11 The Keynesian theory of money

Transactions demand for money

Most people receive their wages and salaries on a weekly or monthly basis. But they have to pay for many goods and services on a daily basis. Therefore they need to hold money. The main factor to determine how much money will be held for transactions purposes, will be the size of the persons' income. Other factors will be how often a person is paid, how frequently they pay various bills, and in general their shopping and spending habits. For example a person paid monthly would be expected to hold more money, at any particular time, than one paid weekly. People used to shopping every day will probably hold more daily cash than those who shop twice per month.

For the economy as a whole it is expected that the total *transactions demand for money* will be a function of the level of *money national income*.

Precautionary demand for money

This is the money needed for unplanned or unexpected expenditures. For example people on a Saturday night out may carry a little extra cash in case they miss the last train and have to get a taxi home. A businessman on an extended business trip may carry extra money in case his plans have to change, a plane or train is cancelled unexpectedly and he needs unplanned overnight accommodation. The higher a persons income the greater may be the value of his transactions and therefore the greater the precautionary balances needed.

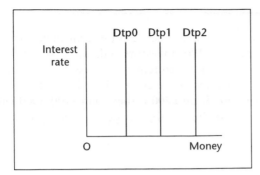

Figure 12.1 Transactions demand and precautionary demand for money

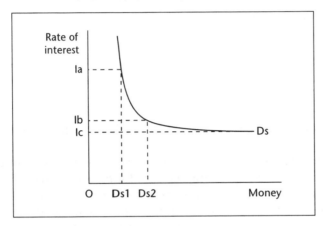

Figure 12.2 Speculative demand for money

The speculative demand for money (D_s) is a function of the rate of interest. An inverse function. This relationship is shown in Figure 12.2.

In Figure 12.2 the speculative demand for money is shown by the demand curve D_s. This is plotted against the interest rate (I) on one axis and the amount of money demanded on the other axis. At the high interest rate of Ia people wish to hold small money balances. (*As the interest rate is high bond prices are low and people will want to buy bonds rather than hold money balances. They will anticipate interest rates falling.*) When the interest rate falls from Ia to Ib the demand for money increases from D_s1 to D_s2. (*As the interest rate falls bond prices will rise and investors can realise capital gains. They will want to hold more money as they anticipate interest rates rising and bonds becoming cheaper again.*) When the interest rate falls to a very low level Ic the speculative demand for money becomes perfectly elastic. (*When the interest rate is so low it means that bond prices are at a peak. Investors will want to hold as much money as they can get, at this interest rate, as they anticipate interest rates must rise and bond prices fall.*)

The total demand for money (D_m) is the addition of D_t D_p and D_s. This is shown in Figure 12.3.

(**Note**   Keynes refers to the total demand for money as **liquidity preference.**)

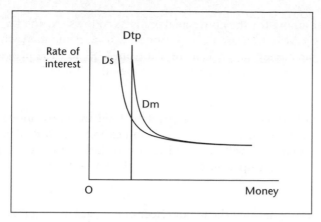

Figure 12.3 **Total demand for money**

The market rate of interest

Keynesian analysis of interest rates is stated in his *liquidity-preference theory of interest*. If there are competitive forces in the money market, then the interaction of demand and supply will determine the equilibrium level of the interest rate. The analysis calls upon what has so far been described of the Keynesian theory, and is as follows.

In Figure 12.4 the money supply MS1 is determined by the authorities in the money market. The interaction of the money supply (MS1) and the demand for money (Dm) will establish a market interest rate of (Ia). If the money supply is increased from MS1 to MS2 this will lead to a fall in the interest rate, initially to (Ib) level of interest. If the money supply is further increased to MS3 there will be no further fall in the interest rate. The general conclusion is that increasing the money supply will have the effect of reducing interest rates. But there comes a point where increases in the money supply will have no effect upon interest rates. This latter position is what Keynes referred to as the **liquidity trap**.

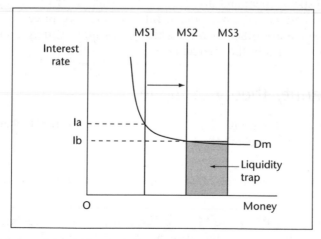

Figure 12.4 **Liquidity preference theory of interest**

187

The Keynesian reasoning for the above analysis is as follows. At the level of money supply represented by MS1 that amount of money will be demanded whilst interest rates are at (Ia). As the money supply is increased from MS1 to MS2 people and firms are forced to hold more money than they wish and they therefore try to spend it. They do this by buying bonds. As the supply of bonds is fixed this extra spending on bonds forces up bond prices. When bond prices rise the interest rate falls. In Figure 12.4 when the rate of interest falls to (Ib) people will want to hold the extra money supply in speculative balances, as bond prices are at a peak and expected to fall. Thus increasing the money supply beyond MS2 will only lead to people holding the extra money and there will be no further affect upon interest rates – the liquidity trap.

> Keynesian analysis implies that the major effect of changes in the money supply is on interest rates.

Exercise

The reverse reasoning applies to decreases in the money supply. You should be sure that you can show the steps that lead from a decrease in money supply to an increase in interest rates (say from MS2 to MS1). **It is important that this reasoning is understood** – all the necessary steps can be reviewed on pages 185–8.

Demand for money, supply of money and prices.

The Keynesian analysis above provides a link with what has been said of the functions of the Bank of England. A stated objective of the Bank of England is to control inflation. It attempts this by influencing the money supply and interest rates. One influence of interest rates is the effect upon the demand for money (see page 181).

It is impossible to speak, meaningfully, only of the demand for or supply of money without considering these effects upon prices. Interest rates are prices – the price of borrowing money. There are other theories which focus more widely upon prices in general, rather than specifically the interest rate.

12.12 The Fisher quantity theory of money

This theory was stated by Irving Fisher and is often referred to as the 'Fisher equation'. It is stated as an identity, namely that:

the amount of money in circulation multiplied by the number of times it changes hands is the same as the number of transactions in the economy multiplied by their average price.

In symbols this is $MV = PT$ where M = the stock of money in circulation: V = the velocity of circulation: P = the average price of all transactions: T = the number of transactions that take place in a time period.

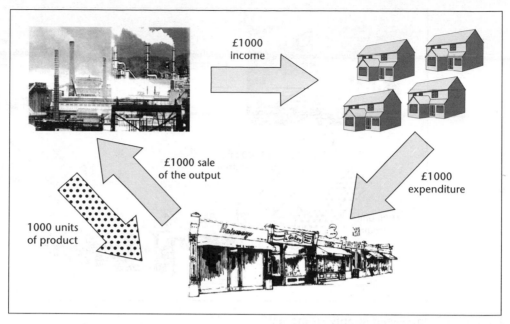

Figure 12.5 **The circular flow of income**

This idea can be seen clearly in the language of Chapter 9. Consider the circular flow diagram in Figure 12.5.

The amount of money which is in the system is £1000. Each week 1000 units of output are available for sale. The money circulates once round the economy and the goods are bought at an average price of £1. If this situation continues then at the end of one year the money will have circulated 52 times (the velocity is 52) and each time (week) 1000 units of product would have been bought for an average price of £1. Thus:

$M =$ money in circulation (which is £1000)
$V =$ velocity of circulation (which is 52 times)
$P =$ average price level for the transactions made (which is £1)
$T =$ number of transactions (which is 52000). For this simple example it is assumed that there are 1000 transactions each week, each involving one unit of output.

$$MV \equiv PT \qquad (M.V = £52\,000) \quad (P.T = £52\,000)$$

Fisher argued that the velocity of circulation (V) and the number of transactions (T) were relatively constant over long periods of time. He therefore held them to be constants in the above identity. This left only the two factors to be able to change; money supply and prices. Changes in the money supply are mainly in the hands of the monetary authorities (Bank of England) and therefore the theory predicts that if the money supply increases this will lead directly to higher prices. This prediction can be seen below.

189

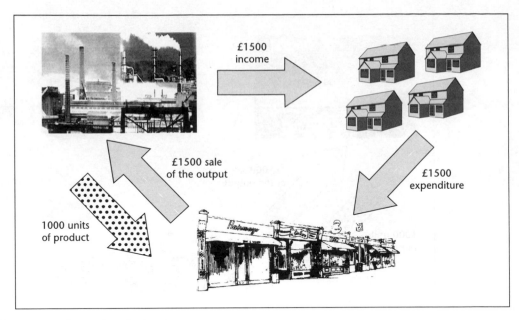

Figure 12.6 **Increased supply of money**

In Figure 12.6 the money circulating round the economy has been increased. Therefore the 1000 units of output will have to sell for £1.50p each in order to soak up this extra money.

Some underlying assumptions made clear.
a. It is assumed that the economy is at the full employment level of output. Otherwise through extra production the extra money could generate extra output.
b. It is assumed that the demand for money is for transactions purposes only. Therefore when the money supply increases consumers find themselves holding more money than they need for their normal level of transactions, and they therefore try to spend the extra money causing the prices to rise.
c. As prices rise the total value of consumer's transactions rise, and therefore the demand for money (*transactions balances*) rises.

12.13 The quantity theory re-stated – Milton Friedman

Milton Friedman's view of the demand for money has been characterised as the 'monetarist' standpoint. In his restated quantity theory he moves away from the idea that the demand for money is purely a transactions demand. He sees money as one of a variety of ways in which wealth can be held. Other means of holding wealth could be financial instruments, property, machines and other consumer durables. The advantage that money has is that it is liquid and therefore convenient for carrying out transactions immediately.

Friedman argues that the real demand for money (the demand for money divided by the average price level) depends on a number of factors. These factors are examined in turn.

THE REAL DEMAND FOR MONEY

The idea of **real** demand for money is a way of expressing what the money will buy. By dividing the demand for money by the average price level the resulting figure is **real** in the sense that it shows how much can actually be bought. This is useful when price levels are subject to constant change.

Example of the real demand for money

Assume a consumer buys articles each week usually costing £50 and that over 3 weeks the prices rise by10 per cent. Further assume that this person usually withdraws £100 each week.

His demand for actual money is £100 but by dividing this £100 by the prices in week 1 the answer is 2. (£100/£50 = 2). This figure indicates that he holds money (or demands money) equal to twice his weekly spend. After 3 weeks he demands the same amount of actual money £100. However when this sum is divided by the price level of £55 the answer is 1.8. This indicates that in **real** terms he is holding less than he held previously. His demand for money was twice the value of purchases previously and now it is only 1.8 times the value of purchases. If he wanted to maintain his **real demand for money** then he would have to increase the actual money sum to £110.

This is a simple example to illustrate the idea. In economic publications it is usual to divide actual money aggregates (and any other aggregate where a REAL value is needed) by an index number, the value of which gives a proxy measure of rising or falling average prices.

Factors upon which the demand for money depends

Total wealth

The value of a person's wealth is the total value of all their assets. Friedman draws the distinction between 'non-human' wealth and 'human wealth' and includes both in the value of total wealth. Money is a component of total wealth, and as total wealth increases the desire to hold money will also increase.

HUMAN WEALTH AND NON-HUMAN WEALTH

Human wealth is the value of a person's intellectual assets. These include knowledge and various skills which can be sold, or used, in order to generate future streams of income. The idea is that people can invest in themselves, by taking various educational or training courses.

Non-human wealth is money and all other physical assets.

Returns on investments

The demand for money will be inversely related to the rates of return (interest rates) on various investments. Additionally Friedman includes expectation of future rates of inflation. As inflation eats away at the value of money balances there will be less demand for money when there is an expectation of high inflation. (See Chapter 13 for a full account of the effects of inflation.)

The ratio of human wealth to non-human wealth

Friedman asserts that human wealth is not easily turned into money and other assets. Thus the higher the ratio of human wealth to non-human wealth the greater will be the demand for money as compensation.

Tastes

This variable is a catch-all for those hidden psychological factors which could influence wealth holders to demand money. The idea, in the previous paragraph, of money balances as a form of compensation will depend heavily upon lifestyles and personal preferences, rather than some obvious known human mechanism.

Some underlying issues made clear

a. There is the problem of trying to measure wealth. This can be briefly illustrated by three simple examples. A house can be valued by different estate agents and a variety of prices suggested. A motor car will have different values depending upon which trader looks at it. Share prices are changing many times each day and are only worth any particular sum when actually sold.
b. A person may take a different view of his/her wealth than merely the sum of the various valuations.

Friedman's answer to the problem of wealth measurement was to introduce the concept of **permanent income** as a proxy for wealth. Permanent income is the present day average value of all past, present and future income from all sources.

Similarities and differences between the three theories

In all three cases the response to an increase in the money supply is that households and firms will seek to spend the extra money. Increased spending leads to higher prices. In Keynes's case higher bond prices; in Fisher's case higher general prices; in Friedman's case higher general prices (but the mechanisms differ from the Fisher equation). It is the differences in mechanisms between Friedman's theory (monetarist) and Keynesian theory that have led to great debate.

Differences between Keynesian theory and Friedman's theory (monetarist)

Keynes says that the demand for money is directly related to (a function of) *current money income*.

Friedman says the demand for money is directly related to (a function of) *permanent income* as a proxy for *total wealth*.

Keynes says that the demand for money is a close *substitute for bonds* and therefore *dependent upon the interest rate*.

Friedman says the demand for money is a close *substitute for a variety of assets* and therefore *independent of the interest rate*.

Keynes says that if the money supply is increased the effect will be for interest rates to fall as spending on bonds will increase. *The demand for money remains the same.*

Friedman says that if the money supply is increased the effect will be for interest rates to fall as some spending on bonds will increase, *and* for prices to rise as there is spending on various other assets as well. *The demand for money will increase in response to the higher prices.*

The different positions in relation to a change in money supply can be shown graphically as in Figure 12.7.

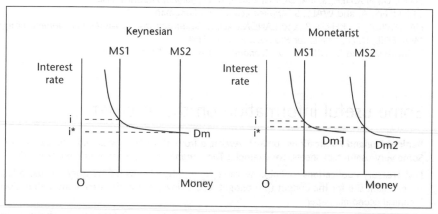

Figure 12.7 **Graphical illustration of Keynesian versus monetarist interest rate reaction to an increased money supply**

Figure 12.7 demonstrates the different effects of the theories upon the interest rate. Keynesian analysis indicates a much larger reaction of interest rates to a change in the money supply from MS1 to MS2. The starting interest rate (i) is the same in both cases. In the monetarist case due to rising prices (because of spending on assets other than bonds) the demand for money has increased from Dm1 to Dm2. The increased money supply MS2 cuts the new demand for money Dm2 at an interest rate of (i*). A much smaller reaction to the increase in money supply.

12.14 ## Summary

It is very important for the government and the monetary authorities to be clear as to the effect of changes in the money supply. The Bank of England has a major task to control inflation, and the government is always keenly aware of unemployment and the external value of the currency. The effects of changes in the interest rate are thought to be considerable (see page 181), and the Bank of England effects change by varying the money supply through open market operations. If the effects of changes in money supply are as predicted by Keynes, then small variations in money supply might be indicated to achieve the desired interest rate effects. If however the effects of changes in the money supply are as predicted by the monetarists then there will be much weaker interest rate effects in the economy and increased consumption of goods and services. This in turn may lead to increased investment in production, but may also lead to short term effects on prices and employment. The government may have to resort to other measures (other then just changes in money supply – monetary policy) to control consumer demand. Measures such as changes in direct and indirect taxation – known as fiscal policy.

Further reading

ANDERTON, A., *Economics*, Causeway Press.
BEGG, D., FISCHER, S. and DORNBUSCH, R. *Economics*, McGraw-Hill.
GRIFFITHS, A. and WALL, S. *Applied Economics*, Longman.
HARDWICK, P., KHAN, B. and LANGMEAD, J. *An Introduction to Modern Economics*, Longman.
McALEESE, D. *Economics for Business*, Prentice Hall.
SLOMAN, J. and SUTCLIFFE, M. *Economics for Business*, Prentice Hall.

Some useful information on the Internet

Bank of England Publications (online). Available from <http://www.bankofengland.co.uk/publica.htm>
Some very useful fact sheets, for example: *The transmission mechanism of monetary policy*.

HM Treasury Publications (online). Available from <http://www.hm.treasury.gov.uk/index.html>.
An excellent site for the budget (pre-budget report November each year); consultation documents; various technical economic papers.

National Statistics – the official UK site (online). Available from <http://www.statistics.gov.uk>.

Test your understanding

(Answers are given at the back of the book)

1. What do you understand by the term **liquidity**.

2. List in descending order of liquidity, 4 different types of financial instruments. Briefly describe each explaining their liquid characteristics.

3. Which of the following is correct.

   A M4 = Private sector holdings of notes and coin + private sector holdings of sterling retail deposits with UK banks + private sector holdings of sterling retail deposits and shares with UK building societies.

   B M2 = Notes and coin in circulation outside the Bank of England + the commercial banks' operational balances at the Bank of England.

   C M4 = M2 + private sector holdings of all other sterling deposits (including sterling certificates of deposit) with UK banks and all other sterling shares and deposits (including sterling certificates of deposit) with UK building societies.

   D M2 = M4 + private sector holdings of foreign currency deposits with UK banks and building societies + sterling and foreign currency deposits held by UK public corporations with UK banks and building societies.

4. The credit multiplier depends upon

   A The banks finding enough suitable customers to lend money to.
   B The total deposits which the bank owns
   C The amount of cash available
   D The reserve asset ratio

5. Even though there is no imposed limit on a bank's ability to create credit, the opportunities to do so may be limited. Why might this be the case?

6. Which of the following statements are correct?

   a. The Monetary Policy Committee of the Bank of England decides the inflation targets and sets interest rates
   b. The Monetary Policy Committee of the Bank of England decides the level of interest rates and instructs the banking system to use the new rates
   c. The Monetary Policy Committee of the Bank of England decides the level of interest rates which they impose through operations in the money markets

   A a and b
   B b and c
   C a
   D b
   E c

7. Which of the following is **not** a function of money?

   i. medium of exchange
   ii. unit of account
   iii. acceptability
   iv. standard of deferred payment

8. You are given the following information.

   The price, last month, of a bond was £100 and it pays an annual interest rate of 8%. The price of the bond currently is £114.

   What is the current level of interest rates in the country, and are they tending to rise or fall?

9. A businessman buys some commercial bonds which are repayable in 12 months time. The amount to be repaid at maturity is £5000. The businessman paid £4628. What is the implied rate of interest that the businessman can expect at maturity?

10. An increase in the interest rate is likely to have the greatest impact upon:
    a. the cost of housing
    b. the cost of food
    c. the cost of motoring
    d. the cost of overseas holidays

11. Which of the following statements are true?
    a. The precautionary demand for money is a function of the rate of interest
    b. The transactions demand for money is a function of the rate of interest
    c. The speculative demand for money is a function of the rate of interest

    A   a
    B   b
    C   c
    D   all of them

12. Explain what is meant by, *the rate of interest is the opportunity cost of holding money*.

13. The diagram below shows the demand for money and two separate levels of money supply. Using the diagram explain what is meant by *the liquidity trap* and explain in detail the mechanism by which it occurs.

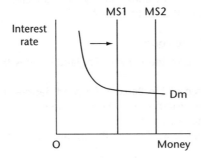

14. What are the main underlying assumptions of the Fisher Equation (MV=PT)?

15. Explain what is meant by the *real demand for money*.

16. Explain how Keynes differs from Friedman in his analysis of the demand for money.

17. Assume that there is equilibrium in the money market. Show, using appropriate diagrams, the effects of an increase in the money supply:

    i.   according to the Keynesian model
    ii. according to the monetarists.

13 Unemployment

Learning objectives

- To understand the official definition of unemployment.
- To be aware of two different measures of unemployment: the claimants measure and the ILO measure.
- To understand the measure of the 'unemployment rate'.
  - To be aware of the different types of unemployment and to understand problems posed for policy makers by each type
- To understand the central features of two different views concerning the causes of unemployment.
  - Demand deficient unemployment – the Keynesian view of unemployment.
  - Excessive real wage unemployment – the monetarist view of unemployment.
- To be aware of empirical data which shows the changing structure of UK employment.

13.1 The importance of employment

Using the format of Chapter 9 it is very easy to see how employment is so important within an economy.

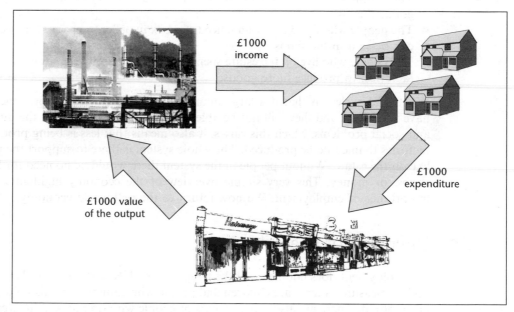

£1000 income

£1000 expenditure

£1000 value of the output

Figure 13.1 Circular flow of income

The people who live on the estate will wish to buy various goods, but they have no money. They go to the factories to work, producing the goods, which they will later wish to buy, and in return they earn wages. The factories, at the end of each week, send the goods, which have been produced, to factory owned shops. The workers go to the shops to buy the goods, with the wages they have received. The shops sell the goods to the workers and pass the money on to the factories in payment for the goods.

The workers are employed in the factory. It may not be possible to give every person, who would like to work, a job. The number of jobs available will depend upon technology (see the chapter on production in the microeconomics section) and upon how much demand there is for the goods. The demand for the goods will be reflected in the amount of money flowing into the factories from the shops. Thus if national income rises there will be more money to spend (creates greater demand) and more money available in the factories to hire more workers. If national income falls there will be less money to spend (demand falls) and less money available in the factories to pay for wages. Thus workers will be made redundant.

Employment depends upon demand for goods and services in the economy. In Figure 13.1 the expenditure in the shops, which is passed on to the factories, is supporting the workers in employment. Therefore any injection into the circular flow has the effect of raising the national income, which leads to raised national expenditure (which is aggregate demand), which leads to pressure on the factories to produce more goods, which leads to the factories wishing to employ more workers. Any withdrawal from the circular flow has the effect of reducing the national income, which leads to lower national expenditure (which is aggregate demand), which leads to the factories wishing to produce less goods, which leads to the factories wishing to employ less workers.

- The people who live on the estate need to work in order to have money to buy the goods they want.
- The people who live on the estate need to work in order to produce the goods, which can be sold in the shops.
- The people who live on the estate spend their money so that it circulates back to the factories, to produce more goods.

What is also clear is that if a large number of residents cannot work, then they will have no money and they will not be able to buy goods. Apart from the humanitarian and social problems, which this raises, it also means that less is being produced in the factories than could be produced. The whole system is there to support the people who live on the estate. Without people in the system there would be no need for factories or shops, or money. This very simple overview of the economy highlights the central importance of employment. We now return to the real world economy.

13.2 Definition of unemployment

Unemployment does not mean all the people in the UK without jobs. This would be a useless measure as there are children and people who cannot work also old people who have retired. There are also other groups of people who do not wish to work. A more reasonable measure of the total numbers unemployed would be: *all those people who are willing and able to work – but have no job*. This idea is translated into an official definition by the government. The number of people unemployed is defined as:

UNEMPLOYMENT – OFFICIAL DEFINITION

The number of people claiming, jobseekers allowance (unemployment benefit) or national insurance credits, on the day of the monthly count; who on that day were unemployed and were willing and able to do any suitable work and actively seeking work.

13.3   Measurement of unemployment

There are two measures.

1. Counting the actual numbers of people who are defined as officially unemployed (claimants) is one measure. This method of producing unemployment statistics has been the traditional method used by various governments up to the mid-1990s. The rules for claiming benefit have changed, and various measures to limit the length of time a person can claim benefit have been introduced at different times, but the basic definition has remained.
2. When the Labour Government came to power in the mid-1990s they introduced their preferred measure of unemployment. This new measure is the International Labour Organisation (ILO) jobless rate. The ILO measure includes claimants plus anyone seeking work.

INTERNATIONAL LABOUR ORGANISATION (ILO) – JOBLESS RATE

Claimants from the official definition plus all people who are available to start work within the next two weeks and have looked for work in the last four weeks or already found a job but waiting to start.

The data are compiled following guidelines set out by the International Labour Organisation, based on surveys, which ask people whether they are seeking work.

Issues concerning measurement No. 1

The accuracy of the first measure can be questioned on a number of grounds.

1. Many people who are unemployed and seeking work do not register as unemployed. They therefore do not become part of the official statistics.

2. There are rules for claiming unemployment benefits. The principal rule being that one has to have worked and paid national insurance contributions to be able to be eligible for benefit. Thus housewives whose children are now able to fend for themselves during the day, and school and college leavers, are not counted as unemployed – even though they are willing and able to work.

3. There are many who are claiming unemployment benefit and who are working in the black economy. The fact that the government has set up detection units, which are enjoying huge success, indicates that this issue is significant.

Issues concerning measurement No. 2

1. The new figures are not really new. The government has always collected them but now they are issued monthly instead of four times a year.

2. The figures should show that unemployment is much higher than measurement 1 monthly figures indicate, as they include the housewives and students excluded from measurement 1.

The differences between the two measures of unemployment can be seen from the graphs in Figure 13.2.

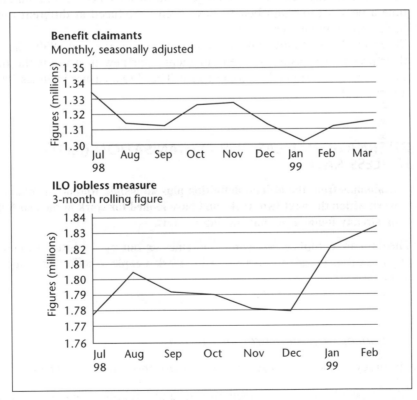

Figure 13.2 Measures of unemployment

The unemployment figures are usually expressed as a percentage of the total working population. This is known as the **unemployment rate.** The unemployment rate is defined as:

> ### UNEMPLOYMENT RATE
>
> **The number of people unemployed expressed as a percentage of the total workforce.**
>
> The total workforce is defined as 'all people in employment, all people self-employed, all people on government sponsored work related training programs, members of the armed forces, all people unemployed'.

13.4　Types of unemployment

There are four types of unemployment which some economists refer to, in total, as **natural unemployment**. The idea of a natural level of unemployment focuses upon the fact that whilst a large number of people may be unemployed, the economy may be booming and the large numbers of workers needed are being identified and employed. The four types are:

1. residual unemployment
2. seasonal unemployment
3. frictional unemployment
4. structural unemployment

These are considered in turn.

Residual unemployment

This is the term used to refer to those people who are disabled (mentally and physically) and therefore only able to perform a limited range of tasks.

This type of unemployment presents policy makers with the problem of trying to encourage employers to identify jobs and widen the opportunities available. There are considerable social costs of this type of unemployment as well as the costs to the exchequer.

Seasonal unemployment

There are a number of people who work in industries where the demand for labour temporarily falls at various times during the year. Examples of this are found in agriculture where workers are employed to pick fruit and vegetables as they mature. During the winter months there is no fruit to harvest. Another example might be in the building industry where bad weather over the winter may mean certain tradesmen, such as plasterers and bricklayers, being temporarily laid off. People working in the tourism industry were traditionally subject to seasonal unemployment but this has changed considerably in recent years as tourism has developed all-year-round demand.

This type of unemployment is a drain on the exchequer. There is very little the government can do to help this group of workers as many find the working conditions desirable and do not wish to change jobs. They just need support during periods of being laid off. Seasonal work is viewed by some people as the opportunity for part-time or casual work whilst waiting for other opportunities to arise. The most important economic consideration is that this group of people represents a pool of under-utilised resources.

Frictional unemployment

At any one time there are a large number of people between jobs. Some people may have left one job and be taking time off before starting another. Some people may have been made redundant or even have been dismissed and are searching for a new job. Others may have left their job and be searching for a more suitable job. They are all searching for a new job, which in the main they are already qualified or experienced to do.

The search can take a number of weeks for someone trying to fit their exact requirements to the job vacancies of which they become aware. Many people have expectations in terms of job content and remuneration. These expectations can be realistic or otherwise depending upon the information available about the job market as a whole. A further problem for the jobseeker is that employers are not always clear in their job specifications or in the personal qualities required to do the job. Thus availability of accurate information is of major importance.

Many economists see frictional unemployment as necessary within the economy. It indicates that the workforce is moving between production possibilities attempting to maximise job satisfaction, and therefore becoming more productive. An adaptive workforce is seen as necessary for improved resource allocation.

The government can help to speed up the process of searching for a new job. Firstly they can support initiatives, which make more information available to the unemployed. This was the reasoning behind the setting up of job centres and job clubs. Secondly they can support the unemployed in their job search by providing facilities, which might otherwise be too expensive for some people, such as computers, telephones, stationery and career counseling advice. These facilities are provided within many of the job centers and job clubs. The more efficient the job search the less the burden on the exchequer. Whilst this group of people are not on long term benefit, there are a lot of them and so any shortening of the time for which benefit is paid, will be of great benefit to the exchequer.

Structural unemployment

This is the most serious form of unemployment. It is caused by fundamental changes in the demand for goods and services and by changes in technology. A few examples will illustrate the problem.

Example 1 The Tyne/Tees region of Great Britain was at one time, a major shipbuilding area. A very high percentage of the regional population were occupied in building ships and had developed the skills necessary for this process. World demand for shipping reduced and the fewer orders were placed with more efficient ship builders overseas. This meant that thousands of people representing a wide range of skills and trades were unemployed. Furthermore they were all resident within the same geographical area where there were no alternative employment prospects. Many families had seen generations start work in the shipyards, bring up families and retire. With children at local schools and family networks all in the region, they were unwilling to uproot and travel away from the region. There were no other major employers in the region so re-training, even if the workers had been so inclined, was not an immediately sensible option.

With no income from employment, families were unable to demand the variety of goods and services that they had previously demanded. Thus shops and businesses in the region, which depended upon this local demand for their living, were also affected. Families forced to live on social security and with time on their hands during the day, became depressed. The social problems associated with long-term unemployment started to appear and added to the already high cost to the exchequer.

Example 2   The analysis is very similar to the example above, so just the situation will be described. In South Wales there were whole communities which depended upon the local coal mine to provide income for the families. In the 1980s many mines were closed as uneconomic and those who had worked in them lost their jobs (and their way of life). There were no other employers, and such is the geography of the region that it is not easily possible to go from one valley to another – even if there had been alternative industries, which there were not.

Example 3   The advance of technology can have a similar effect, though it is unlikely to affect whole regions. The introduction of computerised typesetting in the paper-printing industry is an example. There was massive resistance by well-organised union labour but eventually the jobs were lost and the computers did the work. In this case those losing their jobs had no job and outdated skills but they were not the majority of a geographical region.

Structural unemployment is not easily adjusted because of two main features which are apparent in the examples above. **Geographical** and **occupational immobility of labour**. Geographical relocation for many people is not an option. Their friends and families are all located within an area, and the social structures that they understand are their support. The cost of relocation, for those who might consider it, is often prohibitive. Occupational immobility occurs principally because work skills are not transferable from one occupation to another. Workers are not likely to be aware of which skills are in demand, and they may not have the aptitude or willingness to retrain. To retrain can be very costly.

The governments of the 1960s and 1970s have undertaken many initiatives to try and relieve structural unemployment. Where whole regions are concerned, such as the North East, there is a distorting effect upon demand for goods and services, distribution of wealth and share of the national income. The government has introduced tax concessions, rate relief, employment subsidies, training schemes and financial assistance packages in attempts to relieve structural unemployment. There were also regional policies seeking to make the economically depressed regions of the UK more attractive to prospective employers.

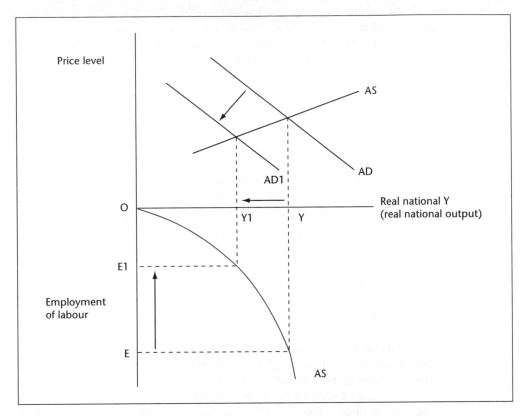

13.5 Demand deficient unemployment (Keynesian unemployment)

The demand for labour is a derived demand. It is derived from the demand for the goods and services which labour helps to produce. Thus if we are to say that unemployment is caused by reduced demand for labour, this is the same as saying that unemployment is caused by a reduced demand for goods and services. The connection between aggregate demand and employment can be shown in Figure 13.3.

Figure 13.3 **Aggregate demand and unemployment**

In Figure 13.3 there are two separate graphs placed side-by-side for convenience. In the top graph aggregate demand and aggregate supply are plotted against real national income and the price level. (See Chapter 11 to revise aggregate demand and supply.) In the bottom graph the demand for labour is plotted against real national income and the number of workers employed.

The production possibility function (PPF) is a technical statement of the proportion of labour necessary to produce a specified level of output. In this case the aggregate level of national output.

Aggregate demand for goods and services in the economy is AD. Aggregate supply of goods and services in the economy is AS. The equilibrium level of real national output (or real national income) is Y. At Y level of national output E number of workers are required to produce that level of output. (Note. Even at E level of employment there will be those people who are part of *natural unemployment*.) If aggregate demand in the economy falls, say to AD1 then the equilibrium level of real national output (real national income) will also fall to Y1. At Y1 level of national output only E1 number of workers are required to produce this new level of output. In Keynesian terms, aggregate demand has fallen causing a fall in the equilibrium level of national income and a rise in unemployment.

You should be sure at this stage that you understand why the following will reduce aggregate demand (see Chapter 12):

a. An increase in the demand for money
b. A decrease in the supply of money

13.6 Excessive real wage unemployment (the monetarist view)

Monetarists argue that demand deficient unemployment does not exist, and that unemployment above the natural rate of unemployment is caused by excessive real wages. They attribute these excessive wages to the power of trade unions. The analysis is shown in Figure 13.4.

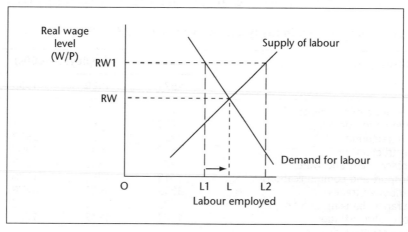

Figure 13.4 **The market for labour**

In Figure 13.4 the analysis is classical market mechanism. The market clearing level of real wages is RW. At this level of real wage L amount of labour would be employed. (Note. At this equilibrium level of L there would still be people unemployed, they would be part of the *natural level* of unemployment). If the real wage level rises to RW1 there would be an imbalance between supply and demand for labour. At this level of real wage L2 labour would wish to be employed but employers would only wish to employ L1. The difference between L1 and L is the amount of unemployment directly attributable to excessive real wages.

The answer to this question of unemployment, say the monetarists, is either to cut money wages or to allow the price level to rise more rapidly than money wages. They see the answer as a more competitive labour market with flexible wages.

The changing structure of UK employment

There have been three major changes in the structure of employment over the last 30 years.

Firstly, there has been the loss of 3.6 million jobs in the manufacturing sector, between 1971–1994. This can be seen in Table 13.1 where the number of jobs in manufacturing fell from 8.2 million in 1971 to 4.6 million in 1994. During this same period the number of jobs in the various parts of the service sector were increasing rapidly, and in total there were over 4.8 million new jobs. The more notable increases being in *insurance, banking and finance* increased 58 per cent; *hotels and catering* increased by 72 per cent; *Other business services* increased by 132 per cent and *education and health* increased by 58 per cent.

Secondly, there has been a great increase in the number of people self-employed. In 1971 approximately 7.5 per cent of the working population were self-employed. By 1994 this figure had grown to 11.5 per cent of the working population.

Thirdly the number of women entering into employment has increased rapidly. In the old industries such as, shipbuilding, mining, and steel the majority of the employees were men. In the newer industries such as, insurance and banking, financial services and electronics the majority of employees are women. Thus the movement of women

Table 13.1 **Employment by main industry group in the UK, 1971–1994**

Industry group	Employees (000s)			
	1971	1980	1990	1994
Agriculture and fisheries	758	647	583	558
Mining and quarrying	409	365	178	93
Manufacturing	8231	7098	5393	4639
Construction	1578	1647	1907	1444
Electricity, gas and water	375	353	277	223
Transport and communications	1618	1580	1570	1411
Distributive trades	3592	3900	4278	4073
Insurance, banking and finance	575	712	986	911
Public administration	1762	1812	1722	1618
Other service industries				
Hotels and catering	814	1083	1436	1398
Other business services	1224	1526	2735	2839
Education and health	2865	3575	4373	4539
Other services	729	1026	1325	1245

Note: This table has been adapted from Johnes & Taylor, p. 38.
Sources: British Labour Statistics, Historical Abstract; *Regional Economic Prospects*, Cambridge Econometrics.

Table 13.2 Full-time and part-time jobs by sex in Great Britain, 1979–1995

	Employment (millions)			
	Males		Females	
	1979	1995	1979	1995
Full-time	14.3	13.0	5.6	6.3
Part-time	0.1	1.1	3.4	5.1

Source: Labour Market Trends, December 1995.

into the workplace has coincided with the decline of the old industries and the rapid development of the new industries. A further aspect of the increased employment of women is the movement towards part-time employment. Part-time employment has advantages for working mothers whilst the advantages to the employer are lower costs and flexibility. The changes in the employment trends for men and women, since the late 1970s, can be seen in Table 13.2.

13.7 Summary

The purpose of this chapter has been to introduce the topic of unemployment so that the student will be able to progress to other texts with more detailed analyses.

The way in which unemployment is defined and measured is a fundamental pre-requisite to further reading.

The different types of unemployment introduce the process and give some idea of the difficulties facing policy makers. The idea that there is a 'natural' (or inevitable) level of unemployment, is understandable; though what the level is – or should be – is controversial in more advanced texts.

The introduction to Keynes's emphasis on aggregate demand as the main factor underpinning employment is contrasted with the monetarist's more liberal market mechanism approach. There is more here than just an argument between two entrenched views. The differences have been building since Chapter 9, and in Chapter 12 with the focus on money the differences were further emphasised. This merely serves to underline the inter-connections between all aspects of the macro-economy (aggregate demand, aggregate supply, money, employment, inflation, etc) and the difficulty of trying to formulate effective control strategies.

The final section attempts to place the subject of unemployment within the framework of a rapidly changing economic structure. The following are just a few of the influences, and part of the changing economic scenery, within which is embedded the issue of unemployment.

- The decline of the old industries (structural unemployment)
- The rise of the new industries (re-training and re-orienting the workforce).
- The rapid rise in the numbers of self-employed and the entry of more women into the workforce.
- The flexibility gained from acceptance of part-time working practices.

Further reading

BEGG, D., FISCHER, S. and DORNBUSCH, R. *Economics*, McGraw-Hill.
GRIFFITHS, A. and WALL, S. *Applied Economics*, Longman.
HARDWICK, P., KHAN B. and LANGMEAD, J. *An Introduction to Modern Economics*, Longman.
SLOMAN, J. and SUTCLIFFE, M. *Economics for Business*, Prentice Hall.

Some useful information on the internet

BUBL UK – Central Government   <http://www.bubl.ac.uk/uk/government.htm>.
This is the site from which publications and papers from various government departments may be viewed. Departments useful for information on unemployment are: Department of Trade and Industry; Department for Education and Employment; Central Office of Information.

National Statistics – the official UK site   <http://www.statistics.gov.uk>.

A good reference article from Wolverhampton District Council   <http://www.wolverhampton.gov.uk/stats/unnotes.htm>.

BBC News Online   <http://www.news.bbc.co.uk/hi/english/business/default.stm>.
An excellent source of general information on topical economic subjects. Search in the *business* section for a variety of topic areas, including unemployment and inflation.

Test your understanding

(Answers are given at the back of the book)

BANK OF ENGLAND responds to excessive wage increases with interest rate increases

During 1999 national statistics showed UK pay levels rising unacceptably quickly from the point of view of the Bank of England. Average earnings rose by 4.7% up to midway through 1999. Whilst this figure was lower than earnings increases in some months, and also lower than City expectations of 4.8%, the Bank of England considered any increase greater than 4.5% to be a threat to its inflation target of 2.5%. For this reason interest rates rose twice during the period August to October 1999.

In October 1999 the Chancellor warned that high pay increases not justified by productivity increases would threaten economic progress. He reiterated that there would be no return to the 'old ways' (implying large cyclical swings in the economy) and he warned businesses that excessive pay awards would attract high interest rates.

National statistics for 1999 showed that average pay increases in the private sector were 4.8 per cent, considerably higher than the 3.9 per cent in the public sector. It should be noted, however, that trends on pay increases were moving downwards. The statistics also showed that unit wage costs fell for the first time in a 5-year period at the same time as productivity rose by 4.3 per cent. This may well have been the result of manufacturing industry shedding jobs in order to remain competitive whilst at the same time output was increasing in line with an expanding economy.

---

1. Explain the connection between interest rates (line 6) and unemployment.

2. '. . . the Bank of England considered any increase greater than 4.5% to be a threat to its inflation target of 2.5%.'

   Explain, using diagrams as necessary, how a monetarist would see the solution to this problem.

3. '[The Chancellor] told business to be sure that inflationary pay awards would simply result in higher interest rates.'

   Explain the connection between interest rates and wage rises which the Chancellor is referring to.

4. 'This may well have been the result of manufacturing industry shedding jobs in order to remain competitive whilst at the same time output was increasing in line with an expanding economy.'

   The above statement in the final paragraph seems contradictory. Industry shedding jobs with output increasing? Explain what is going on here.

5. Which of the following measures may be used by a government in an attempt to *lower* the inflation rate of unemployment?

   A Reducing the rate of interest
   B Decreasing expenditure on capital projects
   C Reducing unemployment benefits in real terms
   D Increasing the rate of taxes on personal incomes
   E Increasing the wages of public sector workers by more than the current rate of inflation

6. The natural rate of unemployment is

   A All those who do not want to work, or are disabled, or are only prepared to work part-time.
   B All those who are frictionally and structurally unemployed.
   C All those who have lost jobs due to factory closures or industry decline, or who are between jobs or who work seasonally or who are disabled.
   D The number of people who are unemployed, for whatever reason, when the total demand for and supply of workers is in equilibrium.

14 Inflation

Learning objectives

- To understand the definition of inflation.
- To be aware of the two principle measures of inflation:
  - the Retail Price Index (RPI)
  - the underlying index (RPIX).
- To understand the effects of inflation.
- To understand the causes of inlation:
  - the Phillips curve.
- To be aware of policy issues:
  - Changing policy objectives
  - Alternative policy measures:
    - Fiscal policy
    - Monetary policy

14.1 Introduction

Definition of inflation

The definition of inflation is not just a question of rising prices. Prices of some goods and services might rise whilst others are falling, leaving the average price level unchanged. Neither is inflation better described as a rise in the general level of prices. The general level of prices may rise during one week or one month and then fall during successive weeks or months, so as to remain unchanged over a period of time. To take account of these points inflation is better described as a *continuous* rise in the general price level over a *period of time*. The period of time is not specified but is longer than just a few months.

INFLATION

A persistent tendency for the general level of prices to rise.

14.2 The measurement of inflation

To try and measure all the prices of all goods and services would be an expensive and pointless task. Pointless because there are many goods and services which only a small fraction of the population can afford. Thus changes in the price of the Rolls Royce motorcar will be less important to the general population than an increase in the price of petrol. It is therefore important to establish a number of goods and services which are relevant to the spending habits of a large percentage of the population. This is done by means of the **retail price index.**

Retail price index (RPI)

A large number of households each year, chosen to be representative of the whole population, are asked to fill in a detailed record of their expenditure over a period of two weeks. This is known as the *Family Expenditure Survey*. From this survey it is possible to select those goods and services which make up the majority of most people's weekly expenditure. The goods and services selected are known as a *representative basket of goods*. The composition of the basket is revised from time-to-time to represent the changing consumption patterns within the economy.

The total value (total of the prices) of the basket, in a particular month or year, is given an index number of 100. Then as the value of the basket changes so the index number changes to reflect the money changes. The changes in the index are a direct measure of inflation. An example will make this clear.

How changes in the value of a basket of goods are measured by an index number

Assume that the basket of goods in year 1 would cost £200. This value is set equal to the index number 100. In year 2 when the value of the basket of goods is measured it is found that it would cost £240. The difference is £40 which is an increase of 20%. The new index number would be 120. In year 3 when the value of the basket of goods is measured it is found that it would cost £250. The difference **from year 1** is £50 which is an increase of 25%. The new index number would be 125. Notice that to get the figure for year 3 inflation we must subtract the year 2 index number from the year 3 index number. Inflation in year 3 was 5%.

Inflation in the UK is measured by changes in the retail price index. However the composition of this index has been subject to criticism. The basket of goods on which it is based includes mortgage interest. Whilst this expenditure is of major importance to many households, being a significant proportion of their total spending, it is not the same as spending money on goods and services. If as the result of increased interest rates, mortgage interest rises; this is not spending on goods and services but a transfer of funds from one group within the economy to another. It is a transfer from borrowers to lenders. This criticism was seized upon by policy-makers who point out that increasing interest rates to try and control inflation, has the effect of increasing the RPI (and thus inflation) – the very opposite of the intended effect. The government therefore decided that its inflation targets will be based upon an index which excludes mortgage interest. This new index is known as the **underlying index (RPIX).** The government considers that this is a better indication of inflation.

TWO MEASURES OF INFLATION

Retail price index (RPI). Known as the **headline** rate of inflation. This measure of inflation is of great importance in the process of wage bargaining. Mortgage interest payments being a major expenditure component for most workers.

Underlying index (RPIX). Known as the **underlying** rate of inflation. This is the measure used by the government to set inflation targets for the Monetary Policy Committee of the Bank of England.

Note: There have been only five occasions since 1979 when the annual rates of change of the two indices have differed by more than 1%.

The following example is an article from *BBC Online News* dated 16th November 1999. Notice how both measures of inflation draw detailed comment. Notice the interesting analysis of the content of the basket of goods, how services are separated from manufacture, and the different cost effects on the RPI.

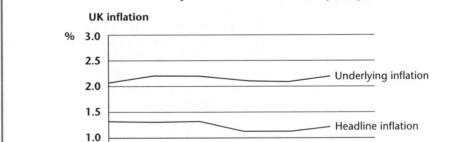

Business: The Economy – UK inflation creeps up

Inflation in the UK rose slightly in October but was roughly in line with expectations. The Office for National Statistics said the headline rate was 1.2%, up from 1.1% the previous month. The key underlying inflation rate – which excludes mortgage interest payments – was 2.2%, compared to 2.1% in September. But it was still well below the government's target rate of 2.5%. The monthly rise in the headline rate was 0.2%, while the underlying rate was up 0.1%.

Influences

The main reason given for the rise in inflation was an increase in motoring costs, with both insurance premiums and petrol prices markedly higher. The headline rate was also affected by mortgage lenders passing on part of the September rise in interest rates to homeowners. Partially offsetting these influences were lower food and household goods costs resulting from intense competition in the retail sector. There is concern among some economists about the widening gulf between inflation in the goods and services sectors, with the latter rising to its highest level since the beginning of 1994. For example, in the past 12 months, the price of clothing and footwear has declined by 3.0% while the cost of leisure services – such as entertainment and holidays – has gone up 4.6%.

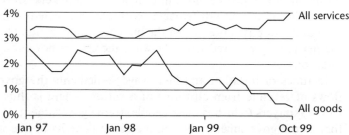

'The split between the two shows once again the extent to which the economy is split,' said Barclays Capital UK economist Adam Law. 'Competitive pressures are such that goods inflation is non-existent but the same level of competition is not yet in evidence in the service sector,' he said.

Philip Shaw of Investec described the data as 'slightly disappointing'. 'If you like, it's a warning shot – a sharp reminder to the markets that they have to look at all constituents of the Retail Price Index.'

14.3 The effects of inflation

Inflation can be either *anticipated* or *unanticipated*. If inflation is anticipated then it is assumed that the various groups within the economy will be fully compensated. However to the extent that the various groups within the economy, say those on fixed price contracts, cannot raise prices to compensate for existing inflation, then inflation is unanticipated. It is also unanticipated if unforeseen or incorrectly forecast. It is the **re-distribution** effects of unanticipated inflation with which we are concerned. The following are those effects.

A re-distribution from LENDERS to BORROWERS

People who borrow money, perhaps to buy consumer durable goods, pay a rate of interest on the borrowed money but obtain the goods at today's prices. They have the satisfaction derived from using the goods immediately rather than saving to buy in the future. The lender gets the interest agreed at the outset. If inflation is above the rate of interest then the borrower is paying back the lender in currency worth less than when it was borrowed. The borrower is better off by having the consumer durable today at yesterday's prices, whilst the lender is worse off because the real value of the money that was lent is not being repaid.

Even if the rate of inflation is less than the rate of interest charged by lenders, it is still eroding their future income returns. That is, the money the lenders receive in repayments is worth less in real terms than the sum of money lent, by the amount of inflation present in the economy. Clearly unanticipated inflation is bad news for fixed rate lenders.

A re-distribution from TAXPAYERS to the GOVERNMENT

As incomes rise people move into higher tax brackets. In the UK there are a series of income levels at which different rates of taxes are levied. A person moving into a higher tax band will pay more tax on the income in that band. This extra tax may mean that the net money received from the wage increase is not enough to fully compensate for inflation.

In times of inflation and high wage settlements the government receives increased flows of revenue from all forms of taxation. There is thus a redistribution of money from taxpayers (which is most people) to the government. It should be noted, however, that as the government pays out increased benefits in line with inflation the net effect of this redistribution is unclear.

A re-distribution from FIXED INCOME EARNERS to STRONGLY REPRESENTED WORKERS

Fixed income earners may be pensioners on fixed pensions, or people dependent on fixed income investments. Clearly these groups of people are unable to gain compensation for inflation. In contrast strongly organised groups of workers, whether by union representation or by professional association, are able to gain full compensation for the inflation. Their share of the total cake therefore increases, and there is a redistribution effect away from the fixed income earners towards those able to defend their wage/salary levels.

A re-distribution from PUBLIC SECTOR EMPLOYEES to PRIVATE SECTOR EMPLOYEES

The government is trying to control inflation and will want to set an example of wage restraint. It is traditional that public sector workers such as, doctors, nurses, teachers, policemen do not get fully compensated for inflation, especially when inflation levels are high. This is in contrast to the private sector where employers are happy to pay much higher wages settlements if they are tied to profit levels or productivity.

Not only is there a redistribution from the public sector workers to the private sector workers, there may also be an erosion of pay differentials within a particular trade or profession between the public and private sectors. For example, a financial accountant working for the health service may fall further behind the pay scales of a similarly qualified and experienced accountant in industry. In this case there is a redistribution effect within professions and trades. Ultimately this issue will have to be addressed or the public sector will lose key workers to the private sector. [Every so often there is a catching up exercise on behalf of certain groups within the public sector. Examples over the last decade include teachers, doctors, nurses, policemen and judges.]

A re-distribution from PROFIT EARNERS to WAGE EARNERS

If wage earners are able to be successfully compensated for inflation then this might increase employers total costs and reduce profit levels. In this case there would be a redistribution away from the profit earner towards the wage earner. However, it must be noted that increased wages/salaries does not invariably mean increased total costs. There may be cost cutting exercises to off-set the increased wage bill. There may be productivity agreements in place. Ultimately any increased costs may be passed on to the consumer – especially if the goods or services are price inelastic.

14.4 The causes of inflation

The main influence is the pressure of demand on the supplies of goods and services and on the supply of labour. When demand exceeds supply there will be pressure on wages to rise. And for retail prices to rise to protect profit margins. This pressure will provide the catalyst necessary for wages to rise, forcing up costs which are then passed on in price rises, whence the whole process starts again. This is the wage-price spiral. M.C. Kennedy estimates that wages are about 66 per cent of total variable costs (in M. J. Artis (ed.) (1997) *The UK Economy* (14th edn), Oxford University Press, Oxford, p. 108). The second main inflationary pressure is the rising costs of imports. Imported goods and materials are about 30 per cent of total variable costs and therefore a major pressure on final prices when the prices of imports are rising. Added to this pressure is the fact that imported goods impact upon consumer demand directly. M. C. Kennedy estimates that 20 per cent of total final expenditure is accounted for by imports.

There are those economists who will claim that it is an increased money supply that causes inflation. Inflation will give rise to an increased demand for money, mainly transactions demand (see Chapter 12). This increase in the demand for money can only be fed by an increase in the money supply. However if the money supply is not increased then the increased demand for transactions balances will have to come from idle balances (precautionary and speculative balances will have to be used for transactions purposes). When these idle balances are used up the inflationary process will end, or output will fall. The conclusion to this line of reasoning is that for the inflationary process to continue there has to be an increase in the money supply. **Increased money supply is a necessary condition for inflation to take place.** This is very different from holding that an increased money supply *caused* inflation. The initial pressure for increased transactions balances was demand related, or price increases due to increased costs of production – both wages and materials.

14.5 The demand for labour and inflation

Keynes argued that if unemployment was high there would be little pressure for wages to rise; but as unemployment reduced and the economy approached its full employment level of national income, money wages would be bid up as employers competed for the best workers. This reasoning suggests a trade-off between wage inflation and unemployment. Professor A. W. Phillips agreed with Keynes' reasoning when in 1958 he published his study on *The Relation between Unemployment and the Rate of Change of Money Wage Rates 1861–1957*.

Phillips examined data on unemployment rates and wage increases, and on the basis of data for the period 1861–1913 he established a relationship between the rate of change of money wages (wage inflation) and unemployment. This relationship is known as the Phillips Curve and is shown in Figure 14.1.

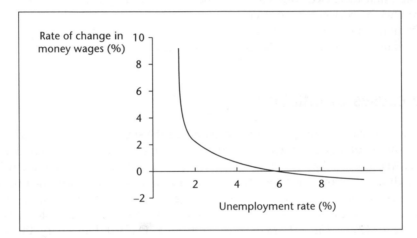

Figure 14.1 **The Phillips Curve**

The Phillips relationship implies that an unemployment rate of 1 per cent could only be achieved at the cost of wage inflation at 8.7 per cent. That zero wage inflation implied an unemployment rate of about 5.5 per cent. Thus there was a trade-off between unemployment and wage inflation. The importance of Phillips' contribution was that here was a relationship with predictive value. Phillips showed in his 1958 paper that wage increases over the period 1948–1957 were almost exactly as predicted by the relationship. The Phillips Curve continued to give accurate predictions of wage increases up to 1965. In 1967 the relationship seemed unable to predict wage inflation. Instead of there being a trade off between unemployment and wage inflation there was both high unemployment and high wage inflation. The main problem was therefore to try and explain the breakdown of the relationship and the co-existence of both wage inflation and unemployment.

The main ingredient missing from the Phillips relationship was *anticipated inflation*. This is hardly surprising as the period between 1861–1913 was one of price stability. However the 1960s saw inflation as a normal aspect of the economy and union negotiators factored into their wage demands a measure of anticipated inflation. This became even more important during the oil crisis of the 1970s and the huge increases in the cost base of many industries.

Another missing ingredient was *pressure of demand for* labour. Pressure of demand for labour is arguably the most important single factor in wage inflation. Both Keynes and Phillips agree that at close to full employment employers will tend to bid up wages in an attempt to hire suitable workers. The categories of workers may be specific, thus there can be general unemployment of unskilled workers whilst there is an auction being conducted, within the economy, for various categories of skilled workers. The critical point is that unemployment figures measure the *excess supply* of workers, not the excess demand for workers in the system. It has been pointed out that perhaps the *vacancy rate* is a more appropriate measure of the excess demand for labour than unemployment statistics. These are figures notified to the government via employers and employers organisations such as the CBI, on a monthly basis. Such data was not available to Phillips.

There have been a number of attempts to revise the Phillips Curve to account for modern circumstances. Friedman introduced an *expectations-augmented* version in which a central theme was money illusion.

14.6 Policy issues

Changing policy objectives

If asked, most policymakers would assert that the main objectives of government policy are to maintain a low level of unemployment and to avoid inflation. Whilst these objectives are usually translated into targets – such as *inflation below 2.5%* and a *reduction* in unemployment – they still present conflicting objectives.

Throughout the 1960s, right up to 1973, there had been relative price stability. Thus successive governments had been able to employ fiscal policies – mainly changes in the levels of direct and indirect taxation – to regulate aggregate demand and establish acceptable levels of unemployment. There was still a trade-off to be had between inflation and unemployment, and small increases in inflation were considered a small price to pay for low unemployment. The problem with this type of demand management was that the various multiplier effects took time to work through the economy, and information on the economy was not as plentiful or a accurate as present day information. Thus there were continual adjustments necessary as information became available, giving rise to what have been called 'stop-go' policies. But for all this, low unemployment was achieved at relatively low levels of inflation.

The oil crisis of 1973, when the price of oil trebled almost overnight, led to serious inflation. The priorities of the government changed from a focus upon unemployment towards the control of inflation. Since the first Thatcher administration in 1979 governments have been almost exclusively concerned with the control of inflation. From time-to-time various policy makers make statements of intent concerning levels of unemployment, or they devise initiatives for certain elements of the unemployed. But no present day political party has presented unemployment targets in the same way that inflation is targeted.

Alternative policy measures

Fiscal policy

The two main aspects of fiscal policy are government spending and taxation. A reduction in government spending (say on schools, hospitals, road building, etc) and an increase in direct or indirect taxation will have a withdrawal effect from the circular flow of income. The multiplier effect will be to reduce the level of national income even further. An opposite effect will be generated by increases in government spending and reductions in levels of taxation. Thus fiscal measures can have a direct effect upon the level of aggregate demand in the economy. If inflation is caused by excess demand for goods and services then fiscal measures should dampen down demand and after a period of time this dampening of consumption demand will feed into the labour markets and restrain wage increases.

Monetary policy

The main instrument of monetary policy is the interest rate. As was shown in Chapter 12 the money supply is manipulated by the Bank of England in its dealings with the money markets. But it is not the money supply itself that is being strictly controlled in order to restrain demand and therefore inflationary pressures. The money supply is not a policy instrument, though it may well be a target of policy. It is the level of existing and expected inflation that is the policy target, and this is the main reason for changes in interest rates. This is explained in detail in a Bank of England (Monetary Policy Committee) paper, an extract of which is given below.

> In the current policy framework, where the official interest rate is the policy instrument, both the money stock and inflation are jointly caused by other variables. Monetary adjustment normally fits into the transmission mechanism in the following way. Suppose that monetary policy has been relaxed by the implementation of a cut in the official interest rate. Commercial banks correspondingly reduce the interest rates they charge on their loans. This is likely to lead to an increased demand for loans (partly to finance the extra spending discussed above), and an increased extension of loans by banks creates new bank deposits that will be measured as an increase in the broad money supply (M4). So the change in spending by individuals and firms that results from a monetary policy change will also be accompanied by a change in both bank lending and bank deposits. Increases in retail sales are also likely to be associated with an increased demand for notes and coin in circulation. Data on monetary aggregates – lending, deposits, and cash – are helpful in the formation of monetary policy, as they provide corroborative, or sometimes leading, indicators of the course of spending behaviour, and they are available in advance of much of the national accounts data. In the long run, monetary and credit aggregates must be willingly held by agents in the economy. Monetary growth persistently in excess of that warranted by growth in the real economy will inevitably be the reflection of an interest rate policy that is inconsistent with stable inflation. So control of inflation always ultimately implies control of the monetary growth rate. However, the relationship between the monetary aggregates and nominal GDP in the United Kingdom appears to be insufficiently stable (partly owing to financial

innovation) for the monetary aggregates to provide a robust indicator of likely future inflation developments in the near term. It is for this reason that an inflation-targeting regime is thought to be superior to one of monetary targeting when the intention is to control inflation itself. In other words, money matters, but not in such a precise way as to provide a reliable quantitative guide for monetary policy in the short to medium term.

14.7 Summary

Inflation is a persistent tendency for the general level of prices to rise. There are two official measures of inflation, the retail prices index (RPI) and the RPIX which is the same index but excluding mortgage interest payments.

Inflation has a number of redistribution effects within the economy and this upsets the sometimes delicate balance between different groups within the economy. The principal problem is for those on fixed incomes or fixed pensions, unlike strongly organised workers, they are unable to get the extra income necessary to offset inflation. There are other important redistribution effects.

The causes of inflation have led to heated debate for many years. On the one hand there are those who believe that excess demand is principally responsible and on the other hand there are those who argue that excessive costs, especially wages, are to blame. The causes of inflation are reasonably well known. The main influence is the pressure of demand on the supplies of goods and services and on the supply of labour. The demand for housing has a particularly widespread and lasting effect. When demand exceeds supply there will be pressure on wages to rise. And for retail prices to rise to protect profit margins. This pressure will provide the catalyst necessary for wages to rise, forcing up costs which are then passed on in price rises, whence the whole process starts again.

Keynes argued that if unemployment was high there would be little pressure for wages to rise; but as unemployment reduced and the economy approached its full employment level of national income, money wages would be bid up as employers competed for the best workers. This reasoning suggests a trade-off between wage inflation and unemployment. Professor A.W. Phillips agreed with Keynes' reasoning and formalised the relationship in the Phillips Curve. This trade-off was a useful insight for policymakers in the 1960s but the relationship did not hold after the late 1960s when high inflation and high unemployment were both present.

The two main aspects of fiscal policy are government spending and taxation. A reduction in government spending (say on schools, hospitals, road building, etc) and an increase in direct or indirect taxation will have a damping down effect on demand and after a period of time this dampening of consumption demand will feed into the labour markets and restrain wage increases

The main instrument of monetary policy is the interest rate. As was shown in Chapter 12 the money supply is manipulated by the Bank of England in its dealings with the money markets. But it is not the money supply itself that is being strictly controlled in order to restrain demand and therefore inflationary pressures. The money supply is not a policy instrument, though it may well be a target of policy. It is the level of existing and expected inflation that is the policy target, and this is the main reason for changes in interest rates. Increases in the interest rate have a damping effect upon demand, especially demand for housing.

The main purpose of this chapter has been to introduce some basic ideas to allow the student to read more advanced 1st year texts on this topic.

Further reading

ARTIS, M. J. *The UK Economy*, Oxford University Press.
BEGG, D., FISCHER, S. and DORNBUSCH, R. *Economics*, McGraw-Hill.
GRIFFITHS, A. and WALL, S. *Applied Economics*, Longman.
HARDWICK, P., KHAN, B. and LANGMEAD, J. *An Introduction to Modern Economics*, Longman.
McALEESE, D. *Economics for Business*, Prentice Hall.
SLOMAN, J. and SUTCLIFFE, M. *Economics for Business*, Prentice Hall.

Some useful information on the internet

Bank of England Publications   <http://www.bankofengland.co.uk/infrep.htm>.
The Bank of England quarterly inflation report can be viewed here.

HM Treasury Publications   <http://www.hm.treasury.gov.uk/index.html>.
A particularly interesting paper published here: Mervyn King, *The Inflation Target 5 Years On* – (Bank of England). This paper looks at six questions.

- Is inflation targeting new?
- What has been the experience of countries with it?
- Does an inflation target mean that monetary policy ignores output?
- What is the role of inflation forecasts?
- Why is openness and transparency important?
- How will the Bank of England be accountable?

National Statistics – the official UK site   <http://www.statistics.gov.uk>.
Especially for consumer prices indices

BBC News Online   <http://www.news.bbc.co.uk/hi/english/business/default.stm>.
An excellent source of general information on topical economic subjects. Search in the *business* section for a variety of topic areas including unemployment and inflation.

Test your understanding

(Answers are given at the back of the book.)

The first 4 questions are based upon the following extracted paragraphs from the Bank of England's Monetary Policy Committee's inflation report for November 1999.

Final domestic demand – especially household consumption – has continued to grow strongly, and was 4.5% higher in the second quarter than a year before. Having significantly lowered overall demand for UK output since mid 1997, net trade – exports less imports – made a positive contribution to growth in Q2, and exports have continued to grow since then as world trade has picked up. Rising demand has been met in part by a rundown in stocks. If net trade and stock building stabilise, the growth rate of final domestic demand will need to ease in order to keep overall demand in line with the economy's supply capacity.

The recovery from last autumn's low points in a wide range of business survey indicators, including manufacturing as well as services, has been maintained. Reports from the Bank's regional Agents confirm expectations of a positive near-term outlook for most business sectors. However, a number of recent surveys point to a pick-up in cost pressures.

Unemployment has fallen further – to 5.9% on the Labour Force Survey measure and to 4.2% on the claimant count. Employment growth, total hours worked, vacancies, and measures of employment intentions have all picked up. Survey evidence and reports from the Bank's regional Agents suggest that recruitment difficulties have increased in some areas and for some types of skill, but not uniformly. Overall, however, labour market conditions have tightened in recent months.

Nominal pay growth as measured by the Average Earnings Index rose to 4.9% in the three months to August, largely on account of higher growth in private sector pay in the services industries. However, wage settlements have on average remained broadly flat. Pay growth in real terms has been rising for some time on most measures, but this might in part reflect lower-than-expected price inflation, as well as labour market tightness.

1. What does the last sentence in the first paragraph mean? Explain and outline the potential risks for UK inflation.

2. With reference to paragraph three.

   a. What are the two unemployment measures referred to in the first sentence? Why is one higher than the other?
   b. What does the evidence in the third sentence suggest for future inflation?

3. Referring to the final paragraph, how does expected inflation affect wages?

4. On the overall evidence of these paragraphs what policy measures would you advocate, remembering that the prime policy objective is to maintain inflation below 2.5%.

5. Changes in the Retail Price Index are an indicator of changes in the

   A standard of living
   B prices of factor inputs
   C cost of living
   D costs of manufactured goods
   E competitiveness of UK industry

6. Real income may be obtained from data on money income by allowing for

   A capital consumption
   B changes in wage rates
   C depreciation
   D inflation
   E transfer incomes

7. Which of the following statements is **incorrect**?

   A Fully anticipated inflation means that all wage earners are able to make wage claims to compensate for inflation.
   B Unanticipated inflation means that there is a general failure in the economy to predict the level of inflation.
   C Anticipated inflation leads to a redistribution effect from certain weak groups to strong groups.
   D Unanticipated inflation means that there is a failure by some groups within the economy to correctly predict the level of inflation so they seek lower money wages than are needed to compensate for the actual level of inflation.

International trade

Learning objectives

International trade

- To understand why there is benefit from extensive world trade. In particular to understand the following ideas:
  - Absolute advantage
  - Comparative advantage
  - Terms of trade
- To appreciate the variety of barriers that can be erected to prevent or reduce foreign trade. Also to understand the justifications made for these barriers.
- To understand the reasons for the setting up the general Agreement on Tarrifs and Trade (GATT).
- To be aware of how GATT went about fulfilling its objectives.
- To be aware of the objectives of its successor body, the World Trade Organisation (WTO).

Exchange rates

- To understand the working of the markets which determine the value of one country's currency in terms of another's.
- To be aware of different exchange rate systems and to understand the advantages and disadvantages of each.
- To understand the system for determining the external value of the pound sterling.
- To understand the concept of the Effective Exchange Rate (EER) and how it is calculated.

Balance of payments

- To understand in detail the structure of the UK's trading accounts with the rest of the world.

15.1 Introduction

This chapter will deal with three major areas; international trade, exchange rates, the balance of payments; which in many textbooks have a chapter to themselves. This is an introductory text, which seeks to give the student a basic understanding of these topics. It is often unclear which should be dealt with first, so for present purposes answering the following questions will determine the order.

1. Why should we trade so extensively with other countries?
2. If different countries use different currencies how is one currency valued in terms of another?
3. Given that there are benefits from trading, how does the UK record its dealings with the rest of the world?

15.2 International trade

The question, 'why should the UK trade with other countries?' is easily answered in the case of bananas or diamonds. The answer is that these products cannot be grown or produced in the UK so they have to be imported. What is not so clear is why the UK buys goods and services which could be produced at home. This question generalises to, 'why should any country buy products and services which could be produced in that country'? The answer is in two parts.

Where one country can produce a product more cheaply and efficiently than another country that country is said to have an **absolute advantage** over the other. Thus for example if the UK can produce 'gaberdine wool' more cheaply and more efficiently than France can produce it, the UK has an *absolute advantage* over France. If France can produce cheese more cheaply and more efficiently than the UK can produce it, France has an *absolute advantage* over the UK. It makes sense therefore for France to concentrate upon producing cheese and the UK to concentrate upon producing gaberdine wool. They can then trade cheese for wool, and vice versa. There is a clear case for trade to take place and a general rule can be stated.

> ### ABSOLUTE ADVANTAGE
> Countries should specialise in producing those products in which they have an *absolute advantage*. In this way the total production of all goods will be greater leading to the possibility of mutually beneficial trade.

What is not so clear is why there should be trade between countries when one country has an absolute advantage in producing **all** products. Thus in the above example, why should there be trade between the UK and France if France can produce both cheese and cloth more cheaply and more efficiently than the UK? The answer was given in the 19th century by an economist named David Ricardo.

Comparative advantage

Ricardo showed that trade was beneficial to both countries even though one had an absolute advantage over the other. This is best explained using an example.

Assumptions
1. Assume there are only 2 countries France and the UK
2. Assume that with 1 unit of labour France can produce 6 bottles of wine or 4 cheeses
3. Assume that with 1 unit of labour the UK can produce 2 bottles of wine or 2 cheeses

The example

Given the assumptions it is possible to state, for both countries, what 1 unit of labour can produce.

- UK   2W or 2C
- France   6W or 4C

where wine and cheese are indicated by W or C

France has an absolute advantage over the UK in producing both wine and cheese.

Another way of stating this is to show that the output of one worker in terms of wine is equal to the output of the same worker in cheese. Thus

- UK   2W = 2C
- France   6W = 4C

Because it is the same worker, he can either produce wine or cheese (opportunity cost). Thus to produce an amount of wine, the cost is giving up the cheese that the worker could have produced. To produce an amount of cheese, the cost is giving up the wine that the worker could have produced. In this sense of opportunity cost the relative costs of producing wine and cheese, for each country, can be stated.

- UK   1W costs 1C   1C costs 1W
- France   1W costs 0.6C   1C costs 1.5W

In terms of cost the UK can produce cheese more cheaply than France (1 cheese costs the UK 1 bottle of wine to produce but the same cheese costs France 1.5 bottles of wine to produce). In terms of cost France can produce wine more cheaply than the UK (1 bottle of wine costs France 0.6 of a cheese to produce but the same bottle of wine costs the UK 1 cheese to produce).

The theory of comparative advantage says that the UK should concentrate upon the production of cheese whilst France should concentrate upon producing wine. More of each will be produced in total allowing mutually advantageous trade to take place.

COMPARATIVE ADVANTAGE

Countries should specialise in producing those goods and services in which they have a **relative** advantage. Put another way, countries specialise in producing those goods and services where they have **the least comparative disadvantage**. In this way world production will increase to the mutual benefit of all countries.

Note: The idea of relative advantage – **comparative advantage** – is to highlight the relative opportunity costs.

This theory can be tested with the use of a few more assumptions and an example of world trade.

Assumptions
1. The world consists of only two countries France and the UK.
2. Each country has 100 units of labour
3. That each country requires 100 cheeses to feed its population.

Example of world trade

Assuming that each country produces both wine and cheese with their labour, Table 15.1 shows the position.

Table 15.1 Each country produces both wine and cheese

	Labour used	Wine	Labour used	Cheese
UK	50	100	50	100
France	75	450	25	100
World production		550		200

Note that 100 cheese have to be produced by both countries to feed their populations. (assumption). Once this amount of cheese is produced the other workers can produce wine. UK requires 50 workers to produce 100 cheeses (the original assumption of what each worker can produce) whilst France only requires 25 workers to produce 100 cheeses. The remaining workers, for each country, then produce wine
Remember the original assumptions:

UK   2W or 2C
France   6W or 4C

Now assume that each country specialises according to their **comparative advantage**. France produces all wine and the UK produces all cheese. The result is shown in Table 15.2.

Table 15.2 Each country specialises

	Labour used	Wine	Labour used	Cheese
UK			100	200
France	100	600		
World production		600		200

The immediate observation is that total world production has increased by 50 bottles of wine. The theory of comparative advantage has been shown to be correct in stating that world production would increase. But what about 'to the mutual advantage' of both countries?

Terms of trade

Continuing with the above example, the UK has 200 cheeses and France has 600 bottles of wine. France needs 100 cheeses to feed its population (assumption). The only question that remains is what will 1 cheese exchange for in terms of wine?

> From France's point of view it could have produced 450 bottles of wine and 100 cheeses – without trade.
>
> From the UK's point of view it could have produced 100 bottles of wine and 100 cheeses – without trade.

So for trade to be mutually beneficial both countries have to be better off. In this case the question is how to share the extra 50 bottles of wine. Let us look again at the opportunity costs of each country.

- UK   1W costs 1C   1C costs 1W
- France   1W costs 0.6C   1C costs 1.5W

The UK will exchange cheese so long as it can get more than 1 bottle of wine for each cheese. (This is the cost of each cheese to the UK.)

France will exchange wine so long as it can get more than 0.6 of a cheese for each bottle of wine. (This is the cost of each bottle of wine to France.)

The *terms of trade* will therefore be:

In terms of wine: 1 bottle of wine will exchange for between 0.6 and 1 cheese.
In terms of cheese: 1 cheese will exchange for between 1 and 1.5 bottles of wine.

Assume that the terms of trade are 1 cheese exchanges for 1.25 bottles of wine (1C = 1.25W). Then in terms of world trade both the UK and France should be better off and world trade increased. The situation after trade has taken place is shown in Table 15.3.

Table 15.3   **The final position after the UK has traded 1 cheese for 1.25 bottles of wine**

	Wine	Cheese
UK	125	100
France	475	100
World production	600	200

Both countries have more wine after trade than they could produce themselves, if they are to feed their populations.

The general conclusion from this simplified example is that all countries would be better off, and world production would increase in total, if each country specialised in producing those goods and services in which it had a comparative advantage. There would be a more efficient world-wide use of scarce resources and every nation would benefit from those countries which enjoy rich natural endowments. This conclusion implies free trade between nations.

World trade

Although there is a clear case for world free trade, many countries erect barriers to trade. These barriers are erected for many different reasons and take different forms.

Reasons for barriers to trade

- Throughout the 20th century there has been armed conflict. Two major world wars together with many other, almost as serious, regionally localised conflicts. Therefore it is not surprising that many governments may wish to protect, and develop, those industries considered to be of **strategic importance**. Examples are armaments, aerospace, power industries, and agriculture. The economic argument for trade is lost in this case as the motive for protection is political.

- When countries are developing their own industrial structures they are vulnerable in their **infant stages**. This is particularly the case with third world countries, where ready and cheap supplies of a good, from the industrialised nations, can undermine their industrial development. They therefore erect tariffs against outside competitors. This is an easily understood argument for protection, and most countries since 1945 have employed this argument to justify a tariff strategy. Nevertheless there are economic costs, in terms of efficiency, resource allocation and social welfare.

- Countries have sought to improve their **terms of trade** by trying to create excess supply and therefore force down price. The argument is that when a country imposes a tariff less of that product is imported. This creates excess supply for the exporting country, which will reduce its price in order to sell all of its output. This is only going to work for a country which is a major buyer of a product and therefore able to have a major effect upon overall supply. It could also work if there was concerted action to impose tariffs by a number of countries. However, the economic costs of reduced world trade and the loss of efficiency and welfare benefits would be enormous.

- From microeconomics we know that firms have a variety of strategies for maximising their revenue or maximising their potential sales. A price discriminating monopolist may choose to sell goods in an overseas market at prices well below those charged in the home market; even allowing for the extra costs involved such as, transport, duties, etc. Another firm may see the overseas market as potentially important within the firm's strategic plans, and may try to sell goods into that market at below cost. This would be written off as marketing expenses by the exporting firm. In both these examples the importing country sees the cheap goods as unfair competition. As far as the importing country is concerned they have been **dumped** upon. The retaliation to dumping is to erect tariffs. Whilst countries may see protection against dumping as justifiable, it should be pointed out that the main beneficiary of dumping is the consumer in the country being dumped upon.

- The most specious of all arguments for protection come from **industries in decline**. Whilst a declining industry can be the cause of unwanted structural unemployment, high claims upon the exchequer and political inconvenience, there can be no justification for protection. Such protection merely distorts the process of re-allocation of resources which is underway and shores up inefficient industry. One form of protection in this type of case is subsidies, by government, to underwrite the inefficiencies of the industry concerned.

Types of barrier to trade

Tariff   This is an import duty levied against goods coming into the country.

Quota   This is a restriction upon the quantity of goods that can be imported into a country, within a specified time period.

Subsidies   These are government payments to firms which have the same effect as reducing the cost structure of a product. They have the effect of making the product cheaper in foreign markets even after tariffs have been imposed. They are difficult to detect as the subsidy can take many different forms.

15.4   The General Agreement on Tariffs and Trade (GATT)

After the second world war there was a perceived need to create a better international order and to avoid the destructive trade policies of the inter-war years. In October 1947, in Geneva, 23 countries signed the General Agreement on Tariffs and Trade (GATT). The signatory countries were pledged to the expansion of multilateral trade and to the reduction of tariffs and quotas. Multilateral trade meant that signatory countries would not enter into exclusive bilateral deals, and that any concession offered to one trading partner would be offered to all other members. This idea was later to be known as the *most favoured nation* clause. GATT grew rapidly over the 25 years since its formation. In 1992 108 countries were signatories.

To further the objectives for which it was founded, GATT organised a number of trading rounds. A trading round was an international negotiating period between members aimed at agreeing reductions in tariffs and quotas. These trading rounds often took many years, rather than months, to complete. The most significant of these rounds have been the Kennedy Round (1954–1967), the Tokyo Round (1973 –1979) and the Uruguay Round (1986–1994). These rounds were successful in that many tariffs were abolished and others significantly reduced. The Tokyo Round, for example, brought the average level of tariffs for the EC, USA and Japan to less than 5 per cent.

There were many problems. Many developing nations felt that GATT worked to the advantage of its members – the developed nations – and they responded to this perceived threat. In 1964 they set up, under the auspices of the United Nations, the UN Conference on Trade and Development (UNCTAD). This was a forum where developing nations could argue for their own trading interests. One particular issue discussed in UNCTAD was the issue of *most favoured nation*. This required GATT members to give equal treatment to all members, but the developing nations felt that they should have preferential treatment in accessing the more prosperous developed markets. This concern was responded to by GATT members when in 1965 the clause was waived to allow preferential agreements with developing nations.

There was a further problem, that as tariffs were reduced countries found other means to protect their interests. These took many forms but the more successful were in the form of restrictive trade agreements between exporters and importers. In this case there could be voluntary agreement to voluntary quotas. The exporter being happier with an ongoing share of the market rather than face a more devious and successful restrictive practice. In addition to this attempt to undermine agreements made within GATT there were whole areas of economic life not covered by the original GATT agreement. These were agriculture, service industries and public sector activities. These further problems were tackled in the Uruguay Round, which started in 1986. The discussions were long and complex and were often reported to be acrimonious. Agreement was finally reached, in 1994, on a number of issues. It was agreed to reduce agricultural protection also to reduce barriers to trade in the financial services sector as well as agreeing to further reductions of tariffs on industrial goods.

The Uruguay agreement included the dissolution of GATT and the setting up of a successor body – the World Trade Organisation (WTO). This new organisation, which came into existence in January 1995, had a very different remit from the original GATT agreement.

15.5   ## The World Trade Organisation (WTO)

The WTO was set up in January 1995 and had the following remit:

1. To promote further reductions in tariffs and other obstacles to trade.
2. To formulate new rules concerning environmental issues, competition policy and trade in services.
3. To arbitrate between members on trade disputes. The WTO has an agreed disputes procedure which GATT never had.

The impetus for nations to move towards the ultimate position of free world trade must surely derive from an acceptance of the predictions of comparative advantage – world production can be increased to the mutual benefit of all. However political expediency and other issues of national interest may make the interim period a very long one. It can be concluded that GATT was moving towards fair trade rather than free trade.

15.6   ## Exchange rates

The value of one currency in terms of another is determined by demand and supply in a free market. In this case pounds or francs or any other currency, are commodities just like fish (see Chapter 3). To show how exchange rates are established and how they may change will be easier if we assume just two countries, the UK and France.

The demand for pounds

The demand for pounds will come about because French importers wish to buy British goods. They have to pay for the British goods in pounds. The demand curve for pounds will be a normal downward sloping curve from left to right. This is shown in Figure 15.1.

At an exchange rate of 10 francs to the £ there will be a certain level of demand for British goods in France. This demand for British goods will give rise to French importers having a total demand for £s. In Figure 15.1 OQ £s are demanded when the price of each pound is 10 francs.

Let us assume that the value of the £ falls to 8 francs. It only costs the French consumer 8 francs now to buy 1 pounds worth of British goods, whereas it cost

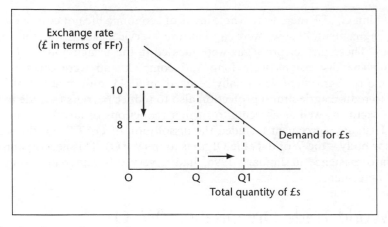

Figure 15.1 **The demand curve for £**

10 francs before. Whilst the cost of the British goods to the French importer has not changed in £s, the goods are cheaper in France to the French consumer because they do not have to pay so many francs for each pound. They will therefore buy more British goods. (This assumes that the French consumer has elastic demand for British imports). If French consumers buy more British goods then the French importers will have to demand more £s to pay for them. Thus in Figure 15.1 when the price of the £ falls to 8 francs total demand for £s increases from OQ to OQ1.

Example

A British product is sold to French importers for £10. When the exchange rate is 10 francs = 1 £ this product sells in the French shops for 100 francs. When the exchange rate falls to 8 francs = 1£ this product sells in the French shops for 80 francs. Because of the pound falling in value French consumers have a cheaper product and they will tend to demand more of the cheaper product.

You should make sure that you understand what will happen to the total demand for £s if the value of the pound was to rise to 12 francs. Will French consumers buy more or less British goods? Why?

The supply of pounds

The supply of pounds will come about because British importers wish to buy French goods. They have to pay for the French goods in francs. The British importers therefore supply pounds as the result of British consumers buying French goods. The supply curve for pounds will be a normal upward sloping curve from left to right. This is shown in Figure 15.2.

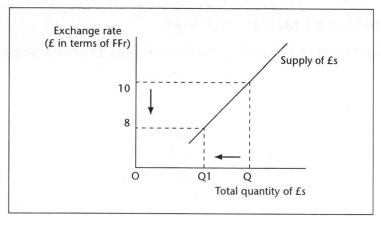

Figure 15.2 **The supply curve for £**

At an exchange rate of 10 francs to the £ there will be a certain level of demand for French goods in British shops. This demand for French goods will give rise to British importers having a total amount of £s that they wish to exchange for francs. They supply these £s. In Figure 15.2 OQ £s are supplied when the price of each pound is 10 francs.

Let us assume that the value of the £ falls to 8 francs. It now costs the British consumer 25 per cent more to buy the same value of French goods as before. (See example below to see how this is worked out.) Whilst the cost of the French goods to the British importer has not changed in francs, the goods are more expensive in Britain to the British consumer because British importers have to pay more £s to buy the same amount of francs. They will therefore buy less French goods. (This assumes that the British consumer has elastic demand for French imports.) If British consumers buy less French goods then the British importers will have to supply fewer £s to pay for them. Thus in Figure 15.2 when the price of the £ falls to 8 francs total supply of £s falls from OQ to OQ1.

> **Example**
>
> A French product is sold to British importers for 80 francs. When the exchange rate is 10 francs = 1£ this product sells in the British shops for £8. When the exchange rate falls to 8 francs = 1£ this product sells in the British shops for £10. Because of the pound falling in value British consumers have a more expensive product and they will tend to demand less of the more expensive product.

> You should make sure that you understand what will happen to the total supply of £s if the value of the pound was to rise to 12 francs. Will British consumers buy more or less French goods? Why?

The equilibrium rate of exchange

This is shown in Figure 15.3, and is where the demand for £s is equal to the supply of £s.

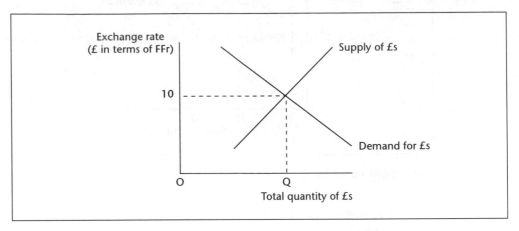

Figure 15.3 **The equilibrium rate of exchange**

This is a stable exchange rate because at any other rate of exchange there is pressure to return to this level. The reasoning is the same as for any market equilibrium, see Chapter 3 page 44.

Note that because the demand and supplies of currencies depend upon demand for goods and services in the different countries, there are a number of more complex market models possible. The above analysis is true where the demand for goods and services overall is elastic. The analysis changes where demand for products and services is inelastic.

Before considering various exchange rate systems, it is important to recall some relationships which have been established.

A rise in the value of the pound

If the value of the pound rises **(appreciates)** then British goods overseas (exports) will be more expensive. This will make it harder for British firms to sell their goods overseas and demand is likely to fall. Provided that the demand for British goods is not inelastic, the fall in demand for exports will mean a decrease in the total demand for £s.

As the pound appreciates then foreign goods at home (imports) will become cheaper. This will mean that demand is likely to increase as British consumers switch their spending to the cheaper imports. Provided that the demand for imports by the British consumer is not inelastic, the increase in demand for imports will mean an increase in the supply of £s.

As demand for £s has decreased and supply of £s has increased this should lead to a fall in the price of pounds. There will be a tendency for the pound to return to its equilibrium value.

A fall in the value of the pound

If the value of the pound falls **(depreciates)** then British goods overseas (exports) will become cheaper. This will make it easier for British firms to sell their goods overseas and demand is likely to increase. Provided that the demand for British goods is not inelastic, the increase in demand will mean an increase in the total demand for £s.

As the pound depreciates then foreign goods at home (imports) will become more expensive. This will mean that demand is likely to decrease as British consumers switch their spending to the cheaper home produced goods. Provided that the demand for imports by the British consumer is not inelastic, the decrease in demand for imports will mean a decrease in the supply of £s.

As demand for £s has increased and supply of £s has decreased this should lead to a rise in the price of pounds. There will be a tendency for the pound to return to its equilibrium value.

The student should be able to draw the necessary graphs to show that the above conclusions are true.

● Demand for £s decreased, supply of £s increased leads to a return towards equilibrium
● Demand for £s increased, supply of £s decreased leads to a return towards equilibrium

---

15.7 ## Exchange rate systems

Three systems are considered. The structure of each system is examined together with any major disadvantages.

Fixed exchange rates

The main feature is that each currency is fixed in terms of all other currencies. Up until the early 1920s the UK fixed the value of its currency in terms of gold – the gold standard. This meant that £1 was worth a certain weight in gold, as was 1$ and 1 franc, etc. Thus for example if £1 was worth 3 grains of gold and the same weight in gold was 4$ in the USA there would be an exchange rate of £1 = 4$.

● This means that there has to be a very strict control of the money supply.
● It can only expand when the gold reserves increase.
● Gold is effectively the only means of international payment.
● There will be a major problem in transporting large amounts of very bulky very heavy gold.
● There is a finite supply of gold, and this creates an upper limit to the value of world trade.

Floating exchange rates

In this system currencies are allowed to establish their own values according to market forces. Therefore an excess supply of £s, because importers had bought more foreign goods than exporters had sold overseas, would put pressure on the £ to fall in value. Similarly an excess demand for £s, because exporters had sold more goods overseas then importers had bought from overseas, would put pressure on the £ to increase in value. Such a system is an automatic adjustment process and requires no action on behalf of the monetary authorities in a country. Some economists have argued for floating exchange rates claiming that the government would not need large reserves of foreign exchange and that they could concentrate upon controlling the domestic problems of inflation and unemployment. Whether it is possible to ignore international effects upon an economy is open to debate, but in terms of the exchange rate mechanism a floating rate has a number of inherent disadvantages.

● *Exaggerated fluctuations in exchange rates 1.* We have assumed that there is an elastic demand for imports and exports. This is probably the case in the long term, but in the short-term market demand may not adjust so quickly to price changes, and that would imply inelastic demand, for a short period. An excess supply of £s would reduce the value of the £. But the excess supply has come about because importers have bought more foreign goods than exporters have sold overseas. So in the short term the cheaper £ would increase the supply of £s and cause the value of the pound to fall even further.

(*Reasoning*: excess supply of £s leads to fall in price of £. Because short-term demand is inelastic, the total spent in foreign currency on imports is greater, and this means a greater supply of the cheaper £s to buy more foreign currency. Because the £ is cheaper exports are cheaper and the total value of the exports will fall, increasing the difference between the value of the imports and exports – *and therefore increasing the supply of £s.*)

In the long term demand is likely to be elastic and demand will adjust to the changing prices caused by fluctuating exchange rates. As the demand for the expensive imports falls (consumers and firms seek alternative supplies) and the demand for the cheaper exports increases (foreign consumers transfer spending to the cheaper goods) there will be an excess demand for £s. This will increase the value of the £, and in the short term this increased value will cause a further increase in value.

● *Exaggerated fluctuations in exchange rates 2.* So far we have concentrated upon trade as the main forces influencing demand and supply of £s. However, with floating exchange rates the activities of speculators may have a marked effect. If they see the £ falling in value they may anticipate further falls by selling £s and buying stronger currencies. The very act of selling £s adds further pressure on the £ to fall. The £ may fall a long way before the speculators sell their strong currencies and buy the very cheap £s. Buying cheap £s puts pressure on the £ to rise. It may rise to a very high level before the speculators sell expensive £s and buy the now cheaper foreign currencies. Then the whole process starts again.

● *Exaggerated fluctuations in exchange rates 3.* If the UK government was to use interest rates to control inflation it may mean that interest rates have to be temporarily high. These high interest rates may be sufficiently above average rates overseas to attract investment capital into the UK. This means a high demand for £s and a subsequent pressure on the value of the £ to rise. *Note: In times of high inflation the costs of producing goods are high, and therefore the prices of goods must be high. Thus exports are already losing any competitive edge they may have had, as they become more expensive due to rising costs of manufacture. The added exchange rate pressure on prices merely causes further concern for exporters.*

● *Exchange rate risk.* Businesses need a stable environment in which to operate. Exaggerated fluctuations in the exchange rate will have a damping effect upon international trade, as businessmen attempt to avoid the exchange rate risk. Many businesses are exposed to this risk in two ways. They import raw materials and part-finished goods as part of the manufacturing process and they export the finished goods. A strong £ will mean cheaper imports and therefore lower costs to such a business. A strong £ will mean higher export prices in overseas markets. But a wildly fluctuating exchange rate could mean imports were bought when the £ was very weak (so imports are expensive – costs of manufacture go up) and the finished goods are being sold overseas when the £ is very strong (higher export prices). This is an extreme case but demonstrates the risk to businesses of a freely floating exchange rate.

Banded exchange rates

This is a system where a country allows its exchange rate to fluctuate within a pre-determined band. Within the band market forces determine the value of the currency. As the currency approaches either the upper or lower boundary the central bank intervenes and either demands £s or sells £s with the aim of keeping the exchange rate within the band.

The currency could be tied to another currency such as the $ and allowed to fluctuate within say plus or minus 3 per cent of the $ value. The currency could be tied to the average value of a basket of currencies, and allowed to fluctuate within a defined band. Or the currency band could be say plus or minus 5 per cent around some ideal central value.

The way that intervention works is as follows. The central bank has a fund of currencies – in the case of the UK this is the *exchange equalisation account*. When the currency (say the £) reaches the upper limit of the band the central bank supplies £s (sells pounds). This puts pressure on the £ to fall in value, back within the band. When the currency reaches the lower limit of the band the central bank demands £s (buys £s). This puts pressure on the £ to increase in value, back within the band. When the central bank is selling £s the exchange equalisation account has a large amount of foreign currency. When the central bank is buying £s the exchange equalisation account has a large amount of sterling. The exchange equalisation account is essentially a chest of money which from time-to-time changes in composition. The value of the chest remains the same, whether it is full of dollars, deutchmarks, francs, or pounds.

- The disadvantage of this system is seen when a currency is being supported at a fundamentally wrong level. The level of support necessary from the central bank may be such as to totally deplete the reserves (the exchange equalisation account). Before this happened the country concerned would try to use fiscal and monetary policies to reduce inflation and to cut home demand for imported goods.
- For countries with high unemployment the necessary fiscal and monetary measures may add to unemployment. Thus there can arise policy conflicts. Which is more pressing domestic unemployment (workers vote governments in and out) or the external value of the currency.
- Speculators, considering that devaluation was imminent, may see little risk in selling the weak currency and buying strong currencies. In this way they add to the downward pressure on the already weak currency.
- Countries have been traditionally slow to devalue their currency.

15.8   The external value of the pound (£)

The pound is currently allowed to 'float' freely against all other currencies. This means that the authorities are not committed to maintaining the market value of sterling within any pre-determined range against any other currency.

From October 1985 interest rate policy was explicitly used to help maintain the external value of the pound within a desired range. This was a very successful policy as the rate of exchange was stable from 1985 up to its entry into the European Monetary System (EMS) in 1990. The cost of this period of exchange rate stability was a continuing deficit on the current account of the Balance of Payments. The value of the pound was higher than at any time since 1985 and it entered the EMS at what was probably too high a level. Sterling was a member of the Exchange Rate Mechanism (ERM) of the EMS from 8 October 1990 until 16 September 1992. During this period the pound was held within a margin of 6 per cent on either side of its agreed central rates against each of the other participating currencies.

The authorities have a number of means of influencing the exchange rate. The Bank of England can *intervene* in the foreign exchange market by buying or selling pounds which would alter the supply of sterling relative to other currencies. However, although intervention could be effective in smoothing short-term fluctuations in the value of the pound, it cannot resolve underlying economic problems, which have to be addressed by more fundamental policy measures. Although monetary policy can influence the level of the exchange rate, the overall objective of monetary policy in the UK is the achievement of domestic price stability, as defined by the inflation target set by the Government.

The Government's foreign exchange reserves are approximately $35 billion; in addition, the Bank of England has approximately $4 billion of holdings of foreign currency and gold. The main method by which the government obtains reserves is to borrow them in foreign currency. The other way to obtain reserves of foreign currency is to intervene in the currency market. When the Bank of England intervenes to buy foreign currencies (and sells sterling), the proceeds will be added to the reserves. On the other hand, sales of foreign currencies to protect the value of sterling will reduce the reserves. However, this does not mean that the reserves have been spent: the foreign exchange reserve 'asset' has merely been converted into a sterling one.

The effective exchange rate (EER)

An *effective exchange rate* is a measure of the value of a currency against several other currencies (a 'basket') at once. It is calculated as a weighted average of exchange rates and expressed as an index number. The weight given to each currency in the basket is related to the trade flows in manufactured goods and represents the relative importance of that particular country, as a competitor, in export markets. Because the effective exchange rate is an average of a currency's exchange rates, it is often a more useful measure, when looking at the value of a currency over a long period, than a single exchange rate (such as sterling-dollar). **The higher the index figure, the stronger the currency**.

15.9 ## The balance of payments

The object of the balance of payments accounts is to identify and record transactions between residents of the United Kingdom and residents of all other countries abroad in a way that is suitable for analysing the economic relations between the UK economy and the rest of the world. In the UK balance of payments accounts, transactions are currently classified into main groups as follows:

Current account: covers trade in goods, trade in services, income – in particular earnings from foreign investors and current transfers.
Capital account: covers transfers of ownership of assets, transfer of funds associated with acquisition or disposal of fixed assets.
Financial account: covers the flows of financial assets and liabilities.Balancing item – Net errors and omissions: a measure of the recording inaccuracies within the system.

Each of these sections of the balance of payments will be explained in detail and the chapter will finish with a complete balance of payments account for 1998 and 1999.

The current account

The current account includes both *visible* trade and *invisible* trade. All transactions are recorded in sterling, thus when transactions are invoiced in a foreign currency the value is converted to sterling using the appropriate rate of exchange.

> **Visible trade**   The import and export of *physical* goods. They can be seen and touched, thus the term visible to describe them.
> **Invisible trade**   The import and export *of services*. These services, which come under a number of different headings, cannot be seen like a physical good, and are thus described as invisible.

Before looking in detail at some of the measurement problems and some of the components of the UK current account, it is important to be clear about the differences between visible and invisible exports and imports. They are summarised overleaf.

Is it an export or an import?

The rule is to **follow the money**. If the money comes into the UK then it is an export. If the money leaves the UK then it is an import.

Visible export   This is where the physical goods leave the UK and *the money comes into the UK*.

Visible import   This is where the physical goods come into the UK and *the money leaves the UK*.

Invisible export   This is where some type of service is provided by a UK business to an overseas resident. The overseas resident pays the UK business and the *money comes into the UK*. An example is a German tourist visiting London. The services are those provided by the hotels and other businesses of London, and in return the German tourist *spends his money in the UK*.

Invisible import   This is where some type of service is provided by an overseas business to a UK resident. The UK resident pays the overseas business and the *money leaves the UK*. An example is a British tourist visiting New York. The services are those provided by the hotels and other businesses of New York, and in return the British tourist *spends his money in America*.

A major error made by many students is to follow the tourist. A British tourist abroad is an IMPORT. Follow the money he spends.

Some issues concerning measurement

Visible trade used to be relatively easy to measure accurately. As imports and exports passed through Customs controls at the border, documents had to be completed. The information on the value of the goods being traded could then be totalled to produce figures for visible trade. However, with the advent of the single market within the European Union (EU) from January 1993, goods no longer have to pass through Customs checks if they are being sold to another EU member. This means that Customs-based information can only be used for trade between the UK and non-EU countries.

For trade with the EU a new recording system, known as Intrastat, has been developed. This involves Customs and Excise asking businesses who trade with the EU to fill in forms giving details of their goods at the same time as they make a VAT return. More detailed forms are returned by the largest businesses. It is reported that some 30 000 firms report their trade every month. Although this represents less than a quarter of all firms trading with other EU member states it covers about 97.5 per cent of the value of trade with the EU.

Customs and Intrastat based figures are on an *Overseas Trade Statistics* (OTS) basis, which are then adjusted by the Central Statistical Office to a *Balance of Payments* (BoP) basis. The adjustment is necessary because imports are measured according to their value as they enter the UK, which includes the costs of freight and of insuring their passage. This is called *the cost, insurance and freight* (cif) value. Exports are measured according to their value before they leave the UK. This is called the *free on board* (fob) value. Goods are value for balance of payments purposes on a *fob* basis. The *fob* value of imports is calculated by deducting from the *cif* value the estimated value of freight and insurance services.

There are timing differences between the EU and the non-EU systems for recording information. For non-EU exports, traders are allowed up to fourteen days, after the day of shipment, to provide Customs with an export document. Thus the recorded export figures for any calendar month relate on average to goods passing through UK ports in a monthly period ending about the middle of that calendar month. Whereas, importers are required to present the relevant documents before Customs will allow them to move their goods out of the ports. This means that import figures should correspond closely to the goods actually imported through the ports during the calendar month. The Intrastat System requires traders to report both imports and exports for the month within ten days, so the recorded import and export figures relate to the same period.

Table 15.4 **UK current account of the balance of payments (summary) (£s billions) (seasonally adjusted)**

	1998	1999
(A) Visible trade balance of which:	−20.5	−26.8
Exports	164.1	165.7
Imports	−184.6	−192.4
(B) Invisibles balance	20.5	15.8

Visible trade

The **visible trade balance** is the value of physical goods exported minus the value of the physical goods imported into the country.

Surplus – where exports are greater in value than imports.
Deficit – where imports are greater in value than exports.

In recent years the UK's visible trade balance has been in deficit. The trade balance deteriorates when domestic demand grows as imports from abroad are often sucked in more quickly than exports can be increased. Economic growth slowed in the early 1990s, and the size of the deficit was sharply reduced, as demand for imports fell. Despite strong economic growth in 1994, the deficit continued to fall. The high level of imports in 1998 and 1999 are mainly due to the high import content in many manufacturing processes; but it is also a reflection of the strength of the economy, with high levels of employment and low inflation.

Trade excluding 'oil and erratics'

All economic transactions vary in size from period to period. Just as each individual household will not spend exactly the same amount of money each day, so visible trade flows fluctuate considerably from month to month. Trade flows can be distorted further when a particularly large value item, such as a jumbo jet, is imported or exported. When considering trade statistics, it helps to exclude some of the more *erratic* items. These are defined to include ships, aircraft, North Sea oil rigs and other installations, precious stones and silver. A month which sees particularly large imports of these items is likely to show a larger than usual deficit on visible trade: but such a deficit should only persist for the duration of the higher level of erratic imports, and does not necessarily indicate an underlying deterioration in the trade position.

From being a net importer of oil before 1980, the UK has been a net oil exporter for the past twenty years. At its peak in 1985, the surplus on trade in oil was £8 billion. But declining output and lower oil prices in the second half of the 1980s reduced the surplus to £1.25 billion in 1991. Since then, the oil surplus has picked up again – the result of increased investment in the North Sea coming on line. The balance reached £4 billion in 1994. In 1998 it was £3 billion and in 1999 it was £4.2 billion. In order to present underlying movements in the visible trade balance more clearly, economists often focus on the non-oil balance.

Invisible trade

The other component of the current account is the balance on invisible earnings. The UK has for many years earned a surplus on invisibles, arising principally from interest, profits and dividend earnings from its substantial holdings of overseas assets, and from London's role as a major international financial centre. In the early 1990s a combination of high interest rates in the UK (which lead to high interest payments to overseas residents investing in this country), and a decline in travel and insurance earnings, resulted in a sharp reduction in the invisibles surplus. It is interesting to note that the net position on travel services in 1999 and 2000 is that there is a continuing deficit. This reflects the increasing numbers of British residents travelling abroad, whilst foreigners visiting the UK are not increasing in number at the same rate.

Unlike the visible trade balance, which is published monthly, most data on invisibles are only available quarterly. Invisibles are also more difficult to measure accurately because, unlike visible trade, there is no common measurement point (such as UK ports) that can be used. The first estimate of the invisibles balance in any quarter is published by the Central Statistical Office (CSO) towards the end of the following quarter, and is only based on partial information. It is therefore liable to revision. We will now consider the three main components of the invisibles balance:

- services
- investment income
- transfers.

Services

The figures for services are shown in detail, for 1998 and 1999, in the box opposite.

SERVICES – ANALYSIS FOR 1998 AND 1999 (£ million)

	1998	1999
Exports		
Transportation	11 582	11 538
Travel	14 302	14 293
Communications	1 277	1 484
Construction	298	267
Insurance	3 228	4 111
Financial	6 438	6 992
Computer and information	1 585	1 928
Royalties and licence fees	4 199	4 387
Other business	16 483	17 083
Personal, cultural and recreational	900	782
Government	1 090	1 117
Total	**61 382**	**63 982**
Imports		
Transportation	13 799	13 930
Travel	20 201	22 634
Communications	1 475	1 694
Construction	111	85
Insurance	585	569
Financial	165	205
Computer and information	451	500
Royalties and licence fees	3 848	3 840
Other business	6 181	6 130
Personal, cultural and recreational	475	490
Government	1 509	2 367
Total	**48 800**	**52 444**
Balances		
Transportation	−2 217	−2 392
Travel	−5 899	−8 341
Communications	−198	−210
Construction	187	182
Insurance	2 643	3 542
Financial	6 273	6 787
Computer and information	1 134	1 428
Royalties and licence fees	351	547
Other business	10 302	10 953
Personal, cultural and recreational	425	292
Government	−419	−1 250
Total	**12 582**	**11 538**

Source: ONS, September 2000.

Net earnings from financial and other business services are strongly in surplus, reflecting the standing of the City of London as a major financial centre and the strength of UK business and consultancy services. Net earnings from transport were in deficit. The main items in this category are earnings by UK shipping operators from overseas customers as against those by foreign operators from UK customers, and trade in aviation services, reflecting mainly the balance of UK airline revenues from tickets sold to overseas residents and overseas airlines income from UK passengers. The deficit on general government services usually arises from spending abroad by UK military forces. The deficit on travel services reflects a continuing shortfall of overseas tourists' expenditure in this country compared with UK residents' spending abroad. Strong growth in real incomes combined with the ready availability of credit led to a sharp rise in spending on foreign holidays, which was not matched by a similar increase in spending by overseas visitors to the UK

Investment income

UK investment income comes from the ownership of overseas assets and includes such items as interest on bank deposits, investment income from shares and bonds, and profits earned by UK companies from their overseas subsidiaries (direct investment). The investment income balance is calculated by subtracting the UK investment earnings of overseas residents. An important influence is interest rates. When they are high relative to other countries' rates, overseas investors earned a correspondingly higher return in this country than UK investors received from abroad.

INVESTMENT INCOME – ANALYSIS FOR 1998 AND 1999 (£ million)

	1998	1999
Credits (money coming into the UK)		
Compensation of employees	840	960
Investment income		
Earnings on direct investment abroad	32 014	33 820
Earnings on portfolio investment abroad:		
Earnings on equity securities	6 214	8 891
Earnings on debt securities	19 706	19 037
Total portfolio investment	*25 920*	*27 928*
Earnings on other investment abroad	49 326	45 230
Earnings on reserve assets	1 132	1 161
Total investment income	108 392	108 139
Total	**109 232**	**109 099**

continued opposite

Debits (money leaving the UK)		
Compensation of employees	850	759
Investment income		
Foreign earnings on direct investment in the UK	11 700	22 302
Foreign earnings on portfolio investment in the UK:		
Earnings on equity securities	10 003	11 363
Earnings on debt securities	18 018	16 456
Total portfolio investment	*28 021*	*27 819*
Earnings on other investment in the UK	54 416	49 887
Total investment income	94 137	100 008
Total	**94 987**	**100 767**
Balances (investment income balance)		
Compensation of employees	−10	201
Investment income		
Direct investment	20 314	11 518
Portfolio investment:		
Earnings on equity securities	−3 789	−2 472
Earnings on debt securities	1 688	2 581
Total portfolio investment	*−2 101*	*109*
Other investment	−5 090	−4 657
Reserve assets	1 132	1 161
Total investment income	14 255	8 131
Total	**14 245**	**8 332**

Source: ONS, September 2000.

Transfers

Transfers are the value of goods, services and financial assets passing between UK residents and overseas residents that are not part of a visible or invisible transaction. They are best thought of as gifts or grants. They cover a range of transactions of which the largest is the Government's net contribution to the European Community. Bilateral aid, in the form of cash grants to developing countries, is also included here. In addition there are substantial transfers by the private sector, such as savings by UK workers temporarily employed overseas, or gifts from UK households to friends and relatives living abroad.

TRANSFERS – ANALYSIS FOR 1998 AND 1999 (£ million)

	1998	1999
Credits (receipts)		
Central government		
Receipts from EU institutions:		
Abatement	1 377	3 171
Other EU receipts	7	5
Other receipts	4 997	6 288
Total central government	**6 381**	**9 464**
Other sectors		
Receipts from EU institutions:		
Social fund	783	434
Agricultural guarantee fund	2 908	2 700
ECSC grant	1	–
Other receipts	5 351	5 680
Total other sectors	**9 043**	**8 814**
Total	**15 424**	**18 278**
Debits (payments)		
Central government		
Payments to EU institutions:		
GNP: 4th resource	3 516	4 403
GNP adjustments	404	229
Other	−1	11
Other payments	2 666	2 635
Total central government	**6 585**	**7 278**
Other sectors		
Payments to EU institutions	6 346	5 881
Other payments	8 863	9 203
Total other sectors	**15 209**	**15 084**
Total	**21 794**	**22 362**
Balances		
Central government	−204	2 186
Other sectors	−6 166	−6 270
Total	**−6 370**	**−4 084**
Of which: EU institutions	−5 189	−4 214

Source: ONS, September 2000.

The summary of the current account given in Table 15.4 is expanded opposite to show the actual summary presentation.

SUMMARY OF THE UK CURRENT ACCOUNT 1998 AND 1999 (£ million)

	1998	1999
Trade in goods and services		
Trade in goods	−20 537	−26 767
Trade in services	12 582	11 538
Total trade in goods and services	**−7955**	**−15 229**
Income		
Compensation of employees	−10	201
Investment income	14 255	8131
Total income	**14 245**	**8332**
Current transfers		
Central government	−204	2186
Other sectors	−6166	−6270
Total current transfers	**−6370**	**−4084**
Current balance	**−80**	**−10 981**

The current account records international flows of money paid for goods and services, earnings on investment and transfers. If the current account is in deficit, then the UK must be paying out more than it receives. This can only be done by running down the UK's stock of assets or increasing UK liabilities to other countries. This is similar to a person who spends more than they earn. To spend more than one earns assets must be run down, such as selling a house or car, or selling stocks and shares (financial assets), or money must be borrowed from someone else (increasing liabilities). These transactions in assets and liabilities for the UK are recorded in the capital account of the balance of payments.

The capital account

The capital account records all capital transfers. These are very difficult to distinguish from current account transfers and therefore most transfers take place in the current account of the balance of payments. Debt forgiveness is where debts are written off and this is similar in idea to a transfer, and thus recorded in the capital account. The capital accounts for 1998 and 1999 are shown below. They give very little additional information and for detail of major movements of capital one has to look at the financial accounts.

CAPITAL ACCOUNT OF THE BALANCE OF PAYMENTS – 1998 AND 1999 (£ millions)

	1998	1999
Credits (receipts)		
Capital transfers		
Central government		
Debt forgiveness	–	–
Other capital transfers	–	–
Total central government	–	–
Other sectors		
Migrants' transfers	967	1144
Debt forgiveness	–	–
EU institutions:		
Regional development fund	357	285
Agricultural guidance fund	56	47
Total EU institutions	*413*	*332*
Total other sectors	*1380*	*1476*
Total capital transfers	1380	1476
Sales of non-produced, non-financial assets	89	86
Total	**1469**	**1562**
Debits (payments)		
Capital transfers		
Central government		
Debt forgiveness	146	10
Other capital transfers (project grants)	182	171
Total central government	*328*	*181*
Other sectors		
Migrants' transfers	531	499
Debt forgiveness	–	–
Other capital transfers	–	–
Total other sectors	*531*	*499*
Total capital transfers	859	680
Purchases of non-produced, non-financial assets	137	106
Total	**996**	**786**

continued opposite

Balances		
Capital transfers		
Central government		
Debt forgiveness	−146	−10
Other capital transfers	−182	−171
Total central government	*−328*	*−181*
Other sectors		
Migrants' transfers	436	645
Debt forgiveness	–	–
Other capital transfers	413	332
Total other sectors	*849*	*977*
Total capital transfers	521	796
Non-produced, non-financial assets	−48	−20
Total	**473**	**776**

The financial account

This is the record of UK investment abroad and overseas residents investment in this country. Investment in this context includes both physical investment spending, such as setting up factories abroad, and financial activities involving the purchase or sale of overseas stocks and shares and other financial instruments. There is a clear distinction between these two groups.

Direct investment (by the UK) involves the setting up and equipping of factories and other productive facilities abroad. It also includes the acquisition or sale of foreign subsidiaries of British firms. Thus direct investment has as its main purpose the production of goods and services in a foreign country. Direct investment in the UK is where overseas investors invest in productive capacity in the UK. Nissan are an example of overseas direct investment in the UK.

By contrast, portfolio investment is undertaken by investors who take no part in the management of the enterprises in which they invest. This type of investment involves buying and selling different types of securities, of overseas companies and governments. The main investors are financial institutions, such as fund managers. Many unit trust funds, for example, have exposure to most of the worlds overseas securities markets. Overseas fund managers are equally as anxious to gain worldwide exposure, and they invest in money market instruments issued by UK banks and private non-financial corporations.

The heading *other investment abroad* is where deposits are made by UK banks, in sterling and foreign currency. UK banks also make loans in foreign currency. Securities dealers and other UK residents have overseas deposits which are accounted for under this heading. Overseas banks make similar deposit in the UK, they also lend money to UK residents. Overseas securities dealers, and other overseas residents, will hold balances in the UK.

One point worthy of mention, concerning the financial account, is that whilst individual and total transactions are very large the net position is, by comparison very small. This point is illustrated with figures for 1998 from the following financial account. The figures are rounded to make the point but are clearly identifiable in the account. In 1998 there was £72 billion in direct investment out of the UK. There was £18 billion in portfolio investment out of the UK. There was £63 billion leaving the UK under the heading of *other investment*. A total of some £119 billion. By contrast £72 billion came into the UK in direct investment, £36 billion in portfolio investment and £16 billion on other investment. A total of some £124 billion. Very large sums, but the net position was just £4.6 billion leaving the UK.

> **Note** Investments by UK residents overseas are shown as money leaving the UK. However in the future these investments will generate profits and dividends. These will be shown as flows of income **into the UK** in the current account of the balance of payments accounts. Similarly although investment into the UK is money coming in to the UK, it will generate future streams of income leaving the UK.

The 1998 and 1999 financial accounts are shown below.

THE FINANCIAL ACCOUNT OF THE BALANCE OF PAYMENTS – 1998 AND 1999 (£ millions)

	1998	1999
UK investment abroad (net debits)		
Direct investment abroad		
Equity capital	47 347	95 024
Reinvested earnings	13 547	19 845
Other capital transactions	11 049	10 419
Total direct investment abroad	*71 943*	*125 288*
Portfolio investment abroad		
Equity securities	2 584	17 915
Debt securities	34 130	−12 483
Total portfolio investment abroad	*36 714*	*5 432*
Other investment abroad	15 918	50 063
Reserve assets	−164	−639
Total	124 411	180 144

continued opposite

Investment in the UK (net credits)		
Direct investment in the UK		
Equity capital	31 199	21 402
Reinvested earnings	1 156	6 875
Other capital transactions	6 078	24 049
Total direct investment in the UK	*38 433*	*52 326*
Portfolio investment in the UK		
Equity securities	36 946	74 341
Debt securities	−19 037	41 261
Total portfolio investment in the UK	*17 909*	*115 602*
Other investment in the UK	63 392	18 069
Total	**119 734**	**185 997**
Net transactions (net credits less net debits)		
Direct investment		
Equity capital	−16 148	−73 622
Reinvested earnings	−12 391	−12 970
Other capital transactions	−4 971	13 630
Total direct investment	*−33 510*	*−72 962*
Portfolio investment		
Equity securities	34 362	56 426
Debt securities	−53 167	53 744
Total portfolio investment	*−18 805*	*110 170*
Other investment	47 474	−31 994
Reserve assets	164	639
Total	−4677	5853

The balancing item – net errors and omissions

This item is a measure of the measurement errors and omissions. As has been explained in the section on trade the recording of exports and imports is by the firms concerned to customs and excise. The reporting and recording of the money flows, which arise from the trade in goods and services, is via statistics provided by banks and other financial institutions. There are inevitably going to be some unrecorded receipts or payments, and other discrepancies in recording economic activity. The main source of errors occurs when information is collected by sample surveys. In many cases respondents have an incentive to over or under report. This is particularly the case in certain services and capital account items. Areas of most concern are the reporting of revenues and expenditures connected with tourism and some private sector capital flows.

The complete balance of payments account for 1998 and 1999 is shown below.

UK BALANCE OF PAYMENTS (£million)

	1998	1999
CURRENT ACCOUNT		
Trade in goods and services		
Trade in goods	−20 537	−26 767
Trade in services	12 582	11 538
Total trade	*−7 955*	*−15 229*
Income		
Compensation of employees	−10	201
Investment income	14 255	8 131
Total income	*14 245*	*8 332*
Current transfers		
Central government	−204	2 186
Other sectors	−6 166	−6 270
Total current transfers	*−6 370*	*−4 084*
Current balance	**−80**	**−10 981**
CAPITAL ACCOUNT (balances)	**473**	**776**
FINANCIAL ACCOUNT		
Direct investment	−33 510	−72 962
Portfolio investment	−18 805	110 170
Other investment	47 474	−31 994
Reserve assets	164	639
Net financial transactions	−4 677	5 853
NET ERRORS AND OMISSIONS	**4 284**	**4 352**

Remember. Balance on current account + Balance on capital account + Balance on financial account + Net errors and omissions (balancing item) = 0.

15.10 Summary

The questions posed at the beginning of this chapter have been answered.

1. Why should we trade so extensively with other countries?
2. If different countries use different currencies how is one currency valued in terms of another?
3. Given that there are benefits from trading, how does the UK record its dealings with the rest of the world?

We trade with the rest of the world because via trade the UK consumer can enjoy a wider selection of goods and services, and more than could be produced by the UK alone. This is clearly the reason for trade. However with national and political interests ever-present countries have been slow to trade freely and often erect barriers to prevent trade. The efforts of GATT over the years since 1947 have led to a wider acceptance of world trade and a steady reduction in barriers to trade. The successor body the WTO will continue the movement towards a more free world wide trade.

Different world currencies are valued in terms of each other by the forces of demand and supply in the price mechanism. In this chapter we have assumed that trade between countries is the main force behind changes in demand for and supply of a currency. There are other very powerful forces which affect currency values, but trade between countries is the underlying factor. The pound is currently allowed to 'float' freely against all other currencies. This means that the authorities are not committed to maintaining the market value of sterling within any pre-determined range against any other currency.

The country's record of all international operations is called the balance of payments. The various sections of the balance of payments have been explained in detail and the student should have no difficulty in understanding any presentation in any other text. This section of the chapter really brings together the first two topics. It should be clear to the student that increasing the value of exports has the effect of reducing the deficit on the current account. Another issue of interest is that if the value of the £ rises and trade levels stay the same, the value of the exports will increase whilst the value of the imports will decrease. Again this will improve the current account balance.

This section links with other topics such as employment and inflation. For example imported goods and materials are about 30% of total variable costs and therefore a major pressure on final prices when the prices of imports are rising. Added to this pressure is the fact that imported goods impact upon consumer demand directly. It was estimated in Chapter 14 that 20% of total final expenditure is accounted for by imports. If the value of the £ is rising imports are becoming cheaper, whilst if the value of the £ is falling they are becoming more expensive.

Further reading

ARTIS, M. J. *The UK Economy*, Oxford University Press.
BEGG, D., FISCHER, S. and DORNBUSCH, R. *Economics*, McGraw-Hill.
GRIFFITHS, A. and WALL, S. *Applied Economics*, Longman.
HARDWICK, P., KHAN, B. and LANGMEAD, J. *An Introduction to Modern Economics*, Longman.
McALEESE, D. *Economics for Business*, Prentice Hall.
SLOMAN, J. and SUTCLIFFE, M. *Economics for Business*, Prentice Hall.

Some useful information on the Internet

Bank of England Publications   <http://www.bankofengland.co.uk/publica.htm>.
The foreign exchange fact sheet. Also papers on foreign exchange markets.

National Statistics – the official UK site   <http://www.statistics.gov.uk>.
The Balance of Payments report quarter by quarter. This information is useful in conjunction with chapter headings allowing the student to be aware of up-to-date figures.
  Exchange rate data is available at this site.

BBC News Online   <http://www.news.bbc.co.uk/hi/english/business/default.stm>.
An excellent source of information on topical issues. Search in the *business* section for articles on Balance of Payments and issues in International trade.

Test your understanding

(Answers are given at the back of the book)

1. Two countries, P and Q, produce cars and butter under the following conditions:

	Factor cost (units)	
	Country P	Country Q
1 car	2	4
1 tonne of butter	1	2

Under these circumstances, which of the following statements is correct?

A   Trade will not take place because P's costs of production are lower for both commodities.

B   Trade will not take place because there is no difference in relative cost advantage.

C   Country Q has an absolute advantage in the production of both commodities.

D   Country P has a comparative advantage in the production of cars.

E   Trade will take place provided that the terms of trade are such that 2 tonnes of butter exchange for 1 car.

2. UK Terms of Trade Index (1985 = 100)

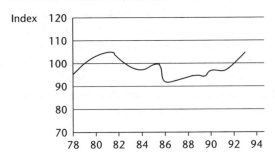

Source: Dataset, 1995.

From the chart it can be deduced that, since 1986,

A   the value of exports has increased relative to the value of imports

B   export prices have increased relative to import prices

C   there has been a deterioration in the current account of the balance of payments

D   more goods must be exported to gain a given quantity of imports

3. The European Union might impose tariffs on goods from outside the EU in order to

   A   increase the budget deficits of member countries
   B   prevent the dumping of goods
   C   maximise the benefits of specialisation
   D   reduce the balance of payments surpluses of member countries

4. A sustained rise in interest rates in Germany is likely to result in

   A   an increase in short term capital flows from Germany to the UK
   B   a fall in the £ sterling exchange rate against the Deutsche mark
   C   an off-setting fall in UK interest rates
   D   an increase in the international competitiveness of manufacturing firms in Germany

5.

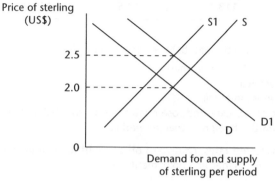

Price of sterling (US$)

Demand for and supply of sterling per period

Other things being equal, which of the following changes is a possible explanation for the dollar price of sterling rising from 2.0 to 2.5?

   A   An increase in tourists from the USA visiting the UK and an increase in UK citizens touring abroad
   B   A decrease in purchases of UK produced cars by US residents and a decrease in car imports from the USA
   C   An inflow of foreign long term capital from the USA into the UK and an outflow of UK long term capital to other countries
   D   An outflow of short term capital to New York and an inflow of long term capital into the UK
   E   An increase in European Union tariffs on imports from the USA and a rise in UK interest rates relative to those in the USA

6. The following table provides a summary of the current account of the UK Balance of Payments between 1990 and 1993. (All values are net.)

Year	Trade in goods (£m)	Services (£m)	Investment income from interest, profits and dividend (£m)	Transfers (£m)
1990	−18 809	3 689	981	−4 896
1991	−10 284	3 709	−217	−1 383
1992	−13 104	4 089	4 293	−5 109
1993	−13 209	4 942	3 063	−5 106

Source: Economic Trends Annual Supplement, 1995, HMSO.

The figures show that

A   in each of the four years the trade in services was in deficit
B   capital flows into the UK were positive for every year except 1990
C   the current account was in deficit throughout the period shown
D   UK official reserves were falling
E   the current account deficit exceeded the balance of trade in goods throughout the
    period shown

7. The following table shows index numbers of UK exports and imports (1990 = 100).

	Exports of goods		Imports of goods	
	Volume	Price	Volume	Price
1990	100	100	100	100
1994	118.1	111.9	110.3	109.1

Source: HMSO.

The data in the table indicate that, between 1990 and 1994,

A   the UK's terms of trade worsened
B   export revenues fell
C   expenditure on imports fell
D   earnings from goods exported rose relative to payments for goods imported
E   sterling rose on the foreign exchange market

8. Explain how high interest rates, relative to other countries, can increase the value of the £
    and exert pressure for higher unemployment levels.

9. You are given the following information:

    There are two countries Peru and Spain. Each country has 100 production units. They divide
    these units equally between production processes. With one production unit they can
    produce the following:

    Peru can produce either   4 tons of beef or 2 tons of grain
    Spain can produce either   2 tons of beef or 2 tons of grain

    i.   Which product should each country specialise in?
    ii. What are the terms of trade?

Answers – test your understanding

Chapter 1

1. C   2. D   3. A   4. A, E   5. C, D

6. Consumers spend their money in order to obtain satisfaction from the goods they consume. If we want to spend more on some goods we have to give up some others. What is consumed is measured in terms of what was given up, as well as the money cost. A farmer can increase the production of one crop only by giving up production of another, or part of another. The local authority may wish to build a school and a car park but only have the funding for one of these. The cost of building the school, in addition to the cash, is the loss of the car parking facilities which the town would have enjoyed. The idea of opportunity cost presumes that all resources are fully used at the time that choices are to be made, otherwise there would be less need to choose. Opportunity cost is the idea that underpins cost benefit analysis, and this is the method frequently adopted by local government and by central government to highlight the hidden costs and benefits of undertaking any one project at the expense of another.

7.
   - Resources are not wasted on competitive duplication.
   - A more equitable distribution of resources can be planned, where all people have access to a standard of living according to their needs.
   - Prices can be set and employment directed thus there should not be the problems of unemployment and inflation.

   These benefits are lost within the sheer social and political complexity of administering such a system. There is inevitably confusion within a command economy because the workers may have no vested interest in working hard or efficiently. They may develop excuses and other defensive skills for self-preservation if things go wrong. The system is seen as more important than the people it was set up to serve, and the workers will eventually lose their collective ability for initiative, invention and problem solving. These problems are not inevitable but to be avoided the workers have to be convinced of the validity of the system, *for them*. As in England during the second world war.

8. Any three of the following:
   - There is an automatic allocation of resources without the need for expensive, or perhaps biased, committee or government interference.
   - The economy produces what consumers want, as consumers reveal their preferences by spending their money.
   - The economy is efficiently allocating production resources to the areas of greatest demand.
   - There is a complex signalling process wherein all parties have a vested interest in making it accurate, efficient and effective.

The advantages of the market mechanism are considerably balanced by a number of criticisms, of which three are most important.

- The market economy is activated, principally, by spending power. Thus those on low incomes, and those on fixed incomes, have very little influence over resource allocation when their social needs may even be the greatest. For example young people with young families very often have heavy family responsibilities at the beginning of their careers when they are earning relatively little. The elderly are mainly on pensions and fixed incomes and have an increased need for resources for health and support services as they get older.
- Firms in industries with little competition, can often dictate to the consumer the qualities and quantities of various products, and leave the consumers to decide who can best afford what is on offer. The production processes that develop within the economy may evolve to counteract the influence of the consumer. Thus there can develop forms of business organisation which are fundamentally against the consumers' interests.
- There is no incentive within the market economy to pay the full costs of production, including the costs of cleaning up pollution, or not producing pollution in the first place. There are many social costs associated with resource allocation, and these include lack of support for the weak or disadvantaged, as well as damage to society in general where economic factors, such as unemployment, are thought to have an influence upon social unrest, crime, illness, etc. These sort of costs can never be recognised and accounted for, by a system which rewards 'low-cost' or 'value for money' as the principle for allocation.

9. a. Non rivalry
   b. Non excludability.
   Non-rivalry means that consumption by one person does not diminish the amount available to another person. Non-excludability means that once they are provided it does not make sense to exclude anyone from benefiting from the good. Pure public goods are rare, but examples might be *defence provision*, or *the Thames barriers* (flood prevention).

10. Examples of private merit goods are education, pensions, health services.
    An example of an external merit good (given in the text) is inoculation against serious diseases.

11. - Reduced accidents from much clearer driving conditions.
    It is almost impossible to put a money value on family distress that is the result of accidents. But it may be more practicable to establish an average cost of treating accident victims in hospital. It may also be possible to establish an average figure for work time lost (and thus production lost) as the result of accidents. There are also the more direct costs of the emergency services who deal with the accidents.
    - Reduced crime in certain areas, such as car thefts, mugging, etc.
    It is impossible to value (in money terms) people's fear or lack of it. However crime often has a direct cost to insurance companies, cost of policing certain areas, costs of replacing damaged windows, walls, street fixtures, etc. These costs rise as crime rises and fall as crime falls. Thus there is a way of allocating specific amounts of money to various crimes, and the financial benefits to society of reduced crime.
    - People living near the road may feel more secure, as their houses are bathed in light.
    This is a difficult benefit to give a money value. Perhaps less police time spent answering calls from nervous residents.
    - The manufacturers of halogen lamps will make a profit and may employ more workers. The extra profits will be spent in the economy. The extra profits will generate extra tax income. The extra employment will reduce benefits paid out and increase tax taken. The workers will spend their money in the local town. Most of these benefits are easy to turn into money.

- The existing workers will feel more secure with the extra demand for their product.
Job security is hard to turn into money. Perhaps fewer days lost to sickness and jobseeking. Most firms have a value they have decided upon for lost working days.
- The existing and extra workers will spend more in the local community.
The local takings will rise. It is hard to predict in advance, by how much. It is probably best to be conservative and take the assumed extra jobs and multiply these by the average wage. This is not very accurate but at least gives a money value which can be understood.
- Old people and females may feel safer when out late at night.
The same as people living near the road.

Some dis-benefits might be.

- The present suppliers of lighting will lose business and may be forced to close.
The loss of jobs can be directly offset against the gain of jobs from the new company. The loss of profits will lose tax revenue, but this again can be offset against the increased tax take from the new company. There may be a cost to local suppliers if the new technology does not use local suppliers. This can be fairly accurately valued.
- The workers for the present suppliers face unemployment or reduced wages.
True. This will become a cost if they cannot find other work or be re-employed by the new company. The costs will be unemployment benefits, other social security benefits, reduced tax, reduced or no council tax, reduced spending in local shops. All these can be given money values.
- Some people may have expensive alarm systems and may not want this level of lighting.
Not an item that can be easily turned into money. It is hard to see the dis-benefit to society. Some people may feel that to light their houses allows the burglar a better chance to evaluate.
This is a matter for discussion and consensus. Cannot be easily turned into a money value, even if true.
- Local home security specialists may find they lose business.
If they do then this can be quantified. Their projected losses can be evaluated and a money value given.
- There will be community dis-benefit from any unemployment or loss of wages.
This has been covered in 2 above.

Chapter 2

1.

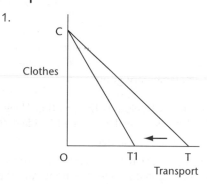

The price of transport has risen by 50 per cent so there is a reduction in what can be bought with the same budget. The new budget line CT1 represents this new price structure. It is likely that total consumer satisfaction will fall as the new budget line CT1 will probably touch a new (lower) indifference curve.

2. The data in the question needs to be extended before the answer can be worked out. The table only gives quantities and MU values. For each product the MU per unit needs to be calculated. This is done by dividing the MU by the cost of each item so as to get the MU per £ for each unit of each item. (The calculations are corrected to the nearest decimal point). The following table gives the necessary additional information.

| | Clothing | | | Videos | |
Q	MU	MU/£	Q	MU	MU/£
0			0		
1	90	4	1	60	4.3
2	78	3.5	2	51	3.6
3	66	2.9	3	42	3
4	54	2.4	4	33	2.4
5	42	1.9	5	24	1.7
			6	15	1.1
			7	6	0.4
			8	3	0.2

The answer is to buy 4 units of clothing and 4 videos. This where the MU/£ for clothing is equal to the MU/£ for videos. Both are 2.4. 4 units of clothing = £90 and 4 videos = £56. Total spending = £146.

3. A consumer should spend money firstly on those goods which give the most satisfaction per £ spent. The consumer will continue to do this until the last penny (or pound) spent on one product brings the same marginal utility as the last penny (or pound) spent on any other product. This is known as the equi-marginal principle and is usually written in shorthand or algebraic form as:

$$\frac{Mua}{Pa} = \frac{Mub}{Pb} = \frac{Muc}{Pc} = \frac{Mud}{Pd}$$

4. Each indifference curve represents a unique level of total satisfaction, for combinations of goods, and the further from the origin the higher the satisfaction represented. If two curves touched or crossed then at that point the satisfaction levels would be equal. The two curves could not therefore represent unique levels of satisfaction.

5. D   6. E   7. A, B, C, D, E.

Chapter 3

1. a. The prices of the various products.
   b. The prices of any substitute or complementary goods.
   c. Changes in income
   d. Tastes: e.g. what summer clothes are in fashion, is the weather likely to remain hot/cold, is it a peer group credibility thing, such as fashion and holidays (Ibiza/Rhodes)

   Examples for each product can be given from the above list.

2. It is usually true that as the price of a product rises demand falls, and as the price falls demand rises. Demand and price are moving in opposite directions, and therefore demand is said to be inversely related to price. If this relationship was not correct then there would be no point in retailers reducing prices for sales, for the purpose of a sale is to sell more products *because* the price has fallen. The line which establishes this relationship is one that slopes downwards from left to right

3. Iii

4. There is a new demand curve to the right of the original demand curve
   There is a movement along the existing demand curve – up the curve
   There is a new demand curve to the left of the original demand curve
   There is a movement along the existing demand curve – down the curve

5. Some possible factors are: weather, fertilizers, wages, consumer tastes, productivity, market prices, production capacity, cost of raw materials

6. GBCM   7. R   8. K

9. Market demand OM is greater than market supply OG. This means that there will be shortages in the shops, and prices will be able to rise to ration out the scarce goods. As prices rise this will not be a problem for those consumers who would be prepared to pay a higher price. Those consumers who do not wish to pay more than OP will cease to demand the good. As the price rises suppliers will be willing to supply more, perhaps from stock or storage. Thus supply will expand whilst demand will contract and the new equilibrium price will be established where $D = S$, at a higher level than OP.

Chapter 4

1. C   2. −1.7   3. B   4. A

5. a. Less units sold
   b. The calculation is:

   existing total revenue (TR) $= 5000$ units $\times 60\,p = £3000$

   $$\frac{\text{The percentage change in quantity demanded}}{\text{The percentage change in the price of the product}} = -0.8$$

   $$\frac{\text{The percentage change in quantity demanded}}{20\,p\ (= 33\%\ \text{or}\ 0.3)} = -0.8$$

   The percentage change in quantity demanded $= -0.8(0.3) = -0.24$

   -0.24 of 5000 is 1200 units.

   He therefore sells $5000 - 1200$ units at 80p each $= £3040$

   Increase in TR $= £40$

6. The calculation

   The formula is:

   $$\frac{\text{The percentage change in quantity demanded}}{\text{The percentage change in income}} = \text{Elast. Y}$$

   $$\frac{\text{The percentage change in quantity demanded}}{3\%} = 1.75$$

   The percentage change in quantity demanded $= 1.75(3)$

   $$= 5.25\%$$

The answer shows the percentage change in demand i.e. demand will rise by 5.25 per cent. The directors will therefore have to make plans to increase production to meet this expected rise in demand. Whether by overtime, etc., in the short-term and larger stocks or by planning increased capacity in the long-term. These are the sort of issues the board will need to consider as the result of an expected increase in demand.

7. The calculation

The formula is:

$$\frac{\text{The percentage change in quantity demanded of seats on BA}}{\text{The percentage change in the price of seats on Eurostar}} = \frac{-30}{-20} = 1.5$$

As the number is positive it shows that these are substitutes. Therefore an increase or decrease in the price of either will have the same effect (increase or decrease) on the demand for the other.

Chapter 5

1. D   2. E   3. B

4.

Factors of production	Rewards
Land	Rent
Labour	Wages, Salaries, Fees.
Capital	Interest
(Entrepreneur)	Profit

N.B. The entrepreneur is part of labour.

5. SHORT RUN   A period of time in which the quantity of at least one input is fixed, whilst the quantity of other inputs can be varied. Thus the firm can only partially adjust to changing market conditions.

LONG RUN   A period of time in which quantities of all inputs can be varied. Thus the firm can fully adjust to changing market conditions.

6.

Total units of output	Total cost	Total fixed cost	Total variable cost	Average cost	Marginal cost
0	300	300			
42	656	300	356	15.6	8.5
100	1050	300	750	10.5	6.8
138	1390	300	1090	10.1	8.9
152	1684	300	1384	11.1	21.0
160	1932	300	1632	12.1	31.0

7.

Total units of output	TC	TFC	TVC	AC	AFC	AVC	MC
0	75	75					
25	325	75	250	13	3	10	10
50	475	75	400	9.5	1.5	8	6
75	975	75	900	13	1	12	20
100	1475	75	1400	14.75	0.75	14	20
125	2200	75	2125	17.6	0.6	17	29

8. This occurs when the marginal product of an additional worker is less than the marginal product of the previous worker. All production processes eventually will reach a point of diminishing returns, *in the short run.* This is because, in the short run, not all inputs can be varied and as extra workers are added they eventually become inefficient without the support of the extra capital or land. This situation has led to the 'law' of diminishing returns.

Law of Diminishing Returns
As more of an input is used, at least one other input being fixed, its marginal output will eventually diminish.

The figures in question 7 can be used to illustrate this. The AVC figures are the ones to use as these represent the extra costs of producing some extra output. As the physical output per worker, or per machine goes down so the average costs of the variable outputs go up. In the above table AVC at first falls (increasing marginal returns) and then rises. This is also reflected in the MC which is the same as Marginal variable costs. (Remember **fixed costs are not part of variable or marginal costs**).

9. D

Chapter 7

1. C   2. B   3. C   4. C   5. A

6.

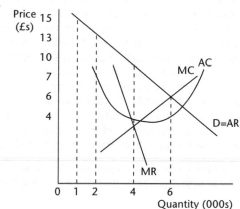

Calculation under price discrimination.
First 1000 units can be sold for £15 each.   revenue =   £15 000
Second 1000 units can be sold for £13 each.   revenue =   £13 000
Next 2000 units can be sold at £10 each.   revenue =   £20 000
Next 2000 units can be sold at £6.50 each.   revenue =   £13 000
                                               Total revenue £61 000

Total cost of the first 4000 units is £16 000
Cost of the last 2000 units is £8000   Total cost   £24 000

Profit is £61 000 less £24 000 = £37 000
Supernormal profit is £37 000

7. D   8. B   9. C   10. 74%   11. C   12. D   13. C

14. Competition as an idea, has two main elements. The first element concerns the number of firms operating within any particular market. The more firms there are, the greater the level of competition, *it is assumed*. This way of looking at competition is often used to construct an index to measure the degree of control that a small number of firms have over the market. The measure is known as a **concentration ratio.** It is all very well knowing how many firms there are in a market, or how much of the total sales is controlled by the biggest five firms; but a far more important question is, 'how do they compete with each other'? To make the point consider the following two extreme hypothetical examples.

Example 1　There is a market characterised by one large firm, which controls 60 per cent of the market sales, and 1500 small firms which between them deliver the remaining 40 per cent of sales. The way in which the market seems to work is that the small firms ignore the presence of the main firm and sell to their own small niche markets. The small firms separate themselves geographically, within pockets of population, so there is no direct competition between them. The small firms take no notice of the prices charged by other small firms, as the cost to consumers in going from one area to another is greater than any small price differences. The small firms cannot compete with the main firm and therefore do not try to.

Example 2　There is a market characterised by four or five firms with approximately equal market shares. They give the appearance of great rivalry. There are many TV advertising campaigns, special offers, and customer loyalty programmes. However, the prices of the products vary only within very narrow bands and the four firms all seem to charge the same price. The profit levels of the firms all seem to be similar.

In the first example the market would be assumed to be competitive: yet there is no realistic competition. In the second example the market would be classified as highly concentrated, i.e. non-competitive: yet there is great non-price competition. From these two examples it is possible to see that there is no natural urge for firms to try and underprice the opposition. There appears to be more of a drive to distinguish each firm's products, service, quality or even geographical territory. This move away from price competition might also be influenced by the height of any barriers to entry into the market. The market could be contestable if barriers were low, and this would effectively keep prices closer to the market equilibrium level, even though the concentration ratio is high. There may even be, on the part of many small firms, a bespoke service or product for a few well known customers, which provides an adequate profit for the sole trader or small limited company.

15. *Sole Trader*　It is up to the proprietor to decide upon objectives, and there will be many who are interested in a variety of objectives other than money – once they have a basic and continuing level of profit.

Partnership　When a partnership becomes very large it is necessary to have management arrangements similar to those in large companies. Thus there will often be an 'executive committee' and a 'remunerations committee' together with various grades of partnership. In this way all the partners agree to be bound by the decisions of these various committees, and the objectives of the business are developed within this sort of structure. It is doubtful that there is a specific intention to maximise profits (i.e. make as much profit as is physically possible) as it is more likely that the executive partners will want to establish a reputation in the marketplace, a presence and reputation within their professional sphere of operations and a basis upon which their future earnings are protected. Provided that most of the partners are satisfied with their share of profits, there may be no major influence for change.

Private limited company　Many companies are very small and the shareholders are the directors and managers. In these cases the legal form of organisation may be different from the sole trader, but the effective management of the business is the same. Thus the question of objectives for the small limited company may be similar to those of the sole trader. As a company gets bigger the question of separating the various management functions becomes more important. In large private companies the shareholders, directors and day-to-day management may all be separate people. There is an obvious potential for conflict as the various groups may have different priorities and conflicting objectives. The potential for conflict of interests is greater the larger the company.

Public limited company   Within the context of the large company (ltd., or plc) the question of 'objectives' or more specifically the main 'objective', becomes very confused.

The shareholders may take a short term view of their investments and may put pressure on the directors (whom they elect) to pay high dividends. These dividends can only be delivered consistently through increasing company profits. Other shareholders, such as the institutional investors, may want long term growth of the share price and the dividend, and be prepared to forego the short term higher dividends. To achieve long term share price growth any company will need to develop its markets, its products and its internal efficiency. As there may be a conflict of interests among the shareholders it is unlikely that there will be an unequivocal message to management.

The directors, once elected, will decide as a body how to run and direct the company. They will formulate the strategic plans for the short and long term development of the company. They will have a number of pressures upon them. They will be aware of the interests of the major shareholders, whose support they will need for re-election at some future point. The question of the company's objective(s), in a strategic sense, are the province of the principal shareholders and the board of directors. It is unlikely that a directive to 'maximise profits' – i.e. make as much profit as you possibly can – would be possible, as it would be difficult to turn such a directive into daily or weekly management tasks. It is much more likely that strategies will be couched in terms such as, 'to be a world class company', or 'to be a market leader', or 'to maintain a % market share'. In all these cases there is the unspoken underlying assumption **and to do it at a profit.** The question will arise as to whether the profit can be improved, over time.

16.   Descriptive elements should include:

- The product is not homogenous. There are different grades of petrol.
- There are a large number of retail sites but a small number of controlling companies.
- As most sites sell similar grades at similar prices, geographical location may be very important.
- Location issues: near to passing traffic; near top large centers of population; near to large shopping centers.
- Overall how concentrated is the market? Does this tell us anything about how various sites compete?
- Is the market competitive? In what sense, i.e. Oligopoly perhaps or perhaps it is contestable. In this case what type of competitive forces ought to be present?

The nature of competition   Price competition or non-price competition or both. A description of how these competitive forces seem to work is necessary.

Chapter 8

1.   A   2.   D

3.

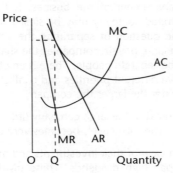

4. C

5.

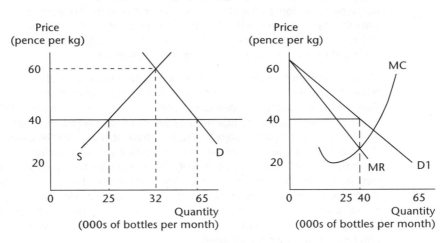

In the above diagrams the small firms can supply 32 000 bottles whilst the dominant firm can supply the market demand above 32 000 bottles. **Total market demand is 65 000 bottles at 40p.**

The dominant firm sells 40 000 bottles per month, where this is the profit maximising output (MR = MC), and we assume that the small firms sell 25 000 bottles per month between them.

TOTAL MARKET DEMAND AND SUPPLY

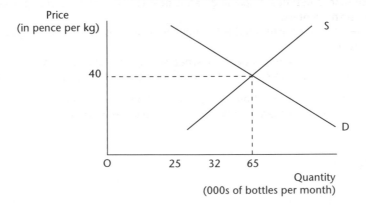

Chapter 9

1. C   2. C

3. In terms of the simple model in Chapter 9 national income is the income that workers derive from producing goods and services. The total value of all the goods and services produced must therefore be equal to what has been paid for them. When the workers spend their incomes on the goods they have produced then their total spending must equal their income and the value of what they have produced.

In practice the construction of national accounts are beset with complications. For an appreciation of these issues students should consult one of the recommended texts from the reading list. Despite the inherent collection problems the identity still holds true: Gross national income = gross national output = gross national expenditure.

4. i. The new government building programme will inject income into the circular flow. This income will be spent and will have the effect of increasing the level of circulating national income to £7000.

   ii. The sale of goods overseas (exports) means that another county's circular flow will pay for the goods and the money will leave that country and be injected into the UK circular flow. This will have the effect of increasing the money available to the factories and they will increase their demand for workers (or pay overtime, etc) so that the extra money finds its way into the circular flow. This will have the effect of increasing the level of circulating national income to £8500.

   iii. The increase in investment (the money to build new factories) will be an injection into the circular flow and will increase the level of circulating national income to £10 000. However the workers will not have this amount to spend as the government is to withdraw 50 per cent of the worker's income in taxation. This means that the level of circulating national income will fall to £5000.

   iv. Savings are a withdrawal from the circular flow. The level of circulating national income will therefore fall to £4000. Only money passed on within the circular flow can keep the circulation going. Savings may re-enter the circular flow at some later stage, but for now are a withdrawal.

5.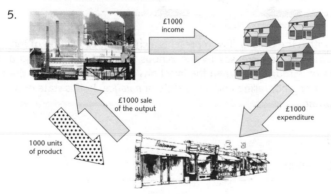

Inflation

Assume in the above diagram that the factories produce 1000 units as a starting position. The goods sell in the shops at £1 each. If the factories are at full capacity and the workers get an injection of funds (perhaps they decide to spend some of their savings) say to £2000 then the price of the goods will rise to £2 each. When there is greater demand for goods than there are goods to satisfy that demand, the shopkeepers cannot immediately meet demand. They therefore soak up the extra money circulating in the circular flow, by raising their prices. If more goods can be produced then there may be no further pressure within the circular flow for prices to continue rising. However if no more goods can be produced, or if productivity falls, then the increase in prices is likely to remain. This is a case of too much money (same as aggregate demand) chasing too few goods.

6. **Employment**

The workers are employed in the factory. It may not be possible to give every person, who would like to work, a job. The number of jobs available will depend upon technology (see the chapter on production in the microeconomics section) and upon how much demand there is for the goods. The demand for the goods will be reflected in the amount of money flowing into the factories from the shops. Thus if national income rises there will be more money to spend (creates greater demand) and more money available in the factories to hire more workers. If national income falls there will be less money to spend (demand falls) and less money available in the factories to pay for wages. Thus workers will be made redundant.

Employment depends upon demand for goods and services in the economy. In the figure for question 5 the expenditure in the shops, which is passed on to the factories, is supporting the workers in employment. Therefore any injection into the circular flow has the effect of raising the national income, which leads to raised national expenditure (which is aggregate demand), which leads to pressure on the factories to produce more goods, which leads to the factories wishing to employ more workers. This pressure on the factories to produce more goods can only result in more employment if there is spare capacity in the factories. If there is already full employment then no more goods can be produced and no more jobs can be created. Any withdrawal from the circular flow has the effect of reducing the national income, which leads to lower national expenditure (which is aggregate demand), which leads to the factories wishing to produce less goods, which leads to the factories wishing to employ less workers.

7.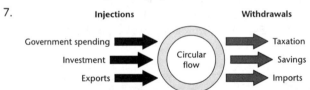

The income within the circular flow represents a changing circulation of money. This flow of national income can be increased by the various forms of injection and decreased by the various forms of withdrawal. When the injections are equal to the withdrawals the circular flow is neither rising nor falling and is in a state of *balance*. In this state of balance it is said to be in **equilibrium**.

Chapter 10

1. 14 000   2. 3500

3.

Aggregate planned expenditure	Consumption	Investment	Government expenditure	Exports	Imports
8 000	4 000	2 000	1 500	3 000	2 500
12 500	8 000	4 000	2 750	1 000	3 250
8 500	3 000	3 500	2 500	750	1 250
14 250	6 000	1 500	3 000	4 500	750

4.

National income (Y) (£bn)	APC	Saving (S) (£bn)	Consumption
150	0.6	60	90
300	0.7	90	210
500	0.74	130	370
750	0.76	180	570

To work out the APC you need to add another column consumption. $Y = C + S$. Therefore consumption must be Y minus the savings figure. The APC is then worked out by dividing each consumption figure by the respective level of national income.

5.

National income (Y) (£bn)	MPC	Saving (S) (£bn)
150		60
300	0.8	90
500	0.8	130
750	0.8	180

Again the consumption figures are needed, and are the same as in the last question. To work out the MPC it is the **difference** between the first and second level of consumption **divided by** the **difference** between the first and second level of national income. Thus $210 - 90 = 120$ and $300 - 150 = 150$ The calculation is 120 divided by $150 = 0.8$.

The student does not need to calculate the rest as all MPCs are the same (see the text). You might just check the next one to prove this to yourself.

6. The multiplier will operate on the injection of government spending. The spending of £50m will be multiplied by a factor which is calculated thus.

Savings are $10\% = 0.1$ Taxes are $60\% = 0.6$ Imports are $25\% = 0.25$
Therefore total withdrawals are $0.1 + 0.6 + 0.25 = 0.95$
The multiplier is $1/0.95 = 1.0526$
This is multiplied by the injection of £50m. Thus $50 \times 1.0526 = £52.6m$
This is added to the original level of national income Thus £350m + £52.6m = £402.6m

7. Government spending is £70m, this is the injection that will be multiplied.

Withdrawals are: Taxation: indirect 20% plus direct $35\% = 55\%$ or 0.55
Savings are 20% or 0.2 (consumption is 80% therefore savings are 20%)
Spending on imports is 25% or 0.25
Total withdrawals $= 0.55 + 0.2 + 0.25 = 1$
The multiplier is $1/1 = 1$. The injection of £70m is multiplied by $1 = £70m$
Thus the **national income rises by the injection £70m**

8. There is a sense in which the chancellor is giving with one hand £70m in government works. This will create incomes for a wide variety of workers and suppliers who will spend their incomes and therefore create incomes for other people. As they spend 80 per cent of income the potential multiplier effect would be great – without any withdrawals other than savings it would be 5 times the original investment. 25 per cent of this extra would go to other economies as spending on imports is 25 per cent, and spending on imports tends to go up as income rises. The intention of the government is to stimulate the home economy not foreign economies. They therefore have to ensure that the extra income generated does not put to much pressure on demand for goods and services which cannot be

produced at home. By increasing indirect taxation the government is allowing people to spend as they wish but they are reining in the multiplier effect of that spending, by increasing the withdrawals. The point to remember is that national income has risen by £70m and hopefully home producers can increase the production of goods and services to match this increased level of income. If they can then employment will increase and inflation will not be present.

Chapter 11

1. Price rises

   ■ A decrease in real income therefore less purchasing power.
   ■ An increase in the current cost of goods and services, leading to a postponing of current expenditure in the hope that future costs will be lower.
   ■ The cost of domestically produced goods increases relative to foreign goods, leading to a tendency to buy more imported goods.

2. Price falls

   ■ An increase in real income therefore greater purchasing power.
   ■ A decrease in the current cost of goods and services, leading to a tendency to spend now as future costs might be higher.
   ■ The cost of domestically produced goods decreases relative to foreign goods, leading to a tendency to buy more home produced goods: also the sale of exports may increase as they are relatively cheaper in overseas markets.

3. Expectations

   When the whole demand curve moves then something other than the average price level has caused the change in demand. One influence on aggregate demand which causes the demand curve to shift is expectations. People tend to tailor their current consumption behaviour to their view of the economy in the future, the so called 'consumer confidence'. There are three areas of expectation which are of considerable importance to people.

   Expected inflation   If people feel generally that inflation is going to increase, they will tend to increase current demand, therefore aggregate demand will increase. As inflation increases future prices are rising, and the value of future income is falling in real terms (i.e. what it will buy). It therefore makes sense to spend 'now' whilst purchasing power is high.

   Expected future incomes   If people expect their future incomes to increase they will tend to increase their current demand patterns in anticipation of the increased future income streams. Households planned spending on consumer durables, cars and holidays are a few of the items which may attract extra demand in anticipation of higher future incomes. If, however, people expect their future incomes to decrease or they perceive their employment prospects to be less than safe, they will tend to decrease their current demand patterns in anticipation of the decreased future income streams.

   Expected future profits   Firms tend to renew their capital, and structure new investment, according to their view of the future prosperity of the industry, and their firm in particular. Prosperity may mean many things but it certainly includes profitability. If there is confidence that future profits will be maintained or improved then investment projects will go ahead and these constitute demand for capital equipment – a major constituent of aggregate demand. If, conversely, there is a lack of confidence that future profitability will be maintained, the investment projects may be postponed or cancelled. Demand for capital goods will decrease and aggregate demand will decrease.

4. D   5. D   6. A

Chapter 12

1. Liquidity is a measure of how **quickly** an asset can be turned into cash. Cash is perfectly liquid as it can always be used immediately to purchase goods and services. Other assets are less liquid because they cannot be used **immediately** to purchase goods and services, but may take time before they can be turned into cash. Some assets are considered to be illiquid because of the long time it may take to turn them into cash, and the fact that in trying to turn them into cash, they may lose capital value and incur transaction costs. A house, for example, may have to be sold when market prices are falling, and there are considerable costs attached to selling a house. A liquid asset is defined as one which can be turned into cash quickly and without capital loss or interest loss.

2. There is a scale of liquidity which runs from liquid to illiquid. At the one end is cash and at the other are assets such as land and buildings, and specialist assets which have few alternative uses. Financial assets rest on the scale between these two extremes, depending upon how quickly their full monetary value may be realised. The following financial instruments are examples of varying liquidity.

    i.   **Current Accounts**   These are considered to be near perfect liquidity.
    ii. **Time Deposit Accounts**   These accounts with banks and building societies are considered to be very liquid. However there may be a 'notice period' before money can be obtained free of any interest penalty. This notice period would measure the liquidity of the particular deposit.
    iii. **Treasury Bills**   These can be issued with 63-day maturity, 91-day maturity or 182-day maturity. The shorter the maturity period the more liquid the Treasury Bill. Those bills approaching their maturity date, regardless of when they were sold, are more liquid than those with more time to run. The fact that Treasury Bills can be traded and turned into cash immediately is of little relevance for the strict definition of liquidity, they would lose interest in so doing and that contravenes the strict definition.
    iv. **Gilt-edged securities**   These usually have original maturity periods from 5 years upwards, with some of the longer dated securities being over 20 years. For most of the lives of these securities they are considered illiquid. But as their maturity date approaches they become more liquid. Thus a 20 year security with only 30 days to maturity would be as liquid as a Treasury Bond with the same period to go to maturity. As with Treasury Bills the Gilt-edged securities are tradeable, but at different times during their lifetimes there is the risk of serious capital loss, when interest rates are rising.
    v.   **Certificates of Deposit**   These normally have original maturity periods ranging from 28 days to 5 years, and for liquidity purposes will cover the issues raised under (iii) and (iv) above.

3. C

4. D

5. In general the commercial banks do not have an unrestricted ability to create credit. Banks may have liquid funds available to support loans but they may have difficulty in finding the quality of borrower they wish to attract. Reducing lending criteria increases the risk associated with lending money and the banks, whilst wishing to make as much profit as possible, do not want to be exposed to high levels of risk. This issue is well illustrated by the slump in house prices during the early 1990s. Many banks had relaxed their lending criteria in the drive for higher profit levels. As the prices of houses rose ever higher, with no end to the boom in sight, banks lent increasing multiples of money secured on property. Thus where prudence indicated that banks should only lend 3 to 3.5 times a person's salary, they

were lending 4 and 5 times salary. They reasoned that the prices of houses had not fallen, in living memory, and if the loan was secured against a property their loan was safe. Then came the crash in the housing market which coincided with a world economic depression. The banks lost considerable sums on many of their loans with forced sales of property, the value of which had fallen below the level of the outstanding debt.

Another example is the way in which banks advertise their credit cards, trying to get as many as possible to apply. This is a clear indication that they wish to extend credit – for they all advertise their low rates of interest, etc. However there are strict credit assessment criteria which are not always made clear, and which are designed to limit the risk of lending to unsuitable people.

6. E

7. iii

8. The amount of money interest paid is £8. This is 7% of £114 the amount the bond currently costs. Therefore we may assume that interest rates in general are about 7% and are tending to fall.

9. He will receive £5000 which is £372 more than he paid. Therefore the implied interest rate is $372/4628 \times 100$. This is 8%.

10. a

11. c

12. If a person chose not to hold money as cash he could deposit it and receive interest on the deposit. Therefore by not depositing the money he loses the interest which would have been paid. This then is the implied cost of holding money. In economic terms the opportunity cost. Opportunity cost is the cost of something in terms of the foregone alternative. In this case interest has been foregone for the privilege of holding cash. *Interest is the opportunity cost of holding money.*

13.

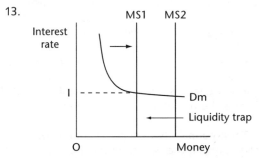

The interaction of the money supply (MS1) and the demand for money (Dm) will establish a market interest rate of (I). If the money supply is increased from MS1 to MS2 this will not lead to a fall in the interest rate. This is because the demand for money at this low level of interest is perfectly elastic. The general conclusion is that increasing the money supply will have the effect of reducing interest rates. But there comes a point where increases in the money supply will have no effect upon interest rates. This latter position is what Keynes referred to as the **liquidity trap**.

The Keynesian reasoning for the above analysis is as follows. At the level of money supply represented by MS1 that amount of money will be demanded whilst interest rates are at (I). As the money supply is increased from MS1 to MS2 people and firms will want to hold the extra money supply in speculative balances, as bond prices are at a peak and expected to fall. Thus increasing the money supply beyond MS1 will only lead to people holding the extra money and there will be no further affect upon interest rates – thus the liquidity trap.

14. ■ It is assumed that the economy is at the full employment level of output. Otherwise through extra production the extra money could generate extra output.
■ It is assumed that the demand for money is for transactions purposes only. Therefore when the money supply increases consumers find themselves holding more money than they need for their normal level of transactions, and they therefore try to spend the extra money causing the prices to rise.
■ As prices rise the total value of consumer's transactions rise, and therefore the demand for money (*transactions balances*) rises.

15. The idea of real demand for money is a way of expressing what the money will buy. By dividing the demand for money by the average price level the resulting figure is real in the sense that it shows how much can actually be bought. This is useful when price levels are subject to constant change. If a person usually holds £100 in cash and continues to do so when prices have risen by say 10 per cent, then although he has the same amount of money the real value (what it will buy) has fallen. To hold the same purchasing power he has to hold £110.

16. There are three main differences.

Keynes says that the demand for money is directly related to (a function of) *current money income*. **Friedman** says the demand for money is directly related to (a function of) *permanent income* as a proxy for *total wealth*.

Keynes says that the demand for money is a close *substitute for bonds* and therefore *dependent upon the interest rate*. **Friedman** says the demand for money is a close *substitute for a variety of assets* and therefore *independent of the interest rate*.

Keynes says that if the money supply is increased the effect will be for interest rates to fall as spending on bonds will increase. **The demand for money remains the same.** **Friedman** says that if the money supply is increased the effect will be for interest rates to fall as some spending on bonds will increase, **and** for prices to rise as there is spending on various other assets as well. **The demand for money will increase in response to the higher prices**.

17. The different positions in relation to a change in money supply can be shown graphically.

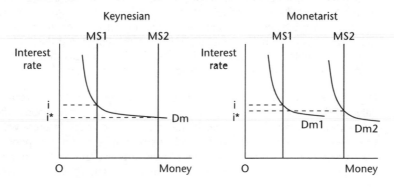

Keynesian analysis indicates a much larger reaction of interest rates to a change in the money supply from MS1 to MS2. The starting interest rate (i) is the same in both cases. In the monetarist case due to rising prices (because of spending on assets other than bonds) the demand for money has increased from Dm1 to Dm2. The increased money supply MS2 cuts the new demand for money Dm2 at an interest rate of (i*). A much smaller reaction to the increase in money supply.

271

Chapter 13

1. Rises in interest rates will have the effect of reducing demand and increasing the external value of the £. Demand for exports as well as home produced goods will reduce. Production will be reduced and probably stocks will be run down. There will therefore be less demand for labour and firms will attempt to cut manning levels to reduce costs.

2.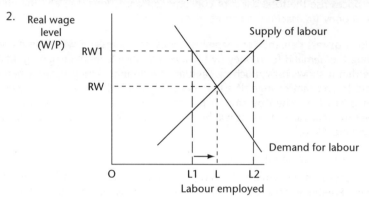

    In the diagram above the market clearing level of real wages is RW. At this level of real wage L amount of labour would be employed. (Note. At this equilibrium level of L there would still be people unemployed, they would be part of the *natural level* of unemployment). If the real wage level rises to RW1 there would be an imbalance between supply and demand for labour. At this level of real wage, L2 labour would wish to be employed but employers would only wish to employ L1. The difference between L1 and L is the amount of unemployment directly attributable to excessive real wages. The answer to this question of unemployment, say the monetarists, is either to cut money wages or to allow the price level to rise more rapidly than money wages. They see the answer as a more competitive labour market with flexible wages.

    The Bank of England (Monetary Policy Committee) cannot allow the price level to rise as this is contrary to their objective of keeping inflation below the target figure of 2.5 per cent. The unemployment which the monetarist model predicts will have some downward influence on aggregate demand, which should reduce the influences upon prices to rise. However the monetarists (in this form) are essentially non-interventionist and the evidence seems to point towards inflexible wages (downwards), which probably means that the Bank's Committee is right to worry at levels of wage settlements far in excess of inflation.

3. Higher interest rates will have the effect of reducing demand and increasing the external value of the £. Demand for exports as well as home produced goods will reduce. A major element in this reduced demand is the fact that mortgage interest will rise, thus taking spending power directly out of the pockets of a large number of people. People tend to take a dim view of the future at times of rising interest rates and high mortgage payments, and they often postpone spending on major purchases such as cars and household appliances.

    Production will be reduced and probably stocks will be run down. There will therefore be less demand for labour and firms will attempt to cut manning levels to reduce costs. People seeing the rising unemployment will take an even dimmer view of their future, and may seek to save rather than spend, just in case they become unemployed. This saving will further dampen demand. General prices will probably fall as firms try to generate some sales, and wages levels may fall if the choice is between work or no work. The depression would have to be severe before this latter stage was reached. Attitudes are changing, however, and people are more willing to see their working career as a process of adjustment to changing conditions.

4. This is explained in terms of the adjustment process over time. As the result of reduced aggregate demand output in the economy fell and workers were laid off (unemployment rose). Those still in employment were working their production processes at less than capacity. The firms had to reduce their costs, and wages are a significant element of final cost. As the economy picks up and demand increases the firms are able to expand their outputs in the short term with the existing workforce and excess capacity. The firms will want to be reassured that the economy really is improving and that the increased aggregate demand is not temporary. It may take some time before they are certain enough to increase production capacity and increase their demand for labour.

Thus it may look as if there is contradiction in the statement quoted in the question, but in the above circumstances both conditions can exist, in the short term.

5. C

6. C

Chapter 14

1. As the demand for exports gets stronger firms will want to produce for their export markets. Given that productive capacity is limited, in the short term, if they are producing for export markets they cannot be producing at the same time for the home market. If demand in the home market is strong then there will have to be extra output to feed this demand otherwise the excess demand will lead to rising prices – the dreaded inflation. The home demand can be fed for a brief period whilst the increased export demand is satisfied by running down stocks. This cannot continue, and either industry will increase productive capacity (if they believe that the strong demand conditions will continue) or the Monetary Policy Committee may have to take steps to reduce aggregate demand and contain prospective inflation before it starts.

2. a. **The claimant count (the official definition)** The number of people claiming, jobseekers allowance (unemployment benefit) or national insurance credits, on the day of the monthly count; who on that day were unemployed and were willing and able to do any suitable work and actively seeking work.

   International Labour Organisation (ILO) – jobless rate Claimants from the official definition plus all people who are available to start work within the next two weeks and have looked for work in the last four weeks or already found a job but waiting to start.
   The data are compiled following guidelines set out by the International Labour Organisation, based on surveys, which ask people whether they are seeking work.

   The second count is higher than the claimant count because there are large groups of people who want to work and are available to start work and are looking for work but do not sign on and claim benefit. Two such groups are housewives (and women returners) and school/college leavers. These unemployed people are not counted in the official measure.

   b. If there are shortages of certain skills in the labour market then it is likely that demand for those workers will exceed supply. In this case the shortage groups will be in a very strong bargaining position and will be able to gain wage increases far in excess of inflation. These wage increases will be viewed by other groups as a bargaining position when their wage reviews are undertaken. The whole process could push up the costs of production and fuel inflation.

3. Expected inflation (anticipated inflation) will be factored in to the wage claims of all workers. The stronger groups of workers will be able to recover their anticipated inflation but the less well organised workers will only recover some of the expected inflation. But the general tendency will be for expected inflation to be reflected in higher wage settlements than would be the case if inflation was not taken into account. If the government is seen to be determined to control inflation, and is seen to be successful, then this perception may reduce future expectations of inflation and in this sense there will be anticipated the results of current interest rate policy.

4. The student should be able to formulate policies at this stage. Monetary or fiscal, or both. There are no right answers, but reasoning is important. Any policy measure must have an intended end result, and you should be able to reason an end result from any chosen policy.

5. C   6. D   7. C

Chapter 15

1. B   2. B   3. B   4. B

5. E   6. C   7. D

8. High interest rates in the UK will attract overseas investment, as investors can see a better return on their money than in their own country. They will therefore demand £s. This extra demand for £s will push up the value of the £. The higher value of the £ will mean that exports are relatively more expensive than previously. If demand for exports is elastic the reduced demand will reduce total revenue for exporters, and they will be under pressure to produce less. If there is not an offsetting extra demand in the home market, producers may reduce capacity and lay off workers in an attempt to protect their profit levels. They clearly cannot maintain existing total costs faced with falling total overseas revenue.

   There is another effect of a high valued £. It means that imports will be relatively cheaper and home consumers may decide to switch their spending to the cheaper imports. If the demand for imports is elastic then total revenue leaving the UKs circular flow will increase. This will have a withdrawal effect upon the level of national income. There will be an added pressure for output to fall as home demand falls due to falling national income.

   These two international effects will combine with the intended direct effects upon aggregate demand.

9. The opportunity costs are: Peru 4B = 2G and Spain 2B = 2G

   For Peru 1B = 0.5G   whilst Spain 1B = 1G
   For Peru 1G = 2B   whilst Spain 1G = 1B

   Therefore Peru should specialise in beef and Spain should specialise in grain.

   If they produce both beef and grain themselves then they produce:

	Workers used	Beef	Workers used	Grain
Peru	50	200	50	100
Spain	50	100	50	100
Total production		300		200

If they specialise then they produce:

	Workers used	Beef	Workers used	Grain
Peru	100	400		
Spain			100	200
Total production		400		200

Total production has increased by 100 tons of beef. The final question is how to share the total production. Both countries will want at least what they could have produced for themselves, plus a share of the extra total output.

For Peru 1 ton of grain costs 2 tons of beef to produce, so it will want to give less than 2 tons of beef for each ton of grain.

For Spain 1 ton of grain costs 1 ton of beef to produce so it will want to receive more 1 ton of beef for each ton of grain.

Terms of trade will be between 1 and 2 tons of beef for each ton of grain. Assume a middle price of 1.5 tons of beef per ton of grain. (This should share out the extra total output equally.)

	Beef	Grain
Peru	250	100
Spain	150	100
Total production	400	200

The final position is that the extra beef was shared equally.

Index